SPARE THE CHILD

Spare the Child

The Religious Roots
of Punishment and
the Psychological Impact
of Physical Abuse

Philip Greven

ALFRED A. KNOPF　　NEW YORK 1991

Owing to limitations of space, all acknowledgments for permission to reprint previously published material can be found on pages 249–52.

Library of Congress Cataloging-in-Publication Data
Greven, Philip J., Jr.
Spare the child : the religious roots of punishment & the psychological impact of physical abuse / Philip Greven—1st ed.
p. cm.
Includes index.
ISBN 0-394-57860-0
1. Corporal punishment—United States—History. 2. Corporal punishment—Religious aspects—Christianity—History. 3. Child rearing—United States—History. 4. Child rearing—Religious aspects—Christianity—History. 5. Child abuse—United States—History. 6. Child abuse—Psychological aspects. I. Title.
HQ770.4.G74 1990
649'.1—dc20   90-53171 CIP

Manufactured in the United States of America
First Edition

FOR HAROLD

CONTENTS

ACKNOWLEDGMENTS

This book has been long in the making, almost an entire lifetime so far. I was raised in a family of Protestants, mostly Methodists, at least on my mother's side. My maternal grandmother, especially, was a quietly devout Christian for whom religion was far more than merely routine church-going. The Bible was the one book that she always read, and she saw to it that we attended Sunday school at the local Methodist church when we lived with or visited her. Being raised as a Protestant has had an enduring impact upon me both personally and as a scholar. *The Protestant Temperament* and this book grew out of my own religious roots as well as reflecting my adult fascination with the personal sources of religious thought and experience. In many ways, no doubt, *Spare the Child* is a sequel to my earlier book, bringing it up to the present in ways that I could not have anticipated many years ago, when I first began my quest for an understanding of these issues.

Equally important is the fact that, like so many other Americans—including many of those whose stories will unfold in the pages of this book—I was physically punished as a child. One memory, representative of many, remains embedded ineradicably in my own mind. When I was about eight years old, we lived in Orlando, Florida, where my father was serving as an officer in the United States Air Force. One day I decided to see how deep a hole I could dig in the sand with a hose gushing full force. The water easily pushed the sand aside, digging a hole many feet deep. The hose disappeared into the ground, burying itself and giving me intense pleasure and satisfaction until I tried to pull it out. Frozen, immobile, absolutely impossible to pull up, the hose seemed to be locked in place forever. Instantly, I knew that I was in trouble; but, since the hose was stuck in the sand, I had no choice but to tell my mother what had happened. She said to wait until my father came home: He would deal with it and with me. I waited, seemingly forever—time can be an eternity to an eight-year-old expecting punishment—until my father returned. I was sent to my room to await my punishment. My father went outdoors, somehow freed the hose from the sand's tight grasp, and came inside to spank me for my misadventure and, presumably, for the difficulties it had caused him.

Many years later, my father reminded me of that incident, acknowledging how angry he had been at the time and recollecting that he had given me one of the hardest spankings of my life. When a man who weighs over two hundred pounds, stands six feet, and has huge hands spanks a small boy hard, it surely must hurt. Yet to this day, I have no conscious memory of the actual pain that he inflicted and I felt. I only can remember the events that led up to the punishment itself. Amnesia has suppressed the pain I must have experienced that afternoon or early evening. The event itself, however, remains vividly imprinted on our family's collective memory. There are certain spankings that one never forgets.

There are also certain stories from childhood that one never forgets. I have often thought about three stories that were read to me again and again when I was small, stories that still resonate to my innermost concerns: Munro Leaf's *The Story of Ferdinand* the bull, "Chicken Little," and Watty Piper's *The Little Engine That Could*. Ferdinand occasionally embarrassed me as an adult when I thought about my own boyhood. Ferdinand, after all, refused to fight in the bullring like the other bulls of his day and time in Spain, and he was sent back to the field in utter disgust by the men who had not had the pleasure of killing him. There he remained for the rest of his life, sitting under the cork tree, smelling the flowers, and being happy. Ferdinand, I now realize, was actually a survivor, a rare bull who refused to fight, who was sensitive to beauty and to the wonderful scent of the flowers in the fields and in the hair of the women at the bullring. Ferdinand was not willing to die for the principle of violence and destruction inherent in the bullring. Chicken Little, on the other hand, was utterly certain that the sky was falling on her head (when, in fact, it had only been a stone falling from the roof of her coop). While she went about warning her friends of the imminent catastrophe, she overlooked the more pressing danger posed by Foxy Loxy. Even at five, I must have sensed some connection between her anxiety and mine since I, too, often felt that the sky might fall at any moment. Chicken Little always has been for me the epitome of an apocalyptic. The Little Engine, on the other hand, set forth the Protestant work ethic for children of the Depression in the 1930s. The small runty engine managed to outdo the bigger, handsomer, and stronger engines that either passed by disdainfully or gave up the task of pulling the train filled with Christmas toys over the mountain. Stories such as these helped me make sense of my life and myself as a boy. They helped me cope with the anxieties and the fears generated by punishments as well as rationalize my own boyhood proclivity toward nonviolence and the life of the mind.

I feel that it is important for readers of this book to know that I write about physical punishment from the perspective of one to whom it was done—by well-intentioned and loving parents, to be sure—and also of one who, as a parent, has done it on at least a few occasions. I doubt that I would have spent so many years exploring and trying to understand the arguments about corporal punishments and the implications of such punishments for myself and for others if I, too, had not experienced them. I believe that scholarship should be brought to bear upon problems that engage our innermost beings. My own scholarship always has been. This book reflects my wish to be a part of the process of changing the ways people rear children. Without the impulse both to change myself and to change others, this study would neither have taken shape nor been completed.

The support and advice of members of my family and of my friends and colleagues who have taken time to read various drafts of the manuscript has been invaluable. I am grateful to each of them, having learned so much from their comments and criticisms and suggestions. Some I have heeded; others I have silently ignored. I have been sustained and assisted by their support of my endeavor for so many years now. I wish to thank Helen Stokes Greven (who read and edited the manuscript at an important juncture); John Greven and Nancy Van Laan, my brother and sister (Nancy now writes books for children, while I write books about children); Catherine Ayoub; Carol Berkin; Paul Clemens; Adrienne Ahlgren Haeuser; Jackson Lears; Brian McHugh; Lorraine (Lori) Pierce; Michael Prokopow; Louis Sass; and Thomas Slaughter. I also wish to thank John Burchard, Edward Carr, and Crighton Newsom for their suggestions and information. Kenneth MacRae, Thomas Kersch,

A. Joshua Sherman, Joseph Cady, Suzanne Heller, Alice Jones, Margaret Engelhart, Daveda Movitz, Edward Movitz, and Gertrude (Trudy) Paddock have been wonderfully sustaining friends as well, as have so many others. I also am grateful to my mother, Sarah Hawkins Greven, for her generosity and support.

I also owe special debts for the insightful readings and suggestions offered by Rudolph Bell, Eileen Jones (who helped shape the final version), and, most of all, Harold Lloyd Poor, to whom my book is dedicated. He has been the best of friends since we were eighteen years old, and continues still to be the ideal friend, colleague, and reader. He has been living with this book nearly as long as I have, and my life and thought have been enriched continually as a result of his presence, conversations, and contributions to our exceptional and enduring friendship.

Hannah Greven and Philip Greven, my children, have enriched my life and understanding beyond measure. Knowing that they will live most of their lives in the twenty-first century has been an impetus for my efforts to fathom the wider implications of punishment and suffering in childhood. My hope is that their world, in the coming decades, can become a much better place in which to live and a less violent and punitive world than the one in which I have lived most of my own life.

I have been privileged to have many students who have shared some of their experiences with discipline and punishment with me and with their fellow classmates. I have learned far more from their questions and doubts and arguments than I have taught, I often suspect, and they have been willing to listen to my speculations and explanations and arguments as I created the patterns that now have taken form in this book. Being a teacher has been a vital part of my own learning.

Over the years, I also have been assisted by many people who have provided me with suggestions, sources, or observations that I otherwise would have missed. Jane Garrett, my editor, has been an unflagging source of encouragement throughout this entire process both as a friend and as a reader and critic. I also wish to express my appreciation for the assistance of Margaret Gorenstein, Gerald Hollingsworth, Bette Keller, and Ann Kraybill. Staci Capobianco, Karen Leh, and Jolanta Benal have been most helpful in sharpening the prose and clarifying the text throughout the book. I appreciated their efforts even when I did not follow their suggestions.

I also wish to pay special thanks to the work of others who have pioneered the exploration of the consequences of physical punishments as well as the practices themselves. Most particularly, the books by Alice Miller have become part of my internal world, so thoroughly have I absorbed them. Miller is one of the few people in her profession of psychoanalysis to grasp the wide range of destructive consequences attributable to physical punishments of children, whose spirits and psyches and behaviors she has explored with enormous insight and empathy. Her work is of profound importance to anyone who cares about reshaping the ways in which we rear and discipline children. Every reader of this book should also be familiar with *For Your Own Good: Hidden Cruelty in Child-Rearing and the Roots of Violence.* It is indispensable.

I have been fortunate to have had the opportunity to spend several months observing children and families and to participate in the discussions concerning these families at the clinic of the Family Development Program at Children's Hospital in Boston, under the sensitive and compassionate guidance of Dr. Eli H. Newberger. Eli Newberger is one of the leading advocates of children in America and one of the most knowledgeable and effective opponents of child abuse in all its guises. Being an observer in his group enabled me, at a crucial time in my writing and thinking, to know that what I had discovered in books and in people's lives, including my own, was being explored in family after family and being assessed continually at the clinic so that children could be spared further hurt and abuse if they had experienced them already. I also learned much from many of the staff at the Family Development Program, especially Catherine Ayoub and Ronald Slaby.

During the many years I spent doing the research for this book, I enjoyed working in archives and libraries whose collections enable us to share the life experiences of people other than ourselves, especially the men and women who have published autobiographies, memoirs, and other self-revealing writings. I have spent much time reading the life stories of Protestants, especially those from evangelical, fundamentalist, and Pentecostal denominations. Many of these life histories provided evidence and insights that helped me create the interpretations and arguments that appear throughout this book.

I wish to thank the librarians at the following institutions especially for their courteous assistance and guidance: Gordon-Conwell Theological Seminary's Goddard Library, Hamilton, Massachusetts; Episcopal Divinity School Library and Harvard Divinity School Library, Cambridge, Massachusetts; Holy Spirit Research Center, Oral Roberts University, Tulsa, Oklahoma; Billy Graham Archives, Billy Graham Center, Wheaton, Illinois; Union Theological Seminary, New York; the Library of Congress; Alexander Library, Rutgers University, New Brunswick, New Jersey; and the Gardner Sage Library, New Brunswick Theological Seminary. I also want to thank Irwin Hyman, director of the extraordinary collection of materials pertaining to physical punishment at the National Center for the Study of Corporal Punishment and Alternatives in the Schools, Temple University, Philadelphia.

Finally, I am grateful to Rutgers—The State University of New Jersey for its support of my research and writing through several faculty leaves during the past decade. Most especially, however, I am grateful to the Rockefeller Foundation Humanities Fellowship in 1982–83, which enabled me to spend an entire year on research on the apocalyptic impulse in American Protestantism, which was the formal origin of this book on punishment. Out of that work came my conviction, hitherto amorphous and intuitive, that corporal punishments were the linchpin of the abuse and violence that have always shaped the desire for the world's end and for the salvation of the few at the expense of the many. The foundation, however, is not responsible in any way for anything that appears in this book, all the arguments and opinions being my own. The same is true for my friends and colleagues as well, since there is no reason whatsoever to assume that they necessarily agree with the opinions and interpretations set forth in the pages that follow.

A child may not be subjected to physical punishment or other injurious or humiliating treatment.

PARENTHOOD AND GUARDIANSHIP CODE, SWEDEN 1979[1]

PART I

The Problem

Billy was always full of pranks; sometimes he carried things a bit too far, and off came his father's belt. Mr. Graham never punished in anger or desperation, but when he did see the necessity for correction, I winced. At such times I had to remind myself of another Proverb: "Withhold not correction from the child: for if thou beatest him with the rod, he shall not die" (Proverbs 23:13). More than once I wiped tears from my eyes and turned my head so the children wouldn't see, but I always stood behind my husband when he administered discipline. I knew he was doing what was biblically correct. And the children didn't die![1]

> MRS. MORROW GRAHAM,
> mother of the Reverend Billy Graham

My father was a gentleman and he expected us to be gentlemen. . . . If we acted disrespectfully, if we did not observe the niceties of etiquette, he took us over his knee and whopped us with his belt. He had a strong arm, and boy, did we feel it.[2]

> PRESCOTT SHELDON BUSH, JR.,
> elder brother of President George Herbert Walker Bush

One of the secrets left to be discovered about American character is revealed by this simple juxtaposition: the North Carolina farmer's son and the Connecticut banker's sons, who seem to have so little in common, shared one experience in childhood—being belted by their fathers. One father belted in the name of the Bible, the other in the name of gentlemanly etiquette. But the pain felt by their children was probably much the same. What was done to them has been done to most Americans, of course, although the actual implements used by parents and other adults range from hands to belts to rods to switches to rulers to boards to paddles to whips to chains and to almost anything else grown-ups might think to use when hitting children and inflicting pain for the purposes of discipline and punishment. Most of us have experienced it; most of us have done it; most of us believe in doing it.

Before this century ends and the third millennium after the birth of Christ begins, surely it would be wise to ask how such commonplace encounters with painful discipline and suffering have influenced our feelings and thoughts, our values and beliefs, and our behavior and actions. How have physical punishments shaped the most private and the most public aspects of American character and culture, past and present? Such questions are asked all too rarely. Perhaps one reason is that physical punishment of children appears to be one of the subjects in America that are still profoundly disturbing, because they are too deeply rooted in our individual and our collective psyches to be confronted directly.

The task that lies ahead, however, is to explore the complicated and diverse experiences, rationales, and implications of the practice of physical punishment of children. We need to begin to chart the maps of the psyche and the self, of culture and society, of religion and politics, of the environment and the world at large from the vantage point of the long-term effects of physical punishment. The astonishing absence of such charts at the present time is itself a fact to be reckoned with, for it reveals the power of the taboo against our acknowledgment of the childhood sufferings experienced by so many people, generation after generation.*

---

* A few remarkable charts do exist already, however. Alice Miller's brilliant analysis of corporal punishment and violence against children in German-speaking countries and Western Europe, *For Your Own Good: Hidden Cruelty in Child-Rearing and the Roots of Violence* (1983), and Ian Gibson's fascinating study, *The English Vice: Beating, Sex and Shame in Victorian England and After* (1978), provide ample evidence of the enduring commitment of Europeans to physical punishment of children. But physical punishment always has been part of the Anglo-Saxon world, brought with the immigrants from Great Britain to America and to the lands throughout Africa and the Pacific. The study of physical punishment in New Zealand by Jane and James Ritchie, *Spare the Rod* (1981), provides remarkable evidence analogous to the explorations by Miller and Gibson,

The pages that follow can be read best as tentative maps, guides to the inner and outer realms of our lives, comparable to the earliest maps of the New World, some bearing witness to what was seen and experienced personally and directly, others observed from a distance, and still others reflecting inferences from stories told of distant lands beyond the boundaries of the familiar and known world. Perhaps, to shift the image, we should think of the pages that follow as being like photos of the night sky, capturing the images left by light generated eons ago, traveling through space and time long after the events themselves ceased to have an actual existence, afterimages of explosions long past. The impact of physical punishment is like this, traveling through time inside our bodies, minds, and spirits and living on long after our individual deaths through the legacies we bequeath to our children and grandchildren and to future generations throughout the world. We now need to recognize the sources and the reasons for such persistent physical punishment of children in the name of love and discipline. We need to create for ourselves charts and maps, however flawed or inadequate they might initially be, so that we can find our way through this maze of punishments that stretch back in time as far as we can see.

Much of the evidence explored in the following pages emerges from an examination of the life histories, thoughts, and beliefs of many generations of white Protestants, especially those from evangelical, fundamentalist, and Pentecostal backgrounds, who have ardently advocated corporal punishment. Mainstream and liberal Protestants have been less enthusiastic supporters of physical discipline, on the whole, yet still have accepted and usually practiced it. In this book I have drawn upon all these diverse voices to reflect the complicated spectrum of opinions and practices among Protestants from the early seventeenth century to the present.*

---

but in the context of English culture in the southern Pacific. Anyone concerned with the experience of and the rationales for corporal punishment in other European-rooted cultures should read these studies.

Also see the compelling evidence and arguments set forth in Irwin A. Hyman's *Reading, Writing, and the Hickory Stick: The Appalling Story of Physical and Psychological Abuse in American Schools* (1990), which provides another perspective on the role of corporal punishments in American education.

* Catholics and many other religious groups have equally sustained traditions of using physical punishments both in families and in schools. But so far very little has been written by or about Catholics concerning their attitudes toward and

Fundamentalists today are among the most outspoken defenders of physical punishments, but they write and say what others believe and practice. To acknowledge the disguised and repressed fundamentalism in those of us who see fundamentalists as "other" is a vital first step in transforming our consciousness and our behavior with respect to active assault and violence against children. While the Bible Belt, long associated with the South and the Southwest, still exists and remains the heartland of fundamentalism in America, no part of the nation is truly exempt from the lure of punishments or free from the consequences of such practices and values. The difference remains a matter of degree, not of kind. So long as children are physically hit in the name of love and authority, fundamentalism will remain a substantial presence in our lives and culture.

So many people share experiences of the pain and suffering undergirding our culture and shaping the character of Americans that there is little to be gained by setting fundamentalists and evangelicals wholly apart from mainstream Protestantism. The spectrum is truly a continuum, not either/or, us and them. Very few Americans have deplored and opposed all forms of physical punishments and violence against children. The rest of us, the large majority, are among those Alice Miller described as " 'decent people who were once beaten,' since such treatment of children was a matter of course in past generations."[3]

The most enduring and influential source for the widespread practice of physical punishment, both in this country and abroad, has been the Bible. Both the Hebrew scriptures in the Old Testament and passages from the New Testament have sustained for centuries the defense of physical punishment and the use of the rod. These biblical texts and the religious rationales used by generations of Protestants to argue the case for physical punishments are explored in the third section of this book.

---

practice of corporal punishments. The subject of discipline among Catholics and Jews needs to be explored. Both religious traditions provide experiences and practices paralleling those among Protestants. One suggestive point of departure is James Terence Fisher's *The Catholic Counterculture in America, 1933–1962* (Chapel Hill: University of North Carolina Press, 1989), which examines the life and thought of Dorothy Day, who was raised as a Protestant, was whipped as a child, and later converted to Catholicism. Day provides a bridge between these two worlds, since suffering, self-denial and self-abnegation, and martyrdom were themes in her life that clearly resonated with many who had been raised and disciplined as Catholics.

Both religious justifications and secular rationales for punishment must be reckoned with and understood before we can begin to grapple with some of the virtually infinite consequences of such physical punishments for ourselves and for all the others who have experienced such forms of domestic and public violence. Given the near universality of such experiences, albeit in varying degrees of suffering and hurt and harm, it should not be too surprising to discover that hardly any aspect of our psyches is free from the imprinting of coercion, violence, and pain.

In the section entitled "Consequences," I have explored some of these complexities, conscious of the vastness of the territory that remains uncharted and unknown to us even now. I also have come to realize that even in those studies that have been done by psychologists and others, the presence of enduring effects from childhood punishments often can be discerned even when the authors themselves did not take note of these commonplace experiences or recognize the persistent implications that childhood punishments have had for the shaping of psyches and characters. Our minds and bodies absorb the blows and pain in childhood and react to them in a multitude of ways for the remainder of our lives, forming a substratum of early experience that continues to be manifested in an astonishing variety of forms in our adult psyches.

My goal in this book is to see some of the subtle and enduring ways in which the mind copes with the anxieties, the fears, and the suffering generated by childhood encounters with discipline. I am seeking to explore and to understand some of the connections between punishment and aspects of our selves, our lives, and our experiences that otherwise might go unnoticed. I am confident that once we begin to ask questions concerning early childhood punishments—and take the answers seriously—we will recognize the enormity of the realm within our adult psyches that remains in bondage to ancient punishments. Old scars can still hurt.

No one is immune from the reverberations of ancient sufferings and hurts, since we see the world in ways shaped by our own personal pasts. Thus theology, so vast and so varied even among Christians, reflects the most ordinary kinds of experiences in childhood, especially those emerging from discipline and punishment. That is why I have paid particular heed to the apocalypticism embedded in Protestant theology and religious life. For many centuries, vast numbers of Protestants have believed that the second coming of Jesus is at hand and that this world is about to come to a catastrophic end. The sense of expectation and the urgent wish to see human history end in the immediate future often emerges from the intense suffering generated by painful childhood punishments.

So much Christian theology has been rooted in the threat of punishment that we need to be aware of the personal experiences that have made such theologies sensible and powerfully appealing to so many people for such a long time. In view of the persistence of physical assaults and violence against children, generation after generation, it is surely no accident that apocalyptic beliefs among Protestants have remained an enduring part of American character and thought for the past four centuries.

Punishment also shapes our attitudes toward authorities of all kinds, and imprints upon our psyches enduring responses, both positive and negative, toward all forms of authority—parental, educational, penal, ecclesiastical, and political. The coerciveness of physical punishments plays an extraordinarily important role in the designs that we construct about the world and our roles in it, designs concerning all forms of authority and all kinds and degrees of obedience. Authoritarianism, which always begins in the home when adults use physical force to teach obedience to authority, needs to be examined since it constitutes one of the most enduring outcomes of physical punishment of children.

Equally enduring has been the legacy of domestic and public violence rooted in physical punishment, the archetype of many other forms of assault and battery. Our country today is one of the most violent in the world, with the highest rates of aggression, crime, and murder to be found in the western world. Television is one of the most powerful expressions of this obsession with and practice of violence. It is sobering to realize that American children who watch television regularly will have witnessed thousands of murders before they reach adulthood. Guns are part of the domestic arsenals of families across the nation. The massive expenditures for nuclear weapons and delivery systems in missiles, planes, and submarines as well as the huge peacetime military establishment that has arisen in the past half-century are indicative of the national obsession with defense and warfare. Aggression and violence are so much a part of our culture today that they seem inevitable, necessary, unavoidable.

All of this grim information is familiar, yet we shy away from recognizing the roots of such collective violence. I share Alice Miller's conviction that the fundamental ground for public violence is always to be found in the personal violence, often long-gone in an individual's life, that has created the feelings, the fantasies, and the needs for aggression that are subsequently expressed in our thoughts, words, and behaviors, both private and public, secular and religious. Virtually no aspect of our lives as a people is untouched by the violence that we do unthinkingly to children.

Most of us hesitate to grapple with the implications of disciplining children by physically assaulting them, whether gently or moderately or severely or brutally. Most of us instinctively defend the practice of corporal punishment, partly out of loyalty to our own parents and grandparents, partly out of anxiety about ourselves (especially if we as parents have used physical punishments in rearing and disciplining our own children, as most of us have), and partly out of an unwillingness to think that something so common and so ordinary could be so consequential and so damaging to so many of us. We also know now, as never before, that physical abuse and sexual abuse are realities and we fear, therefore, that the lines separating abusers from ourselves might not be as sharp and as clear as we would like them to be. That is entirely understandable and reasonable, I believe. Many of us would agree with Alfred Kadushin and Judith Martin that "The problem lies in distinguishing discipline which is 'legitimate violence' toward children from abuse which is excessive and inappropriate and, hence, unacceptable violence toward children."[4] But, as this entire book will seek to make clear, there actually is no way such a distinction can be sustained. All levels of violence against children, including all the varied forms of physical punishments, are hurtful and harmful.

Child abuse takes many forms. One of them is physical punishment.[5] Few of us believe this yet, but more and more undoubtedly will, once we begin to recognize the implications of physical assaults against children, the ordinary kinds of pain that invariably result from being struck. Without pain, without assault, without coercion, physical punishment cannot and will not be possible.

It is hard for most of us to imagine alternatives to such normal violence, so ingrained and so familiar is it to so many of us. But I invite you to consider the evidence and the arguments that unfold in the following essays, keeping an open mind and being aware of the possibility that surprising—perhaps disturbing—feelings, thoughts, and responses may arise while you read this book. How could it be otherwise, given the resistance so many of us experience when confronting the shadows of our own childhood encounters with pain and punishments?

The past holds a powerful grip upon the future by shaping feelings, actions, and beliefs in the present. The pain and suffering experienced by children who have been physically punished resonate through time, first during the seemingly endless days and nights of childhood and adolescence, and later through the lives we lead as adults. The feelings generated by the pain caused by adults' assaults against children are mostly repressed, forgotten, and denied, but they actually never disappear. Everything remains recorded in our innermost beings, and the effects of punishment permeate our lives, our thought, our culture, and our world.

The evidence is everywhere—surrounding us, engulfing us—yet, like the air we breathe, usually invisible to us. Once it becomes visible, surely we will begin to see ourselves and our world differently. Then we will be in a better position to consider alternatives to coercion, hitting, and painful discipline and to make choices that will be more nurturing, loving, and life-enhancing than those associated, generation after generation, with physical punishment.

PART II

Experiences

Stories about childhood experiences with discipline and punishment abound both in our personal memories and in those shared in print through autobiographies, memoirs, and biographies.[1] Often only one or two are recollected or described, yet they are frequently emblematic of many others silently passed over or forgotten. These stories have a curiously timeless quality. It hardly seems to matter when, or where, or by whom they are told. They often seem familiar even when they involve people other than ourselves. Of course, the kinds of punishments, the levels of pain, the forms of suffering, the degrees of physical and emotional harm vary enormously from person to person, ranging from the mildest to the most severe. These stories can tell us far more about the individuals who share them with us than most people realize. That is why they are so vitally important, both personally and historically. That is why we must begin our exploration with a series of recollections about punishments in childhood.

From the early seventeenth century to the present, Protestants have written about their encounters with parental and other forms of discipline and punishment. Just as within the larger society and culture there has always been a wide spectrum of experiences with discipline, so too among Protestants there always have been varied encounters with punishments and discipline in childhood, from little or no physical hitting to brutal batterings and fatal assaults. The diverse experiences of individuals in childhood mirror the larger configurations of belief and theology among Protestants during the past four centuries, from the most liberal and flexible to the most conservative and rigid manifestations of piety and doctrine. Patterns of punishment correspond closely to people's conceptions of God and to their attitudes toward the most basic theological issues.

These conceptions and attitudes have divided people into many disparate groups and denominations throughout our history.[2] This, however, is not our concern here. We need to pay heed to the stories themselves.

The experiences recalled and observed in the following pages are parts of a seamless continuum which reflects a subtle but constant escalation of levels of coercion, force, assault, violence, pain, and suffering. Although the progression unfolds here from the least severe to the most severe, it could just as easily unfold in the opposite direction. Most Americans can locate their own experiences as children and their experiences as parents or grandparents somewhere along this spectrum. Very few of us have never had any experience whatsoever with any kind of physical punishment. Thus it is important to begin with some stories about people whose childhood discipline either was not physical at all or only rarely involved being hit and physically hurt.

Moral Suasion and Nonviolence

The Reverend Lyman Abbott was born in Massachusetts in 1835, the son of the Reverend Jacob Abbott whose books on child-rearing were among the most influential in the post–Civil War era. Lyman Abbott recalled in his *Reminiscences* (1915): "I do not remember that he ever punished me. Yet I not only do not recall that I ever thought of disobeying him, but I do not remember ever to have seen a child refuse him obedience, and I have seen him with a great many young people of all ages and temperaments." He attributed this compliance to his father's *"moral power,"* which clearly did not depend upon physical force to be effective.[3] Throughout his long and active career, Lyman Abbott was among the most liberal preachers of the post–Civil War era, an advocate of evolution and a believer in the immanence of God. According to his biographer, "Moderation and mediation were the secrets" of his "character."[4] Given his father's views on discipline, however, it is entirely possible that Abbott experienced some form of corporal punishment early in his life, before his conscious memory began; or his memories, when in his eighties, might have been glossed over.[5] But the evidence of both his character and his career suggest the truth of his conviction that discipline in his own childhood was benign and unphysical.

One of Abbott's contemporaries, the Reverend Dwight Moody, who became the most famous evangelist of the late nineteenth century, was one of those rare parents who do not discipline their children as they themselves have been disciplined. Although he had been whipped as a boy, he did not choose to inflict similar pains on his own children. As his son William noted:

> To these whippings Mr. Moody always referred with great approval, but with delightful inconsistency never adopted the same measures in the government of his own family. In his home grace was the ruling principle and not law, and the sorest punishment of a child was the sense that the father's loving heart had been grieved by waywardness or folly.[6]

Dwight Moody's son, Paul, later confirmed this observation in his autobiography. One of Paul Moody's most vivid memories was of an incident that occurred when he "was quite young." He was playing in the kitchen with a friend who had stopped by after his normal bedtime hour. His father observed this, and then returned shortly and commanded him to go to bed. Paul Moody recalled:

> This time I retreated immediately and in tears, for it was an almost unheard-of thing that he should speak with such directness or give an order unaccompanied by a smile. But I had barely gotten into my little bed before he was kneeling beside it in tears and seeking my forgiveness for having spoken so harshly. He never, he said, intended to speak crossly to one of his children.[7]

Paul Moody's childhood experience remained embedded in his consciousness years later, and he acknowledged the impact that this encounter with his father had upon his religious life thereafter:

> Half a century must have passed since then and while it is not the earliest of my recollections I think it is the most vivid, and I can still see that room in the twilight and that large bearded figure with

the great shoulders bowed above me, and hear the broken voice and the tenderness in it. I like best to think of him that way. Before then and after I saw him holding the attention of thousands of people, but asking the forgiveness of his unconsciously disobedient little boy for having spoken harshly seemed to me then and seems now a finer and a greater thing, and to it I owe more than I owe to any of his sermons. For to this I am indebted for an understanding of the meaning of the Fatherhood of God, and a belief in the love of God had its beginnings that night in my childish mind.[8]

In the Moody family, the pattern of corporal punishments, undoubtedly passed from generation to generation on his mother's side, was broken with the children who wrote with such affection and loyalty about their eminent evangelist father, whose ministry reached vast numbers of people on both sides of the Atlantic. Dwight Moody's experiences with pain and punishment were not transmitted to the generation to come. The Moody family, however, was an exception to the general rule, which has shaped American family life, that we do to our children what was done to ourselves.

Harry Emerson Fosdick, one of the most prominent and influential liberal preachers of the twentieth century, grew up in a household very similar to the one described by the Moody sons. Fosdick was minister to the Riverside Church in New York, writing and preaching for decades as one of the most outspoken opponents of fundamentalism of his generation. His memories depict a childhood in which pain was minimal and terror virtually unknown:

Many a time in later years, hearing expounded some new, progressive idea concerning the rearing of children, I have wondered why it was called new, because it was the familiar method of my childhood's home. We were a democratic family from the start. Among my earliest recollections are family conferences where all of us were called together to talk over some problem which concerned the whole household. We youngsters were invited to say what we thought. I never recall feeling that commands were handed down to me by a dictator. . . . So from the beginning we were trained for independence. That was the end and aim of our upbringing—to throw us on our own and enable us to handle ourselves.[9]

Fosdick's own memories, however, are supplemented by family stories that modify his recollections in important ways. He described his experiences with authority and discipline in some detail:

> Far from lessening paternal authority this method strengthened it. To feel that by unwise, wrong behavior we had let down our parents who had trusted us to be wise and right was in itself so severe a punishment that other kinds were superfluous. I recall no corporal chastisement, although tradition has it that when I was a mere toddler my father spanked me for strewing a set of Shakespeare on the floor after he had told me not to; and once I remember being shut up in a closet until a spell of bad temper was under control. Paternal authority, however, was uniformly of another sort. Starting for school one morning my father turned to my mother, who was waving him good-by, and said: "Tell Harry he can cut the grass today, if he feels like it." Then after a few steps he turned back and added: "Tell Harry he had better feel like it!"

Fosdick believed that this was "the best advice ever given me."[10]

As Fosdick's biographer, Robert Miller, observes, the Fosdick family was typical of Moderates—and bending the will rather than breaking it was the pattern discernible in all their lives.[11] Corporal punishments played no significant role in the lives of the Fosdick children. But it is notable, nevertheless, that Fosdick's own memory did not include the one story told over the years in the family that reveals the presence of physical punishment and pain in very early childhood. Not remembering is no guarantee that such punishments never took place.

Harry Emerson Fosdick's memories of childhood were shared by his brother, Raymond B. Fosdick, who became president of the Rockefeller Foundation in 1935. He recalled that the

> fascination [of his father's] life was children. To his own children he was a source of endless delight, entering into their games, wrestling with his sons and even with his daughter, fishing with them on the Niagara River or in the deep pools of the Chautauqua Gulf. Anything that children did seemed to interest him.

Raymond Fosdick also noted that "no children ever took advantage of him. He expected obedience and obtained it without difficulty. Punishments he abhorred. There was something about him—a dignity, a presence, a sudden steely look in his eyes—which instantly froze any tendency to impertinence."[12] Raymond Fosdick, too, recalled no experiences with corporal punishments. In the autobiographical memories of these two sons, physical discipline played no significant role in the shaping of their characters or lives.

The power of moral suasion, as well as its potential coerciveness, was evident in the memories of Benjamin Spock concerning discipline in his own childhood. Although baptized an Episcopalian, he went to a Congregationalist Sunday school as a boy. He notes that his "Mother was not strongly religious in the sense of being a church-goer," although she did attend Easter services, among others.[13] In terms of discipline, he observed:

> I remember having been spanked only once or twice when I was a child. It was done gravely by my father—on the recommendation of my mother—with the back of a hairbrush to the palm of my hand. I can still recall the awful fear and guilt that hung over me between the time when my mother pronounced the sentence and the hour when my father came home from work and carried it out.

Ordinarily, however, he was disciplined without physical punishments. He remembers that

> for all the rest of my childhood I was held firmly in line by my mother's stern rulings and even sterner disapproval. She didn't just disapprove of an act. Her facial expression was intended to convey withdrawal of love—for the time being, anyway—and the substitution of condemnation and some anger. It's what I call moral discipline, used in an unnecessarily severe form in my mother's case, its purpose being to make the child feel guilty.[14]

Fear, anxiety, and guilt can be induced in many children without the application of physical force, especially when "moral discipline" threatens to make a child, like young Spock, feel unloved. He, at least, became convinced that he and his six siblings "grew up with a more severe conscience and a greater sense of guilt than was necessary or healthy."[15] Moral suasion, in this form, at least, can have enduring effects just as surely as can physical discipline, even one or two instances of which, however, caused Spock to feel fear as a boy.

Before Conscious Memory Begins

When painful blows are inflicted upon infants, not even memory suffices to tell the stories firsthand. Accounts must be provided either by those who chose to inflict the pain or by witnesses who observed the punishments. The body and the brain probably encode such pain, but none of us has any conscious recollection of blows experienced very early in life. Yet we know now, as never before, just how frequent such physical punishments are. The battered-child syndrome, brought to public awareness by C. Henry Kempe and his colleagues in 1962, has roots that reach back centuries.[16] Assaults against infants in the name of punishment and discipline have been taking place seemingly forever.

John and Charles Wesley, the founders of Methodism in the mid-eighteenth century in England, were undoubtedly victims of painful blows by their mother and other adults from early infancy. We know this because their mother, Susanna Wesley, herself the daughter of Puritans and the wife of an Anglican rector, wrote a letter to her son John in 1732 detailing her personal methods of child-rearing for his edification and use. Even today, her letter is widely quoted among evangelical Protestants concerned with child-rearing and discipline. Her viewpoint still has a receptive audience, two and a half centuries later.

Susanna Wesley recalled that her infants had been "put into a regular method of living" from the outset, in their patterns of sleeping, eating, and dressing, an experience that was to have profound consequences for the characters of John and Charles Wesley, who reshaped the contours of English and American Anglicanism into the rituals and beliefs that ultimately became part of the Methodist Church. But Susanna Wesley was insistent upon harsh physical punishment from a very early age: "When turned a year old (and some before) they were taught to fear the rod and to cry softly, by which means they escaped abundance of correction which they might otherwise have had: and that most odious noise of the crying of children was rarely heard in the house, but the family usually lived in as much quietness as if there had not been a child among them."[17] Her hostility toward her infant children and her willingness to enforce her control through assaults and violence in order to silence them through fear of pain is clear.

The use of the "rod," begun with the physical assaults in infancy, persisted throughout John's and Charles's childhoods, and the pain and repressiveness that began in the cradle continued to dominate the experiences of children in Susanna Wesley's household. Beatings were a normal part of daily life. She observed: "Drinking or eating between meals was never allowed, unless in case of sickness, which seldom happened. Nor were they suffered to go into the kitchen to ask anything of the servants when they were at meat: if it was known they did so, they were certainly beat, and the servants severely reprimanded."[18] She insisted "that no sinful action, as lying, pilfering at church or on the Lord's Day, disobedience, quarrelling, etc., should ever pass unpunished."[19] Punishment thus was a central theme in the Wesley household, dominated for years by the mother who shaped the characters of her children through the persistent use of pain and rigorous control from infancy. She was intent upon the domination of her children's wills from the cradle, convinced that only through the use of the rod and the infliction of pain could such submission and obedience be obtained.

Contemporaneously, across the Atlantic in New England, Jonathan Edwards and his intensely pious wife, Sarah, were raising their children in a remarkably similar manner, beginning in infancy and continuing until the children's wills were entirely under parental control. Edwards's grandson, Sereno Dwight, wrote about the child-rearing methods used by Sarah Edwards:

> She had an excellent way of governing her children; she knew how to make them regard and obey her cheerfully, without loud angry words, much less heavy blows. She seldom punished them; and in speaking to them, used gentle and pleasant words. If any correction was necessary, she did not administer it [physical punishment] in a passion; and when she had occasion to reprove and rebuke, she would do it in few words, without warmth or noise, and with all calmness and gentleness of mind.

He added the crucial observation, parallel to Susanna Wesley's method of inflicting pain on infants while still in the cradle, that

Her system of discipline, was *begun at a very early age*, and it was her rule, to *resist the first*, as well as every subsequent exhibition of temper or disobedience in the child, *however young*, until its will was brought into submission to the will of its parents: wisely reflecting, that until a child will obey his parents, he can never be brought to obey God [emphasis added].[20]

The methods of discipline implied in this grandson's account are detailed explicitly in the words of Jonathan and Sarah Edwards's daughter, Esther Edwards Burr, who became the wife of the Reverend Aaron Burr, president of Princeton. In 1754 she reported to her best friend, Sarah Prince:

I had almost forgot to tell you that I have begun to govourn Sally [her firstborn child]. She has been Whip'd once on *Old Adams* account, and she knows the differance betwen a smile and a frown as well as I do. When she has done any thing that she Surspects is wrong, will look with concern to see what Mama says, and if I only knit my brow she will cry till I smile, and altho She is not quite Ten months old, yet when she knows so much, I think tis time she should be taught.[21]

By starting her physical discipline of her daughter when the child was nine months old, Esther Burr surely was repeating the experiences she had had as a child herself, thus following her mother's practice of resisting "the first, as well as every subsequent exhibition of temper or disobedience in the child, however young."

In the Edwards and Burr families, corporal punishments began in infancy, and thus pain was encountered before conscious memory began. In this family, at least, the observations recorded many years later were confirmed by the mother's actual testimony to her most intimate friend, revealing in one rare document what appears to have been a consistent practice within the Edwards family over at least two generations. Painful punishments, so central to the theology of her father, the most articulate rationalizer and defender of eternal punishment in American history, began in his family before the first year of life had been completed. By the time the Edwards children, like the Wesley children, had conscious memories, they had already experienced much pain purposefully inflicted by the mothers who loved and cared for them. Infancy was the beginning but rarely the end of such punishments.

Memories of Pain and Punishments

The puritanical preoccupation with discipline and obedience characteristic of the Wesleys, the Edwardses, and the Burrs was evident throughout
the childhood of Dwight Moody, the post–Civil War American revivalist
whose own disciplinary methods have been described already. Born in
1837 in Northfield, Massachusetts, the son of "a stonemason with a small
farm" who "was a genial, shiftless, lazy fellow" and also "addicted to more
whiskey than was good for his heart," and a mother (described by her
grandson as "completely the Puritan") who "seemed to be afraid of spoiling us, for she was certainly never remarkably demonstrative and . . .
suffered our filial kisses with a sort of grim resignation," Dwight grew
up knowing the pain of physical punishments.[22] His eldest son, William,
who became his official biographer after his death, observed:

> While the mother was truly kind and loving she was withal a strict
> disciplinarian. Order was enforced by rules, with old-fashioned whip-
> pings as a penalty. These events were more or less frequent in the
> case of Dwight, who was the leader in all kinds of boyish mischief.
> In later years he described these punishments and his futile attempts
> to escape them:
> "Mother would send me out for a stick, and I thought I could fool
> her and get a dead one. But she would snap the stick and then tell
> me to get another. She was rarely in a hurry, and certainly never when
> she was whipping me. Once I told her that the whipping did not hurt
> at all. I never had occasion to tell her so again, for she put it on so it
> did hurt."[23]

Although his mother later lived nearby and he never once criticized her
methods of punishment, he himself chose not to use physical punishments with his own children.

Nearly a century later, the Reverend Jack Hyles, a successful
fundamentalist Baptist evangelist-preacher, first in Texas and later in
Indiana, remembered encounters with his mother's switch throughout

his childhood. In his book, *How to Rear Children* (1972), he described his experiences as a small boy:

> When I think of the old peach tree I think of Mother walking back from it with a branch in her hand, peeling the leaves off as she came. I then recall her using that switch to spank my little bare legs. I can still see the stripes often left by that switch, and I thank God for every one of them. Today I call her "blessed" because of her faithfulness to the teaching of God and her willingness to obey Him. Placing stripes on me as a child kept me from bearing more painful ones as an adult.[24]

His experiences and Moody's were virtually indistinguishable, switching being a common method of discipline throughout the land.

The experiences recollected by the Reverend Nickels J. Holmes, one of the earliest Pentecostals in the South in the late nineteenth century, were very similar to those recalled by Dwight Moody and Jack Hyles, although the implement was different. Holmes was born in 1847 in Spartansburg, South Carolina, the eldest son of a transplanted New Yorker who became a Presbyterian preacher and slaveowner. He lived his early life on a large plantation surrounded by numerous brothers and sisters and a large group of black slaves. Holmes's earliest memory of school was that "I was a bad boy, hard to manage, and that there was another boy at school who was worse than I was. We used to get whippings together." His experiences with switchings at school mirrored those at home, where corporal punishment was taken for granted as the proper biblical method of discipline. Holmes recalled:

> My father was a real Presbyterian preacher and believed that children should be taught to do right, corrected when wrong, and memorize the Shorter Catechism. My mother was an earnest, pious Christian woman who loved her children and was good to them, but she wanted them to be good, and had read what Solomon said about spoiling the child; and she did not want her children spoiled, so she did not hesitate to use the remedy which Solomon suggested. In fact, our parents thought that the older children should be made models or examples for the younger ones to follow, and they undertook the task with the fear of God in their hearts. They were never harsh or angry with their children, but with firmness and decision settled matters with them.

They used the same rod with their children that they did with their little colored slaves. They were kind to their slaves and thoughtful of their comfort and welfare, but they taught them obedience and righteousness.[25]

Physical punishments were an integral part of the childhood memories of Aimee Semple McPherson, who became one of the most flamboyant Pentecostal evangelists in the first half of this century and the founder of the Foursquare Gospel Church in Los Angeles, California. Her parents were Canadian; her mother was raised in a family active in the Salvation Army and her father, a farmer in Ontario, was raised a Methodist. Born in 1890, Aimee McPherson grew up in an intensely religious household. She later recalled:

Like all other restless youngsters, I was constantly getting into dilemmas and difficulties. After similar outrages to the dignity of my household, I would be banished to my room and told that in exactly one-half an hour I would be spanked. I was thoroughly familiar with those whippings. They were no gentle love pats, and my parents never stopped till I was a thoroughly chastised girl.

The time of waiting for the footsteps on the stair, the opening of the door, and the descending palm was the worst of all. On one such occasion I stood looking wildly about for a way out of the dilemma. No earthly recourse was nigh. Taught as I was about heavenly intervention, I thought of prayer. Dropping to my knees on the side of my bed, I began to pray, loudly, earnestly. "Oh, God, don't let mama whip me! Oh, God, dear, kind, sweet God, don't let mama spank me!"[26]

On this one occasion, at least, her prayers were answered and she was spared the whipping she had anticipated so anxiously. But such punishments were evidently familiar experiences throughout her early childhood. Her son, however, reported that she herself did not repeat such punishments when she became a parent, choosing to rear her own children "diplomatically rather than through any means of punishment."[27]

Billy Graham, one of the most influential evangelists of this century, also has vivid memories of the punishments inflicted upon him as a child. Graham was born on a farm in North Carolina in 1918, the eldest son of Frank and Morrow Coffey Graham, a descendant of many generations of

Scottish Presbyterians whose roots reached back to prerevolutionary Carolina. His parents were not particularly devout Christians during his early life. He recalls that " 'They went to church, but beyond that they never talked religion. They never acted religious.' "[28] His encounters with discipline, however, persisted throughout his childhood. As Marshall Frady, Graham's biographer, observes:

> His father would sometimes withdraw a wide leather belt to apply to him, once when he was discovered with a plug of chewing tobacco bulging in his cheek, another time snatching him up from a church pew where Billy had been fretfully squirming, shoving him on out into the vestibule and there strapping him thoroughly. Over all the years since then, Billy maintains, what he still remembers most about his father is the feel of his hands against him: "They were like rawhide, bony, rough. He had such hard hands." In one instance, after Billy had gained some size, his father stood over him flailing away with the belt as Billy was lying on his back, and "I broke two of his ribs, kicking with my legs."[29]

Such resistance, however, must have been quite rare, since the central memories are not of opposition, but submission to the pains being inflicted by his father and mother.

> He was also occasionally whistled with a long hickory switch by his mother—"But," he says, "I never fought back with her." Mrs. Graham reflects now, "Mr. Graham was right stern, I suppose. Perhaps we were both a little too strict, perhaps we whipped them more than we should have. But it was just that we had to work so hard then, we had little time for anything else, we had too little patience. We thought that little disobediences, you know, were terrible things."[30]

Her son learned this lesson well, for he has spent much of his life convincing others that "little disobediences" are "terrible things," with consequences that eventually will lead sinners to eternal life in hell, suffering the torments of the damned forever.

The possibility of going too far, of hurting or maiming a child, crossed Graham's mother's mind on at least one occasion. At times, though, she must have thought that her husband was being too harsh, since she "winced" and cried when she saw what her husband was doing to their children. Yet she apparently did not intervene to halt the punishments being belted out. Although she obviously felt empathy for their pain and suffering, she also believed that her children's suffering was deserved and necessary.[31]

Billy Graham later recollected these childhood punishments while he stood preaching before several thousand people. On one occasion in 1976, captured on a videotape, Graham stood alone on a high platform surrounded by a vast audience while preaching on the topic of Christian homes and family life. He told them about his experiences with punishment, both in terms of his own children and himself as a child. At one point in his sermon, Graham, Bible in hand high in the air, suddenly pretended to whip off his belt, just as his father must have done so many times in the years long past. Seeing him mime his childhood experiences of being belted by his father is an unforgettable image.[32]

Oral Roberts, born in Arkansas in 1918, shares Billy Graham's experiences with childhood pain from corporal punishments. Oral Roberts has vivid memories of being strapped by his Pentecostal-preacher father. In his autobiography, he recalls a particularly painful incident, which began during one of his father's sermons. While Oral and his brother Vaden lay on a pallet, listening to their father preach, another boy pulled on their pallet, which angered them. Then, Oral Roberts recalled, "Vaden said, 'If you touch our pallet again, I will cut your ear off.' " When the boy replied that Vaden did not have " 'the nerve,' " Roberts later commented that "He didn't know Vaden like I did." After being provoked again, "Vaden had his knife out and was cutting the little boy's right ear off" while Oral held him. Their father heard the boy's scream, stopped preaching, and "said 'Boys!' I knew the judgment had dawned," Roberts recalled.

> We sat down on the altar bench and awaited the verdict of the judge. In a moment he pronounced the sentence. "When I get you two boys home," Papa said, "I will tend to you."
>
> Papa believed in the stars and stripes. He put on the stripes and Vaden and I saw the stars. When he got us home he took down his big razor strap. It was made in two pieces. When he got through with us, we believed it had a thousand pieces.[33]

Corporal punishments continued to be the rule in the Roberts family when Oral and Evelyn Roberts became parents. Evelyn Roberts also spent most of her childhood in a Pentecostal family (her stepfather, too, was a preacher). In her autobiography, she recalled experiences with punishments during the years their children were growing up:

> I know our children felt Oral and I were hard on them, but they never doubted our stand on what we felt was right. When we had family discussions, all of this came out.
>
> Usually I disciplined the children because I had to. But there were times when I waited for Oral to come home. He often accused me of meeting him at the door with, "Here's a switch. Whip these children."
>
> He said, "My children hate to see me come in the door because they know you are going to say, 'Switch these children. They've been acting bad since you've been gone.'"
>
> I'm sure it may have seemed that way at times, but there were some things for which I felt *he* should discipline them. I wanted the children to know that their father didn't approve of some of the things they were doing. And I wanted them to know that he was as much of a disciplinarian as I was.[34]

In the Roberts family, as in so many others, physical punishments were passed on from generation to generation.

If the Roberts children had reason to feel, as their mother believed, that their parents had been "hard on them," Kathryn Kuhlman surely had equal cause for such a conviction. Kuhlman became one of the rare women evangelists of the mid-twentieth century. Both as a healer and as a preacher, on stage and on television, Kuhlman had an extraordinary career, preaching the doctrines of the Holy Spirit, acting as a conduit for the healing grace of God while ministering to thousands across the land, and awaiting the imminent end of the world in an apocalyptic holocaust. Her character and her faith were shaped by the memories of her conflicted childhood, with its pains and its longings.

Kathryn Kuhlman was born in 1907 near Concordia, Missouri, of German descent on her father's side. Her father was a well-to-do businessman and a nominal Baptist.[35] Her mother was a Methodist, a churchgoer, and an obsessive person who never allowed herself to be seen casually dressed, even at breakfast. Although Kuhlman's father appar-

ently never spanked her, her mother often did. According to Jamie Buckingham, her biographer, who interviewed her at length about her
childhood experiences, including those involving discipline, "There
seems to be ample proof that Kathryn deserved all those spankings she
got as a child." Once, when Kuhlman was about nine years old, she gave
her mother a surprise birthday party, which happened to coincide with
washday, a ritual in her household. Her mother was totally unprepared
for the arrival of women bringing gifts, and her anger toward her daughter
was immense. According to Buckingham, "Emma Kuhlman had the rest
of the afternoon to plan her punishment." Later "that evening, as soon
as the last woman departed, mama grabbed the guilty culprit by the arm
and yanked her down the cellar steps. Kathryn later said that even though
they had enough cake to eat for two weeks, she had to do most of her
eating standing up, so great was mama's wrath." Buckingham adds that
Kathryn Kuhlman's father "never understood Emma's harsh disciplinary
treatment."[36]

The irony was that Kuhlman from early childhood had a desperate
need to please others. Nevertheless, her childhood was punctuated by
encounters with punishment and pain, those sessions in the basement
remaining imprinted upon her memory years after the handprints on her
body had faded and disappeared. Her psyche and her spiritual life would
bear the marks of these early encounters with pain, inflicted by a mother
who was never once able to acknowledge any love for her daughter.

Physical discipline was common in the Wilkerson family, according
to the recollections of the Reverend David Wilkerson and his sister, Ruth
Wilkerson Harris. David Wilkerson, an apocalyptic Pentecostal evangelist
like his father and grandfather, still has vivid memories of his boyhood
experiences with punishments. He often went to the top of a small mountain near his home, particularly when he was in trouble and needed a
refuge, and he recalls:

> From Old Baldy, I could look down on our house and watch Mother
> and Dad and the other children running around the neighborhood
> trying to find me. Sometimes I would stay up there for the better part
> of a day, thinking through the problems a boy has to conquer. When
> I got back, I always got a licking, but Dad's switch never kept me
> from making my journey again, because up there I found an aloofness
> and a detachment that I needed.[37]

His sister, Ruth Wilkerson Harris, tells another version of the same story. She recalls in her history of the Wilkerson family that "We had some classic spankings in our Hall of Disfame." One day her brother David, angered at having to wash "dishes," left home and went up to the top of the mountain, while his family looked for him in vain. When he finally returned, he was given nothing to eat and was ignored by everyone. "Finally, Dad walked out the front door and said, 'Alright, son, up to the room.' As always, King Solomon's discipline theory brought about a painful, but peaceful settlement."[38]

Both Ruth Wilkerson Harris and David Wilkerson have written about their persistent memories of encounters with their father's leather strap. Ruth Harris described her childhood experiences in detail:

> I do believe that ours was the only parsonage that could boast of personalized prayer, monogrammed with a razor strap. Dad never took a course in child psychology, but the very personal prayer sessions he used with his discipline methods proved he was master of the subject. His motto for these therapy sessions was: "Spare the rod and spoil the child," and he spared not because of our crying, either! Those who have married into our family are inclined to disbelieve me when I say we definitely were not the typical P. K. Rascals. They don't seem to know how much a three-inch-wide leather strap can hurt![39]

The pains she recalled so vividly were remembered with equal clarity by her brother. Despite his efforts as a boy to avoid being hit and despite his loud vocal outbursts when being disciplined, his protests did not stop his father's blows.[40] Immediately after being strapped, the Wilkerson children were expected to seek the forgiveness of both their Father in heaven and their own father, who had just punished them.[41] As Ruth Wilkerson Harris recollects:

> Dad used prayer both as a soothing balm and to make sure the whipping took. We just weren't allowed to cry and go off then, and pout. No! Our rebellious spirits were humbled even more when we were told to put our arms around Dad's neck and say, if we *could* in our grief, "I love you, Daddy. Forgive me for disobeying." Then Dad would tell us, "I love you too, but now we must ask God to help you overcome your stubbornness."[42]

Love and pain, rebellion and submission, disobedience, punishment, and
forgiveness thus were intertwined in a powerful mixture of opposing
feelings and experiences.

Sometimes punishments with belts, rods, and other implements used
by adults on their children do visible physical harm to their bodies. Images
of bloody weals and loosened skin recur in a number of recollections and
descriptions of childhood punishments. The Reverend A. E. Humbard,
a Pentecostal preacher who grew up poor on the Arkansas farm of a
hardworking father (who married three times and had a total of thirteen
children), remembered that "Once, after my father and stepmother had
some trouble and there was trouble between the children, why, to please
her he had taken a spite out on me and whipped me till I could not talk,
and my clothes were all bloody." He also remembered that "The night
before this happened I had awakened and at the foot of my bed saw a
man standing, with a bloody sheet wrapped around him. I saw this three
times and then it disappeared. Of course," he concluded, "this was a
warning to me of what would happen to me the next day."[43] Walter
Mondale's father, a Methodist preacher, used various punishments for
his son, including corporal punishments. Once "Reverend Mondale
marched his son into the brush, let him pick a keen switch, and then
whipped him until blood appeared."[44] Frank Norris, one of the most
aggressive and violent fundamentalist preachers of the early twentieth
century, was brutalized by his father, an impoverished alcoholic share-
cropper. "Poverty, punishment, and pain characterized the lad's youth
and appear to have molded his personality," a biographer noted. "On one
occasion Norris' father disciplined his son so severely that the boy's nose
was broken and his body severely lacerated."[45] Tammy Bakker remembers seeing her stepfather "beat" her brother and stepbrother "with a belt
until he drew blood on their backs" for having thrown "a hammer" at
their "pet duck." "To this day," she noted in her autobiography, "I can
see my mother, tears streaming down her face, wiping the blood off my
brothers' backs, and my father hating himself for beating them like he
did."[46] Although she says nothing about her own experiences with discipline, seeing her brothers being beaten bloody remained indelibly imprinted in her memory from childhood. A child does not have to bear the
scars and marks in order to be traumatized by witnessing the infliction
of such severe and bloody discipline on others.

Family violence often accompanies the infliction of harsh physical punishments. In countless instances, poverty, hunger, humiliation, and shame combined with recurrent domestic conflicts, fueled but not caused by alcohol, have warped and embittered the early lives of individuals, generation after generation, century after century. One such person was Asa A. Allen, who later became a popular and successful Pentecostal evangelist and healer. The punishments that he encountered as a boy took place in a drunken, violent, and often terrifying family. Allen began his autobiography by remembering that

> I wasn't raised, just jerked up by the hair of the head, backwoods style.
> The only training I got was to hate people.
> I loved nobody, not even my mother and father.
> Nobody loved me.
> I never knew anyone that loved anyone else.[47]

Allen was born in 1911 on a failing farm in Arkansas, the youngest of seven children; his mother had married at fourteen and his father was "an alcoholic of Scotch-Irish descent whose pathetic forty acres was too small to support a family of nine."[48] His father soon gave up farming and moved to town, while his mother surreptitiously entertained other men in his father's absence. Both parents and children drank whiskey constantly. Allen recalled: "When my father was home his drinking triggered violence. He would rage at my mother and pick up chairs and fling them at her. Anybody who was in the way got hit. 'Run, children, run,' my mother would scream on these occasions."[49]

Allen's memory of these early years was that "the good moments were far outweighed by the bad."[50] When he reached the age of five, his mother, having divorced his father, took him to another town to live. Her second husband, like the first, was an alcoholic. Allen recalled that "If I ever forgot one of my chores, which I did occasionally," his stepfather "whacked the tar out of me."[51] Since he never had "a real mattress" until his adolescence, he would often lie down on his mother's bed to "enjoy its cloudlike softness, always careful afterwards to smooth out the covers so that John wouldn't have the excuse of beating me for disturbing his bed."[52]

The enduring poverty left permanent scars, as Allen and his brothers and sisters "developed inferiority complexes because we seemed to be the poorest kids around," with no shoes, ragged clothes, and inadequate food. His mother, in addition, was a violent and unpredictable woman who always carried "the armor of a bandit" whenever she left the house.[53] Allen was always expecting his mother and her husband to kill one another. "The battles between them had a punishing effect on me," he recalled. "By the time I was eleven, I felt I could no longer live in an atmosphere that was more akin to an armed camp than a home."[54] He also remembered "arguments so terrifying that I took to slipping out of the house and spending nights with a neighbor or a friend rather than witness yet another pitched battle."[55] In such a family, being beaten and punished were so much a part of the scene that Allen himself mentions them only incidentally, in passing, so much does he take his own personal suffering and bodily pain for granted. But A. A. Allen's story could be repeated countless times across the land and through the generations.

Most children suffer the pain of punishment inflicted by adults within their own families and households, without public knowledge, concern, or protection. Occasionally, however, the assaults and violence against children done in the name of discipline become public knowledge, and the courts or other public officials intervene to protect the interests of the child or children being assaulted and abused in the guise of discipline. Two remarkably similar cases, more than half a century apart in time but surprisingly alike in their commitment to severe and painful corporal punishments, focus the issues latent in domestic experiences of cruelty and abuse. Both cases involve apocalyptic fundamentalist sects in northern New England—one in Durham, Maine, the other in Island Pond, Vermont—and in both situations public authorities intervened in an effort to protect children from alleged abuse arising from corporal punishments.

At Shiloh in Durham, Maine, during the late 1890s and early 1900s, the Holy Ghost and Us Bible School, housed in a sprawling wooden Victorian building, provided the center for the Reverend Frank Sandford's apocalyptic sect, known after 1904 as The Kingdom. The Church of the Living God, as it was also called, was founded and dominated by Sandford alone. His authoritarian rule, based upon biblical principles in a literalist and Pentecostal mode, provided the core of repressiveness evident in so many aspects of the lives of the men, women, and children—for many families lived there—who gave all their worldly possessions and wealth to the church when they came to live at Shiloh. Corporal punishments and the beating of children were apparently daily experiences. Fasting by everyone, from infants to the elderly, was also frequent. The entire community submitted their wills to that of Frank Sandford, their prophet and leader. Obedience to authority was the central premise of the entire school and community, but the rule of God was interpreted by one man alone. Through him the voice of God spoke, and his followers obeyed.

Life at Shiloh in the early 1900s was portrayed vividly in a remarkable memoir written by Arnold White, whose entire family moved there when he was a boy of twelve. He notes that "the rigid, even harsh, training often meted out to Shiloh children was not long in taking form. Some of the young women who were engaged as nursemaids for children of the ministers, including Sandford's own family, have told heart-wringing stories of brutal punishment meted out to children too small to understand what it was all about." His wife told him of

one of those first ordained ministers who whipped his baby boy of two years again and again until he was so bruised she, the family nurse-maid at the time, wept as she bathed the child's cruel welts. Apparently the baby did not understand his father's repeated commands. Lack of obedience resulted in the conclusion that the child was "stubborn." This young father thought it important to "break a child's spirit," beginning at an early age.[56]

Similar experiences were reported by a woman who had come from Tacoma, Washington, in 1902 to join the group in Shiloh with her husband and three children. In 1904, after leaving Shiloh, she observed that "There is no natural affection among the people or families. All are cold, uncompromising and terrible. No pity is shown for each other, nor mercy in any respect." She recalled that

When the babies fasted they went forty hours without food or water. This included all the nursing babies. I should think there must have been about forty in all. In the room right over my head I could hear them crying and it sounded like a flock of little lambs. I called one of the ministers to the door to listen to them, but he laughed and said it was the devil in the babies. I was sick at the time with nervous prostration brought on by hearing a boy being whipped by somebody, his father, I assume.

He was made to get up at 1 o'clock in the night and whipped until

someone went in and stopped it. His screams awoke most of the people
in that section. Almost any time you could hear some children being
whipped, and the rules were that he must be whipped until there was
no doubt in the mind of anyone that he was conquered.[57]

On another occasion, a minor act of impertinence on the part of Frank
Sandford's six-year-old son, John, ultimately led to a charge of cruelty
and child abuse by the state of Maine "under the statute that makes it
criminal for a parent to cruelly treat a child or abuse it in such a manner
as to cause it unnecessary pain and suffering."[58] After John's sixth birthday, his father "expressed to him a desire that the following year he live
a perfect Sabbatical life and approach as near as possible to perfect holy
living." His father later "found him associating" with people of whom
"he did not approve," which "displeased" him.

John was also said to have been impertinent to his mother. John
was accordingly taken and told in substance that he should undergo
a severe whipping; that it didn't make any difference what the whipping was to be, whether severe or not he must come to believe that
he must accept it. The upshot of it was that John was ordered to fast
until willing to walk up and submit to the whipping. And furthermore
it was to be [an] absolute fast—no food, no water. This fast was begun
Feb. 14th, 1903.

It endured 72 full hours. During the fast John stayed in this room
where food and water or water at least was in sight. He continually
cried or asked for water. The evidence is that this water was not refused
to him when he called for it but there was ever before him that in-
genious method of indicating the whipping ahead of him and the
species of control over the mind of the little child that he was constantly
impressed with the question if he hadn't better go through and put
the whipping off until the next day.

After fasting three days and "growing weaker," Sandford's son was

taken to the room with his father and in the presence of others asked
if he was willing to take the whipping. He had reached a state of mind
where he was willing to take any thing for a change. He was told then
that the whipping might be severe. He was informed that if it touched

and hurt his hands[,] he must remember that the hands of Jesus were pierced by nails; if it beat his arms[,] that Christ's arms were stretched upon the Cross; that if it was on his feet, Jesus' feet were nailed; that if it was upon his back[,] so upon the back of Jesus was laid the scourge.

The boy decided to take the whipping just the same rather than the continued fast. He had been brought to a terrible tension for a six-year-old babe. He was willing to take the punishment and accordingly was informed that the Lord had taken the punishment for him and that he would himself be excused.[59]

Although Sandford's son was spared the actual whipping, the total fast continued until the following day. Subsequently, the Reverend Sandford was convicted of cruelty to his child and fined $100. Immediately following this trial, however, he was indicted for manslaughter in the death of a fifteen-year-old boy at Shiloh, who had died of diphtheria while being forced to fast. No judgment was reached in this case, but the prosecutor for the state clearly believed that Sandford had been responsible for the death of his young follower.[60] The state of Maine was prepared in 1904 to seek to protect children from abuse and cruelty by parents or parental surrogates.

Seventy years later, on June 22, 1984, a large group of Vermont state officials, including police officers and social workers, participated in an early-morning raid on houses associated with the Northeast Kingdom Community Church at Island Pond, Vermont. This was the result of several years of intense but frustrating investigation by the Department of Social and Rehabilitation Services, which is responsible for cases of alleged child abuse and neglect within the state. After being issued a warrant by District Court Judge Joseph Wolchik, the police took into custody 112 children in anticipation of their being examined for signs of physical and emotional abuse. Almost immediately, however, a second judge, Frank Mahady, declared the action to be unconstitutional, and the children were returned to their parents and community. In a previous case, in 1983, involving four children whose parents had been participants in the Northeast Kingdom Community Church, Judge Mahady had declared his opinion that " 'At all material times while the children have been residing at the religious community, they have been subjected to frequent and methodical physical abuse by adult members of the community in the form of hours-long whippings with [wooden] balloon sticks. These beatings result from minor disciplinary infractions,'" the judge noted.[61] Dr. John D. Burchard, commissioner of the Vermont Department of Social and Rehabilitation Services at the time of this incident, observed that "Physical abuse is defined in the law as permanent or temporary disfigurement or impairment of any bodily organ or function by other than accidental means. Any person who reads the published accounts of the disciplinary practices of the church must believe there is reasonable evidence that child abuse may have occurred."[62] Despite the official concern that abuse of children may have occurred at Island Pond, by the end of 1989 the Vermont state authorities had taken no further legal action to ascertain whether such abuse occurred within the Northeast Kingdom Community Church at Island Pond. The complex constitutional issues raised by this action and the failure of the Vermont state legislature to enact new laws which would permit such interventions, together with the political controversy arising from the experience, apparently have combined to prevent further investigation by state authorities or other interventions on behalf of the children at Island Pond.

The Northeast Kingdom Community Church is a small apocalyptic sect, founded in 1972 in Chattanooga, Tennessee, as the Vine Christian Community under the leadership of Elbert Eugene Spriggs. According to various observers, the members are convinced that the end of the world is imminent, and that they alone will be spared the holocaust to come. Their biblical fundamentalism undergirds their commitment to corporal punishments. A statement published by the group declares that "we discipline our children according to the Word of God. We love our children; we do not abuse them; we discipline them." Citing biblical texts from Proverbs, Ephesians, and Hebrews, they observe that "In light of all this the infliction of pain upon a child's rear end with the use of a reedlike rod is not child abuse, but rather their salvation. It is consistent and given with *controlled* severity by the loving hands of the child's parents, unless the parents ask someone else to help and to support them in discipline."[63]

Reports from journalists, observers, and participants agree, however, that harsh corporal punishments are daily routines within the community. Sharon Sexton, a journalist, observed that "The beatings begin when the children are six months old, although infants younger than that have been disciplined. The weapon of choice is a rod, and many members employ thin, flexible sticks—identical to the kind used by street vendors who sell balloons at parks and at zoos. The method of discipline has been prescribed, in exact terms, by the group's leader."[64] Sexton described the experience of one twenty-eight-year-old man who punished a small girl repeatedly for four hours:

> the little girl in the diapers, would not receive her discipline. She cried and cried and [he] kept hitting her, trying to make her tears stop. "I wasn't sure of myself," he recalls, "so I kept calling [a fellow church member]. I'd say, 'She's doing the same thing. I don't know what to do.' He told me, 'You spank her till she breaks.' So I spanked her and I spanked her and I spanked her. I was crying. She was crying. Her parents were crying. I called again. He said: 'Spank her till she breaks.' But [she] didn't break and, after four hours, [he] couldn't continue.[65]

One investigator from the Vermont inquiry into possible abuse at Island Pond interviewed a woman who was formerly a member of the sect concerning the physical punishment of a girl:

> Q: What was [her] condition [after the punishment]?
> A: She was pale, she had red marks all up and down her back and on the backs of her legs, and welts, and she was totally exhausted and her spirit was completely broken.
> Q: All this was because of . . .
> A: A strawberry.[66]

Similar physical marks were alleged to have been left on the body of another child. Her mother provided evidence from a doctor who examined the child and reported " 'positive findings of multiple long, narrow, dis-colored scar-tissue areas of the child's buttocks and posterior thighs— the result of severe blows to this area with a rod-like instrument.' "[67] Her mother said that "She told me she was beaten almost every day" and "was beaten for asking for a second helping of food, for biting a blister in the inside of her mouth. The worst beating she got was when she gave them a flower and said, 'Oh, doesn't this flower smell beautiful?' They told her she was lying, and they stripped her and beat her back, the bottoms of her feet, her stomach, her head."[68]

Such beatings seem to reflect convictions such as the one voiced by an ex-member of the community, who said: " 'You can never over-

discipline. You can under-discipline.' " He described the governing premise of the group: " 'Better that you should beat a child within an inch of
its life than that they would be cast into the Lake of Fire for all eternity.' "[69]
According to the acting leader of the Island Pond community in 1984,
"We do what Jesus requires us to do. . . . We are perfectly prepared to
be judged by our children."[70]

Disciplined to Death

Sometimes assaults and beatings done in the name of discipline are not
only painful and physically harmful, with marks, bruises, welts, and
bloody breakings of skin, cartilage, and bone; they can and do cause the
deaths of children. In recent years, we have become increasingly aware
of the frequency with which both infants and older children die as a
result of blows inflicted by adults. Pediatricians and other doctors, especially those working in emergency rooms in hospitals, see the terrible
injuries too often caused by the infliction of punishments. Death, accidental or intended, is the endpoint on the continuum of coercion, force,
hitting, and violence inherent in physical punishments.

In 1985, a jury found Dorothy McClellan of West Virginia "guilty of
involuntary manslaughter and conspiracy to commit the unlawful wound-
ing of Joseph Green," a twenty-three-month-old boy who had died after
being paddled for two hours by his parents. At the time of Joseph's death,
both Dorothy McClellan and the Greens were residents of Stonegate, a
fundamentalist Christian community established in 1974 by the Mc-
Clellans in a twenty-seven-room Victorian house. Individual families lived
in separate spaces "and children were raised solely by their parents."[71]

The scene that culminated in the boy's death is set forth in some
detail in the appeal McClellan's attorneys made to the Supreme Court:

> On October 5, 1982, two year old Joseph Green died from a spank-
> ing by his parents, Stuart and Leslie Green. Leslie Green began spank-
> ing her son Joseph when he refused to apologize to another two year
> old after striking him. After a period of spanking, Stuart Green, Jo-
> seph's father, entered the room and continued to spank him with a
> paddle while both parents unsuccessfully tried to force Joseph to apol-

ogize to the other boy. After approximately two hours of intermittent spankings, petitioner, who had been out of the sight and sound of the room where the spanking was occurring throughout the two hour period, was summoned to the room by another. As soon as petitioner Dorothy McClellan arrived, she told Stuart Green to stop the paddling. Petitioner and others rendered first aid to Joseph, and he was later taken to a local hospital. Shortly thereafter Joseph Green died from shock and hemorrhaging.[72]

The jury in the circuit court that considered the evidence and the judge who tried the case ultimately held Dorothy McClellan responsible for the death of the boy since she was the leader of the fundamentalist religious community and allegedly the primary advocate of corporal punishments for children. According to her petition to the United States Supreme Court, "The State's theory of the case was that [McClellan] had brainwashed the adults residing at Stonegate into following her fundamentalist Christian beliefs and way of life, a central tenet of which was child obedience enforced, when necessary, by reasonable corporal punishment. The State's contention was that [McClellan's] expression of these beliefs made her a conspirator with the Greens in the beating death of their child, Joseph."[73]

Testimony was presented during McClellan's trial to persuade the judge and jury that the actions resulting in the child's death were part of a context of severe corporal punishments within the Stonegate community. According to McClellan's lawyers, the State theorized that she "was responsible for Stuart and Leslie Greens's acts, and Joseph's death, because it was her religious beliefs, and her domination over the free will of the Greens, that caused them to act as they did." In their brief to the Supreme Court, her lawyers argued unsuccessfully that the State's contention "is wholly repugnant to the Constitutional guarantee of the free exercise of religion."[74]

The judge who sentenced Dorothy McClellan stated that "Of those responsible for the death of the young boy," she was the "most culpable" despite the fact that "the Defendant did not actually participate in the physical abuse which brought about the death." The judge declared further that

Dorothy McClellan is an extremely strong-willed and manipulative woman who was unquestionably the leader of the Stonegate group.

She instituted therein a policy of child discipline which ultimately
encouraged the acts which brought about Joey Green's death, and
thus is just as surely responsible as if she had wielded the paddle
herself. One only has to realize that her teachings created an atmosphere in which each set of parents had their own monogrammed
paddles, which were carried openly and used frequently. Indeed,
through her leadership there evolved a system of child abuse which
was mistakenly justified under the guise of religion.[75]

In January 1987, the United States Supreme Court refused to hear an
appeal by Dorothy McClellan. It let stand the prior convictions and jail
sentences.

The issues raised by this case are profoundly disturbing. First, there
is the death of a small child whose paddling and "discipline" mirrored
the convictions of the fundamentalist religious community in which his
parents lived and practiced their beliefs. Second, the leader of this religious community was considered responsible for the child's death because of her advocacy of corporal punishment, not because of any specific
act she had done. She had not been physically present during the beatings
and she had intervened to stop them when apprised of the situation.
McClellan's conviction appears to have been grounded in large measure
upon her expression of certain views about discipline and punishment
and upon her alleged power over the minds and actions of the adult
members of her community. The judge's conviction that "through her
leadership there evolved a system of child abuse which was mistakenly
justified under the guise of religion" appears to overlook the larger, cru-
cially important issue implicit in this case: the pervasiveness of such
views about physical punishment among fundamentalist, evangelical,
and Pentecostal Protestants as well as many Americans of other persuasions, both religious and secular.

In retrospect, the Supreme Court's denial of Dorothy McClellan's
appeal and refusal to reconsider her case were most unfortunate, since
the issues raised by this case merit conscientious and informed consideration by both the courts and the public at large. McClellan's commitment to physical punishment as biblically based discipline in no way set
her apart from millions of other Americans who share similar beliefs and
who practice similar forms of punishment on children of all ages.

What appears to be missing from the West Virginia court's decision—

and from the Supreme Court's refusal to act upon McClellan's appeal to reconsider this case—is a full awareness of the religious, ideological, and historical contexts surrounding such beliefs about discipline. Had the judges and the courts been more amply informed about the rationales for physical punishments that successive generations of Christians have advocated for centuries, the decision to imprison Dorothy McClellan surely would have been made more difficult and complex.

The arguments are vitally important if we are to understand both the historical roots of physical punishment in American life, society, and culture and the reasoning that has sustained such modes of discipline for so long. Before considering the many complex consequences of physical punishments, we must first explore some of the religious and secular rationales for inflicting painful punishments. Only then will we begin to understand some of the intellectual sources—as well as the experiential roots in the early lives of many individuals—for our persistent collective commitment to hitting children in the name of discipline.

PART III

Rationales

Each generation, feeling compelled to justify suffering arising from discipline, has set forth a continuous series of rationales and arguments in favor of bodily assaults and pain inflicted by adults upon children. For many Christians, the Bible has provided the primary basis for arguments advocating corporal punishments, and the religious rationales thus require careful scrutiny. Equally central have been secular defenses of physical punishments, in both domestic and public contexts, especially education. The law and the nation's courts have been consistent supporters of physical punishment, and the rationales that have sustained some of these legal justifications for continued violence against children need to be examined also. For many decades now, the behavioral sciences too have used punishments and have argued in favor of the purposeful infliction of pain to modify and alter behavior in both animals and humans. Without an awareness of the conscious defenses of punishment set forth for so long by so many people on both sides of the Atlantic Ocean, we can never hope to grasp the full complexity of the emotional, intellectual, religious, educational, and legal roots of physical violence against children.

RELIGIOUS RATIONALES

Biblical Roots

For centuries, Protestant Christians have been among the most ardent advocates of corporal punishment. The Bible has provided fundamental texts that have served successive generations as primary guides to child-rearing and to discipline. These ancient writings, in both the Old and New Testaments, have justified and shaped the practices of corporal punishment in the discipline and rearing of children. Even in the late twentieth century, the words written by Prophets, chroniclers, and others centuries before the birth of Jesus remain the major sources for Christian rationales for physical discipline and punishment of children, casting a shadow of pain and suffering over the lives of vast numbers of people for more than two millennia.

The God who appears throughout the Old Testament was known to the Israelites as "the LORD, whose name is Jealous," and "is a jealous God" (Exodus 34:14).[1] But God was also Jehovah or YHWH, a god above all other gods. The Israelites' God constantly sought to demonstrate his power and authority, often through acts of violence, vengeance, and murder that recur throughout the accounts of the history of the Hebrew people. Jehovah punished when enraged and jealous, not hesitating to kill and destroy those he considered disobedient to his commands and will. God clearly was not bound by the commandments he had given to Moses and thence to the Israelites.

Jehovah's ability and willingness to destroy both individuals and whole groups of people is apparent throughout the Old Testament. During the Israelites' flight from Egypt, Moses was told by the Lord, "I will bring you to a land flowing with milk and honey, but I will not journey in your company, for fear that I annihilate you on the way; for you are a stubborn people" (Exodus 33:3–4).[2] God evidently did not trust himself to control his violent temper.

On at least one occasion, Jehovah tempted a father to murder his son

in order to sacrifice him "for a burnt offering upon one of the mountains,"
to which God directed him. Abraham led his trusting son Isaac up the
mountain, in obedience to the command from his God. "And Abraham
stretched forth his hand, and took the knife to slay his son," whereupon
an angel called to him and said, "Lay not thine hand upon the lad, neither
do thou any thing unto him: for now I know that thou fearest God, seeing
thou hast not withheld thy son, thine only son from me" (Genesis 22:1–
2, 10, 12). However, Abraham clearly had intended to carry out the will
of God even though in doing so he himself would kill his only son. Familiar
as this story is, it remains one of the most profoundly disturbing examples
of Jehovah's willingness to destroy human life in order to assure himself
of the unquestioning and absolute obedience of his subjects.*

Sons' obedience to fathers is a recurrent biblical theme, of course.
Consider the advice Moses gave his people after having delivered Jehovah's commandments to them: As Moses declared, "Thou shalt also consider in thine heart, that, as a man chasteneth his son, so the LORD thy
God chasteneth thee. Therefore thou shalt keep the commandments of
the LORD thy God, to walk in his ways, and to fear him" (Deuteronomy
8:5–6). Moses added this threat to his admonitions: "As the nations which
the LORD destroyeth before your face, so shall ye perish; because ye would
not be obedient unto the voice of the LORD your God" (Deuteronomy
8:20). Subsequently, when Jehovah spoke through his Prophet Nathan,
his message to King David was: "I will be his father, and he shall be my
son. If he commit iniquity, I will chasten him with the rod of men, and
with the stripes of the children of men: But my mercy shall not depart
away from him . . ." (II Samuel 7:14–15). Jehovah's punishments thus
provided the paradigm for parental discipline of children, a model that
became most explicit in the proverbs attributed to Solomon, the king of
Israel.

For many centuries, the Book of Proverbs has provided parents,

---

* Alice Miller has explored the implications of this story in *The Untouched Key:
Tracing Childhood Trauma in Creativity and Destructiveness*, translated by Hildegarde and Hunter Hannum (New York: Doubleday, 1990), pp. 137–45. Her
analysis of paintings of this scene is acute and she, unlike most commentators,
is well aware of the murderous abuse inherent in this story. As she notes
(p. 141): "Our awareness of the child's victimization is so deeply rooted in us
that we scarcely seem to have reacted at all to the monstrousness of the story of
Abraham and Isaac."

preachers, and teachers with the basic aphorisms that have justified their commitment to corporal punishment of children. The verses are so familiar that they have become part of both Christian and secular culture, generation after generation, century after century. Ironically, the one aphorism that epitomizes the commitment to corporal punishment— "Spare the rod and spoil the child"—is not from the Bible at all, though it has that familiar proverbial ring.[3] But the other aphorisms attributed to Solomon are equally well known and commonly cited, most often in the language of the early-seventeenth-century King James translation:

Train up a child in the way he should go: and when he is old, he will not depart from it (Proverbs 22:6).

Correct thy son, and he shall give thee rest; yea, he shall give delight unto thy soul (29:17).

My son, despise not the chastening of the LORD; neither be weary of his correction: For whom the LORD loveth he correcteth; even as a father the son in whom he delighteth (3:11–12).

In the lips of him that hath understanding wisdom is found: but a rod is for the back of him that is void of understanding (10:13).

Chasten thy son while there is hope, and let not thy soul spare for his crying (19:18).

Judgments are prepared for scorners, and stripes for the back of fools (19:29).

A whip for the horse, a bridle for the ass, and a rod for the fool's back (26:3).

He that spareth his rod hateth his son: but he that loveth him chasteneth him betimes (13:24).

Foolishness is bound in the heart of a child; but the rod of correction shall drive it far from him (22:15).

The rod and reproof give wisdom: but a child left to himself bringeth his mother to shame (29:15).

The blueness of a wound cleanseth away evil: so do stripes the inward parts of the belly (20:30).

> Withhold not correction from the child: for if thou beatest him with
> the rod, he shall not die. Thou shalt beat him with the rod, and shalt
> deliver his soul from hell (23:13–14).[4]

More than two thousand years of physical violence and painful assaults
against the bodies, spirits, and wills of children have been justified by
these proverbs, scattered through the Old Testament collection of sayings
attributed to Solomon.

Other Old Testament texts lend additional support to the punishment
and violence against children advocated in the name of King Solomon.
In the book of Deuteronomy, for instance, Moses told the Israelites that

> If a man have a stubborn and rebellious son, which will not obey the
> voice of his father, or the voice of his mother, and that, when they
> have chastened him, will not hearken unto them: Then shall his father
> and his mother lay hold on him, and bring him out unto the elders of
> the city, and unto the gate of his place; And they shall say unto the
> elders of his city, This our son is stubborn and rebellious, he will not
> obey our voice; he is a glutton, and a drunkard. And all the men of
> his city shall stone him with stones, that he die: so shalt thou put evil
> away from among you; and all Israel shall hear, and fear (Deuteronomy
> 21:18–21).

Thus, the price of filial disobedience is death. Moses' injunctions clearly
mirrored the will of Jehovah, who often killed those he judged to be
disobedient or rebellious. Chastisements, in the form of physical punishments with the rod, were often only the first stage in the progression of
discipline from pain to death.

One of the most profound and consequential transformations wrought
by Christianity has been the radical change in the nature of God from
Jehovah to Father. Christianity from the outset has emphasized the familial context of religious experience and belief, casting the central nar-
ratives of the life of Jesus in terms of the relationship of a father in heaven
to his only son on earth. No relationship in history has been more closely
examined than that of Jesus to his heavenly Father.[5] Yet hardly anything
survives in the Gospels to inform us about Jesus' own childhood as the
son of earthly parents. Even at the age of twelve, however, Jesus evidently
realized that his true father was not on this earth. Doing his Father's will

became the central motif of Jesus' life, a motif that has provided Christians with a central religious paradigm for children's obedience to parental will and authority for centuries. For Protestants, patriarchy has always been at the core of theology, since the mother of Jesus, adored and worshiped by Catholics for centuries, has played little or no role in the religious experiences and doctrines shaping the multitudinous forms of Protestantism in America for the past four centuries.

One of the most perplexing questions confronting many Christians is surely this: If the Israelites' Jehovah was also Jesus' Father in heaven, as most assume, did he then apply his harsh discipline of the rod and demands for obedience to his own only son?[6] Was Jesus crucified and put to death in fulfillment of his Father's will and command, as Jehovah once arranged for the sacrificial murder of Isaac, Abraham's son? Jonathan Edwards, the great eighteenth-century American evangelical theologian, believed that the Crucifixion "was willed and ordered by God," a condition that made "one of the most heinous things that ever was done" by men, "one of the most horrid of all acts," into "the most admirable and glorious of all events." For Edwards, at least, "the crucifixion of Christ was not evil, but good."[7] This argument, however, implies that God the Father was directly responsible for the death of his only earthly son.

Since the Gospels are silent concerning so much of Jesus' infancy and childhood, no one knows for certain whether Jesus was subjected to the rod and the pains of physical punishments by his earthly parents, as so many children of his time and place certainly were. But the Gospels do reveal that Jesus' Crucifixion was preceded by the physical chastisements inflicted upon him by his captors during his last days on this earth. Pontius Pilate responded to the crowd seeking Jesus' death by asking: "Why, what evil hath he done? I have found no cause of death in him: I will therefore chastise him, and let him go" (Luke 23:22). When describing the beatings he received at the hands of his captors, Matthew, Mark, and John report that Jesus was "scourged" (Matthew 27:26, Mark 15:15, John 19:1). Surely we must wonder if it is likely that the chastisement and scourging of Jesus before his Crucifixion would become the model for Christian parents to follow with their children in the centuries to come?

Christians who advocate physical punishment for children rarely inform readers or listeners about Jesus' views on the disciplining of children. From the Gospels, it is clear that Jesus loved children and used children often in his parables and speeches as models for others to follow. When children were brought to him to be touched and prayed for, his "disciples rebuked them. But Jesus said, Suffer little children, and forbid them not, to come unto me: for of such is the kingdom of heaven. And he laid his hands on them, and departed thence" (Matthew 19:13–15).

For many Protestants, the crucial text concerning Jesus' attitudes toward children is this:

> At the same time came the disciples unto Jesus, saying, Who is the greatest in the kingdom of heaven? And Jesus called a little child unto him, and set him in the midst of them, And said, Verily I say unto you, Except ye be converted, and become as little children, ye shall not enter into the kingdom of heaven. Whosoever therefore shall humble himself as this little child, the same is greatest in the kingdom of heaven. And whoso shall receive one such little child in my name receiveth me. But whoso shall offend one of these little ones which believe in me, it were better for him that a millstone were hanged about his neck, and that he were drowned in the depth of the sea (Matthew 18:1–6).

Jesus clearly felt a deep love and compassionate concern for children, adding that his disciples and others should

> take heed that ye despise not one of these little ones; for I say unto you, That in heaven their angels do always behold the face of my Father which is in heaven. For the Son of man is come to save that which was lost. . . . Even so it is not the will of your Father which is in heaven, that one of these little ones should perish (Matthew 18:10–11, 14).

When a Christian parent tells a child who is about to be punished that "Jesus teaches that you must receive the rod," he cannot justify this with any text from the Gospels.[8] Jesus never advocated any such punishment. Nowhere in the New Testament does Jesus approve of the infliction of pain upon children by the rod or any other such implement, nor is he ever reported to have recommended any kind of physical discipline of children to any parent.

The arguments for corporal punishment as the Christian method of discipline thus must be drawn from New Testament texts other than the Gospels. Yet given the persistent Christian obsession with corporal punishment, remarkably few passages anywhere in the New Testament advocate physical discipline and painful assaults by parents upon children. The only words attributed to Jesus that appear to justify chastisements of any sort were recorded long after his death by the John whose vision from an angel became the basis for the Book of Revelation. According to Revelation, Jesus said: "As many as I love, I rebuke and chasten: be zealous therefore, and repent" (Revelation 3:19). In this single passage, however, he said nothing specific about children.

The context of Jesus' remark, it should be noted, is the most violent and punitive book in the New Testament, the apocalyptic conclusion of the Bible, which has had a profound impact upon Christian thought and practice for the past two millennia. The setting of this one instance of chastening is the violent and murderous end of the world and the Last Judgment, in fulfillment of the wrath and punishments yet to be inflicted according to the will and word of God himself. According to Revelation, the whole earth and all sinners are to be chastised, while those whom Jesus loves and who obey him will be saved from the anger, judgments, and tribulations to come. Given the fact that the book was written long after Jesus' death, no one can be certain that these words, ascribed to Jesus via an angel and a man named John on the island of Patmos, reflected the views of Jesus himself.

The key text in the New Testament cited in favor of harsh physical discipline of children is Hebrews 12:5–11, which many Christians assume to have been written by the Apostle Paul, who converted to Christianity after Jesus had been crucified. Modern scholars, however, have concluded that Paul was not the author of this book, which thus remains anonymous.[9] Although no one actually knows who wrote Hebrews, this unknown author has had, and continues to have, an incalculable impact upon the lives of children. The text is familiar to Christians concerned about the discipline of children:

> And ye have forgotten the exhortation which speaketh unto you as unto children, My son, despise not thou the chastening of the Lord, nor faint when thou art rebuked of him: For whom the Lord loveth he chasteneth, and scourgeth every son whom he receiveth. If ye endure chastening, God dealeth with you as with sons; for what son

is he whom the father chasteneth not? But if ye be without chastisement, whereof all are partakers, then are ye bastards, and not sons
(Hebrews 12:5–8).

This anonymous author then drew upon his own experience as a boy,
using his personal memories of pain and suffering under punishment as
a guide to those whom he was addressing:

Furthermore we have had fathers of our flesh which corrected us,
and we gave them reverence: shall we not much rather be in subjec-
tion unto the Father of spirits, and live? For they verily for a few days
chastened us after their own pleasure; but he for our profit, that we
might be partakers of his holiness (Hebrews 12:9–10).

He knew from experience the actual suffering felt during a beating,
however justified and proclaimed necessary, and drew from the Book of
Proverbs for his admonition:

Now no chastening for the present seemeth to be joyous, but grievous:
nevertheless afterward it yieldeth the peaceable fruit of righteousness
unto them which are exercised thereby (Hebrews 12:11).

The justification of corporal punishment by the author of Hebrews
thus drew upon an ancient history filled with instances of divine chastisements and pains, while he himself supplied memories of the personal
anguish that once felt "grievous" to him and to others. But at no point
does the author of Hebrews cite words spoken by Jesus to confirm his
beliefs about the necessity for scourging sons. If any such text existed
in his own time and place, the anonymous writer does not make use
of it.

Apart from Hebrews, the only passages in the New Testament often
cited on behalf of corporal punishment are from texts generally ascribed
to the Apostle Paul.[10] In the Epistle to the Colossians, Paul commanded
children to "obey your parents in all things: for this is well pleasing unto
the Lord." However, he immediately added his injunction to fathers,
whom he urged to "provoke not your children to anger, lest they be
discouraged" (Colossians 3:20–21). In the Epistle to the Ephesians, Paul
again urged:

> Children, obey your parents in the Lord: for this is right. Honour thy
> father and mother; which is the first commandment with promise;
> That it may be well with thee, and thou mayest live long on the earth
> (Ephesians 6:1–3).

Once again, though, he advised fathers to "provoke not your children to
wrath: but bring them up in the nurture and admonition of the Lord"
(Ephesians 6:4).

Taken together, these are Paul's only admonitions concerning discipline and the obedience of children. In neither Epistle, however, does
Paul explicitly advocate corporal punishment or the use of the rod.* Instead, he emphasizes the necessity for paternal restraint and care of
children to prevent "anger" and "wrath" from arising. Surely this indicates his compassion for children and his desire to have them nurtured
rather than punished, knowing, as he did from his own experiences, that
punishments, especially beatings with rods, produce wrath, not love.

Corporal punishment is not and cannot be grounded in words ascribed
either to Jesus or to Paul. In the New Testament, only two unknown
men—one the author of Hebrews, the other the author of Revelation—
can be cited by even the most literal-minded Christians (who believe that
the Bible is the inerrant word of God) as justification for corporal punishment of children. The practice thus rests upon only the most fragile
New Testament foundation. Why, then, has physical punishment been
considered "Christian" at all?

---

* Perhaps this reflects his own experience with rods as an adult evangelist. In
the Second Epistle to the Corinthians, Paul describes the beatings he had experienced: "Of the Jews five times received I forty stripes save one. Thrice was
I beaten with rods, once was I stoned, thrice I suffered shipwreck, a night and
a day I have been in the deep" (II Corinthians 11:24–25). Is it likely that Paul
would have urged parents to use rods on the backs of their children when he
himself suffered great agony from the beatings with rods that he describes here?
Paul's experience as an adult who was beaten with rods is usually passed over
in silence by Christian advocates of the rod for punishing children.

Eternal Punishment

Punishment is embedded in most Christian theology. The threat of future and eternal punishment has provided the ineradicable core of violence, suffering, and pain that has perpetuated anxiety and fear in the minds of vast numbers of people throughout the world for two millennia. Although the Old Testament provides most of the verses and texts used to advocate the physical punishment of children, the New Testament Gospels and Epistles and the Book of Revelation provide the basis for terror contained in a single word: *hell.*[11] For believers in the literal reality of hell, salvation means escape and rescue from the eternity of suffering that many Christians believe awaits the bodies and souls of unsaved sinners (those who have not received the divine grace essential to their salvation and indispensable for eternal life in heaven).

For many Christians, and virtually all fundamentalist Protestants, hell is an actual, physical place of punishment, the locale of future suffering so vast, so extreme, and so permanent that our minds can hardly grasp the enormity of the threat. But for centuries, preachers and theologians of various persuasions have sought to convey in both speech and writing something of the horrible suffering that faces everyone who does not submit or surrender entirely to the will of God and his only son, Jesus.

In seventeenth-century New England, the apocalyptic end of this world often seemed very close at hand and the threat of imminent punishment and torment for sinners was continuously present in the minds of people throughout the northern colonies. Michael Wigglesworth, whose parents were among the first generation of settlers in New England, wrote an extraordinarily popular poem about the approaching "Day of Doom." Punishment and affliction were the central themes shaping the obsessions of this anxious and tormented Puritan preacher, whose poem vividly portrays the final days on earth before the Last Judgment and the ultimate separation of the saved from the damned. Wigglesworth pictured the scene at the Last Judgment, with God's throne surrounded by

all Christ's afflicted ones,
Who being chastised, neither despised
nor sank amidst their groans:
Who by the Rod were turn'd to God,
and loved him the more,
Not murmuring nor quarrelling
When they were chast'ned sore.[12]

Wigglesworth was certain that God afflicted those whom he loved and had chosen to be his own children, destined for salvation and eternal life in heaven. Although the sufferings of the saints while on earth would eventually be recompensed in heaven, the sufferings of sinners had barely begun. Wigglesworth acknowledged the question that arises in many people's minds when they are confronted with the prospects of the torments of hell:

How can it be that God should see
his Creatures endless pain,
Or hear the groans and rueful moans,
and still his wrath retain?
Can it agree with Equitie?
can mercy have the heart
To recompence few years offence
with Everlasting smart?[13]

Wigglesworth imagined Jesus replying with these harsh words:

It's now high time that ev'ry Crime
be brought to punishment:
Wrath long contain'd, and oft restrain'd,
at last must have a vent:
Justice severe cannot forbear
to plague sin any longer,
But must inflict with hand most strict
mischief upon the wronger.[14]

The day of judgment is the focal point of the poem, for punishment is the obsession that shapes Wigglesworth's paean to pain and torment of sinners in hell, which he delineates in vivid detail:

> *(That dismal place far from Christ's face,*
> *where Death and Darkness dwell:*
> *Where Gods fierce Ire kindleth the fire,*
> *and vengeance feeds the flame*
> *With piles of Wood, and Brimstone Flood,*
> *that none can quench the same,)*
>
> *With Iron bands they bind their hands,*
> *and cursed feet together,*
> *And cast them all, both great and small,*
> *into that Lake for ever.*
> *Where day and night, without respite,*
> *They wail, and cry, and howl*
> *For tort'ring pain, which they sustain*
> *in Body and in Soul.*
>
> *For day and night, in their despight,*
> *their torments smoak ascendeth.*
> *Their pain and grief have no relief,*
> *their anguish never endeth.*[15]

In his depiction of the hell to come, Wigglesworth left little to the imagination of his readers; he expressed a fantasy mirroring a lifetime of suffering that, for him, was grounded, both personally and theologically, in the experience and imagery of physical punishment.[16]

Like Wigglesworth, Jonathan Edwards was obsessed with punishment and with the terrors of hell.[17] No one has ever spoken more precisely about, or described with greater explicitness, the suffering that awaits non-Christians and sinners of all descriptions than Edwards, the most eloquent defender of divine punishments, pain, and torment in American history.[18] He was convinced that God is absolute and sovereign and, while in total control of everything and everyone, simultaneously holds each person fully responsible for his or her actions, thoughts, and feelings. For those who could not surrender themselves to the will and the grace of God and become reborn as Christians, eternal torments after death would be inevitable and inescapable. Edwards's fantasy elaborated the tortures awaiting sinners with exquisite detail:

> But to help your conception, imagine yourself to be cast into a fiery oven, all of a glowing heat, or into the midst of a glowing brick-kiln, or of a great furnace, where your pain would be as much greater than that occasioned by accidentally touching a coal of fire, as the heat is greater. Imagine also that your body were to lie there for a quarter of an hour, full of fire, as full within and without as a bright coal of fire, all the while full of quick sense; what horror would you feel at the entrance of such a furnace! And how long would that quarter of an hour seem to you! . . . And after you had endured it for one minute, how overbearing would it be to you to think that you had it to endure the other fourteen!
>
> . . . O then, how would your heart sink, if you thought, if you knew, that you must bear it forever and ever! That there would be no end! That after millions of millions of ages, your torment would be no nearer to an end, than ever it was; and that you never, never should be delivered!
>
> But your torment in hell will be immensely greater than this il-lustration represents. How then will the heart of a poor creature sink under it! How utterly inexpressible and inconceivable must the sink-ing of the soul be in such a case![19]

The horror of hell is so immense, the danger so acute and omnipresent for everyone not yet reborn and thus saved for eternity, that Edwards returned to the theme of suffering and pain again and again. In another sermon, he warned:

> Do but consider what it is to suffer extreme torment for ever and ever; to suffer it day and night, from one year to another, from one age to another, and from one thousand ages to another . . . in pain, in wailing and lamenting, groaning and shrieking, and gnashing your teeth; with your souls full of dreadful grief and amazement, with your bodies and every member full of racking torture, without any possibility of getting ease; without any possibility of moving God to pity by your cries; without any possibility of hiding yourselves from him; without any possibility of diverting your thoughts from your pain; without any possibility of obtaining any manner of mitigation, or help, or change for the better.[20]

Endless pain and torture throughout eternity will be the fate of everyone who fails to heed Edwards's invitation to become a true Christian,
saved by the grace of God from the horrors of hell forever. For Jonathan
Edwards, as for so many other Christians, the reality of damnation was
a continuous threat without the knowledge and assurance of having been
truly converted and saved.

Many Christians, both before and after Edwards, have had similar
visions and fantasies of eternal punishment. As a fifteen-year-old convert,
the twentieth-century evangelist Morris Cerullo had a vivid out-of-body
experience and a vision of hell. His mother died when he was small; he
was left in the temporary care of an alcoholic father prior to being placed
in foster care and in an orphanage, where he was beaten with paddles
regularly. Feeling himself to be in the presence of God's light, he recalled
looking through a hole in the sky and seeing

> the very flames of hell. I saw them rising and rising until they were
> literally burning right underneath the hole which had been made by
> the presence of God. In the midst of those flames were multitudes of
> lost souls. No mortal tongue can describe the anguish. If a messenger
> were sent straight from hell to warn the sinner, man still would not
> comprehend the awful anguish and torment that awaits the unsaved
> in that dreadful place. Oh the screams and the cries of these anxious
> souls! . . . Throughout the endless ages of eternity these souls would
> be continually reminded through the torment of their souls of the
> awful sin of rejecting God's love and mercy.[21]

A strikingly similar vision was experienced by Lester Sumrall in the
1930s during the early days of his ministry in the South:

> In the vision, God lifted me up until I was looking down upon that
> uncountable multitude of human kind. He took me far down the
> highway until I saw the end of the road. It ended abruptly at a precipice
> towering above a bottomless inferno. When the tremendous unending
> procession of people came to the end of the highway I could see them
> falling off into eternity. As they neared the pit and saw the fate that
> awaited them I could see their desperate but vain struggle to push
> back against the unrelenting pressure of those to the rear. The great
> surging river of humanity swept them ever forward.
>
> God opened my ears to hear the screams of damned souls sinking

into hell. God brought me nearer. As men and women of all nations plunged into that awful chasm, I could see their faces distorted with terror. Their hands flailed wildly, clawing at the air.

As I beheld in stunned silence, God spoke to me out of the chaos. "You are responsible for those who are lost."[22]

His life mission suddenly became clear and the twenty-year-old man became an evangelist to the world, intent upon saving souls while remaining haunted by this terrifying vision of hell. He was one of those Christians whose lives have been transformed by such visions of terror, torture, and torment awaiting every person who does not submit to God's word and will.

Though these are only visions, images created by the mind to convey something of the horror of hell evoked by the language of the Bible, for every literalist such fantasies bear the weight of fact, of physical reality. Although such Christians remain aware that they are seeing visions, imagining the horror without yet experiencing it themselves or witnessing it engulfing others, they cannot forget that hell exists and that the danger is ever present.

The terror of eternal punishment has always been at the root of much suffering on this earth as well. Incalculable suffering and pain have been inflicted on children because of the belief in the physical reality of hell. Many Christians have heeded and acted upon the words of Proverbs 23:13–14: "Withhold not correction from the child: for if thou beatest him with the rod, he shall not die. Thou shalt beat him with the rod, and shalt deliver his soul from hell." The threat of eternal punishment remains one of the greatest sources of anxiety and terror ever known, and must be recognized as a primary basis for the rationales for painful physical discipline and punishment advocated and practiced by so many Americans for centuries.

Breaking Wills

Anglo-American Protestants have always been among the most vocal public defenders of physical punishments for infants, children, and adolescents. They have provided many generations of listeners and readers with a series of theological and moral justifications for painful blows inflicted by adults upon the bodies, spirits, and wills of children. These defenses remain crucial to any understanding of the earliest sources of suffering and violence in our lives and culture. It is no accident that the shelves of evangelical and fundamentalist Protestant bookstores through-out the land are filled with books advocating physical punishments as the "Christian" method of discipline, essential to the creation of morality, spirituality, and character, and vital, ultimately, to the salvation of souls.

The basic premise shaping contemporary fundamentalist-Protestant rationales for corporal punishment is simply that God has willed it and requires it. As Roy Lessin, author of *Spanking: Why, When, How?* (1979), notes:

> Spanking is God's idea. He is the one who has commanded parents to spank their children as an expression of love. Spanking is not optional. It is an issue love cannot compromise. The question we face as parents is this: do we love God enough to obey Him, and do we love our children enough to bring into their lives the correction of spanking when it is needed?[23]

Larry Christenson, whose book *The Christian Family* (1970) has sold more than a million copies throughout the world, observes in his chapter "God's Order for Parents":

> *God holds you accountable for the discipline of your children.* If you discipline and bring up your children according to His Word, you will have His approval and blessing. If you fail to do so, you will incur His wrath.[24]

Christenson also insists that "The Scriptural method of discipline is simple and unequivocal: *the rod.*"[25] Similarly, J. Richard Fugate, a former administrator of a Christian school in Texas, the head of the Foundation for Biblical Research, and the author of *What the Bible Says about . . . Child Training* (1980), answers the question "Why must we use a rod to chastise our children?" as follows: "The first and only reason that should be necessary is because God's Word says to use a rod. God has specifically established the rod as the symbol of human authority."[26]

Many advocates of corporal punishment are convinced that such punishment and pain are necessary to prevent the ultimate destruction and damnation of their children's souls. Susanna Wesley was certain in 1732 that

> religion is nothing else than doing the will of God and not our own: that the one grand impediment to our temporal and eternal happiness being this self-will, no indulgence of it can be trivial, no denial unprofitable. Heaven or hell depends on this alone; so that the parent who studies to subdue it in his child works together with God in the renewing and saving a soul. The parent who indulges it does the Devil's work; makes religion impracticable, salvation unattainable, and does all that in him lies to damn his child body and soul forever.[27]

Similarly, two and a half centuries later, the Reverend Jack Hyles wrote in his book *How to Rear Children* (1972):

> *The parent who spanks the child keeps him from going to hell.* Proverbs 23:14, *"Thou shalt beat him with the rod, and shalt deliver his soul from hell."* A child who is spanked will be taught that there is a holy God Who punishes sin and wrong. Hence, he will learn to heed authority and obey the laws and rules. When he hears the Word of God he will obey what he hears and will accept the Gospel as it is preached. The parent has kept his child from hell by teaching him truths that can be learned only by discipline and the use of the rod.[28]

The possibility of future punishments thus justifies the infliction of present pain. As Larry Christenson observes, "God has ordained issues of the greatest importance to hinge upon the discipline of the rod—even involving the child's eternal salvation."[29]

Implicit in such convictions is an assumption that permeates the literature on Christian child-rearing: the belief that God is a father. The prayer repeated by Christians throughout the world begins, "Our Father, who art in heaven." But what kind of father is God? The answer clearly depends upon the experiences, the beliefs, and the images of parenting present in the minds of those who seek to describe God.

Given the pervasive threat of hell and the conditional promise of heaven—the only alternatives available to most Protestants, who generally reject the concept of Purgatory in the life to come—fear and love are the two most powerful and most common emotional responses to God as Father. If God is both loving and punitive, if he both embraces and hurts those he considers his own children, then love and fear are the keys that unlock many of the secrets of evangelical and fundamentalist commitments to painful forms of punishment. Roy Lessin writes, for example, that "The heavenly Father is the proper example of parental authority."[30] He acknowledges the ambivalence inherent in the kind of love God exhibits towards his human children:

> Because God is holy, He seeks to change us so that we will become like Him. As His children, He wants us to be a reflection of *both* His love and His righteousness. . . . Since God is holy love, it is perfectly consistent with His nature to both embrace us and to chasten us.[31]

Parents are often advised to tell their children that they are acting as God's surrogates when they inflict pain. As Jack Hyles notes: "So God is like a father and He chooses fathers and mothers to represent Him in the punishing of little children." He advises parents:

> Explain to him that you are a child of God and if you refuse to obey God in the execution of His judgment upon your children, God will pour out His wrath upon you. For you to be a good child of God requires that you be a good parent to the child. Let him understand this. He will get the idea that God is a holy and just God, One Who loves and yet One Who wants us to become our best. For this to be so He must punish us when we are deserving.[32]

Such sentiments can be found time and time again among Protestant writers. The Reverend John Abbott, whose 1833 book *The Mother at Home* was one of the early nineteenth century's most popular treatises on evangelical child-rearing, advised mothers to be "affectionate and mild" with their children and to "punish them in sorrow, but not in anger." He acknowledged, however, that "Fear is a useful and a necessary principle in family government," and noted that "God makes use of it in governing his creatures. But," he added, "it is ruinous to the disposition of a child, exclusively to control him by this motive." Abbott told mothers that "In all cases in which it can be done, children should thus be governed by kindness. But when kindness fails, and disobedience ensues, let not the mother hesitate for a moment to fall back upon her last resort, and punish as severely as is necessary."[33] For Abbott, these injunctions to painful physical assaults by mothers against children mirrored the relationship of God to his children on earth. Abbott urged that

> the child should be taught to regard God as that being who, while he loves his creatures, cannot look upon sin but with abhorrence. . . . It is to be feared that many deceive themselves in thinking they love God. They have in their minds a poetic idea of an amiable and sentimental being, whose character is composed of fondness and indulgence. Such persons are as far from worshiping the true God, as is the Indian devotee or the sensual Moslem. . . . He is a God of mercy and of justice. He is a God of love, and a consuming fire. He is to be regarded with our warmest affections, and also with reverence and godly fear. Let, therefore, children distinctly understand that sin cannot pass unpunished.[34]

Larry Christenson sounds remarkably like Abbott when he declares that "A spanking combines the twin aspects of love and fear, and in this it is patterned after our relationship to the Heavenly Father." He adds that "Some people have trouble with the idea of *fearing* God because a certain brand of sentimental humanism has crept into our thinking."[35] Christenson, however, has no doubts whatsoever about the fact that "God's discipline of us, His human children, is calculated to inspire fear. And this does not signify a failure or withdrawal of love," he insists, because "Fear acts as a catalyst for love. He who fears God most will love Him best. If God, the perfect Father, so disciplines His children as to inspire fear, then we should follow the same pattern in dealing with our children."[36]

Susanna Wesley, Jonathan Edwards, and countless other evangelical and fundamentalist Protestants for the past four centuries would have agreed: Fear is as essential to Christian parenting as love, since it mirrors the relationships of twice-born Christians to their Father in heaven. Without fear, they insist, there can be no true love. Always, however obscured, there is the knowledge and the certainty that eternal punishments await those who do not obey their heavenly Father. Fear arises from the punitive responses of parents to infants' and small children's first displays of self and self-will.

The focal point of evangelical and fundamentalist Protestant child-rearing always has been the emerging wills of children.* Breaking the child's will has been the central task given parents by successive generations of preachers, whose biblically based rationales for discipline have reflected the belief that self-will is evil and sinful. From the seventeenth century to the present, evangelical and fundamentalist Protestants have persistently advocated the crushing of the will even before a child can remember the painful encounters with punishment that are always necessary to accomplish such goals.

The theme of breaking children's wills was voiced even before the Pilgrims had taken firm root in America. John Robinson, who had been their minister in Holland but did not accompany them on their voyage to the New World, acknowledged in his essay of 1628 on the education of children that "It is much controverted, whether it be better, in the general, to bring up children under the severity of discipline, and the rod, or no. And the wisdom of the flesh out of love to its own," he recognized, "alleges many reasons to the contrary. But say men what they will, or can, the wisdom of God is best." Citing Proverbs to confirm his point, Robinson noted that

> surely there is in all children, though not alike, a stubbornness, and stoutness of mind arising from natural pride, which must, in the first place, be broken and beaten down; that so the foundation of their education being laid in humility and tractableness, other virtues may, in their time, be built thereon. This fruit of natural corruption and root of actual rebellion both against God and man must be destroyed, and no manner of way nourished, except we will plant a nursery of contempt of all good persons and things, and of obstinacy therein.[37]

Robinson's language of breaking, beating, and destroying is no accident, as his advice concerning children's willfulness makes clear:

---

* In *For Your Own Good*, Alice Miller extensively quotes German and other European sources from the eighteenth century to the present concerning the breaking and controlling of children's wills. The texts' interchangeability with those from English and American sources is indicative of the omnipresence of such views throughout both Europe and America for many centuries. They are so much alike that any reader who compares the quotations in this book with those in Miller's surely will be conscious, as never before, of the pervasiveness of what Miller labels "poisonous pedagogy."

For the beating, and keeping down of this stubbornness parents must provide carefully for two things: first that children's wills and wilfulness be restrained and repressed, and that, in time; lest sooner than they imagine, the tender sprigs grow to that stiffness, that they will rather break than bow. Children should not know, if it could be kept from them, that they have a will of their own, but in their parents' keeping: neither should these words be heard from them, save by way of consent, "I will" or "I will not."[38]

A century later, Susanna Wesley used the same harsh language while recommending a similar course of action to Christian parents in her famous letter to her son John: "To inform the understanding is a work of time, and must with children proceed by slow degrees, as they are able to bear it; but the subjecting the will is a thing that must be done at once, and the sooner the better," she insisted. Her advice still resonates:

When a child is corrected it *must be conquered*, and this will be no hard matter to do, if it be not grown headstrong by too much indulgence. And when the will of a child is *totally subdued*, and it is brought to revere and stand in awe of the parents, then a great many childish follies and inadvertencies may be passed by. . . . I insist on the *conquering of the will of children* betimes, because this is the only strong and rational foundation of a religious education, without which both precept and example will be ineffectual. But when this is thoroughly done, then a child is capable of being governed by the reason and piety of its parents till its own understanding comes to maturity, and the principles of religion have taken root in the mind [emphasis added].[39]

Subduing and conquering wills in the Wesley family required repeated infliction of painful beatings, beginning in the cradle and continuing throughout childhood, a process Susanna Wesley also recounts in considerable detail in this letter. Physical punishment clearly seemed to her indispensable to her aim of conquest.

The echoes of the seventeenth- and eighteenth-century evangelicals' insistence on the breaking of children's wills are audible in this observation, from an anonymous author's essay on "The Importance of Family

Discipline." The essay appeared in the November 1841 issue of *The Mother's Magazine*.

> I have sometimes thought that parents of the present day were too indolent or too feeble to exercise family government. But I am sure that if half the breath spent in repeating commands or coaxing obedience, or reasoning about the propriety of the thing required, were used in the application of the rod according to divine appointment, until submission and a prompt compliance with a command once given were gained, there would be a great saving of time, of strength, and [of] broken-hearted parents. We used to hear of parents breaking their children before they reached a certain period—after which the child understood that the will of the parent was to be implicitly obeyed, and all contests were easily settled. This breaking or subduing the will was considered a most important event in the history of the child. The process was conducted with coolness, patience, and much prayer to God for his blessing, while it was pursued with an inflexible firmness. The result could not but be happy. After this the rod was seldom, if ever, called for.

This evangelical's conviction that "we have fallen on evil times" and that "there is a fearful decline of family religion" clearly shaped the plea for rigorous use of the rod on children, without which their souls would not be saved. But the rationale for breaking their wills remains the same as it had been a century earlier: Obedience to God requires the infliction of pain upon children in order to make them obedient both to parents and to God.[40]

The obsession with children's wills and willfulness characteristic of evangelicals in previous centuries remains as powerful today among fundamentalists and other Protestants who advocate corporal punishment.[41] For J. Richard Fugate, it is clear that "The only issue in rebellion is will; in other words, who is going to rule—the parent or the child. The major objective of chastisement is forcing the child's obedience to the will of his parents."[42] The same preoccupation with the child's will is visible in the advice offered to parents by Jack Hyles:

> *The spanking should be administered firmly.* It should be painful and it should last until the child's will is broken. It should last until the

child is crying, not tears of anger but tears of a broken will. As long
as he is stiff, grits his teeth, holds on to his own will, the spanking
should continue.[43]

But how long is long enough? When will the child's will be truly broken?
What sounds indicate to a parent "not tears of anger but tears of a broken
will"? Hyles does not say. What is remarkable, though, is the imagery of
breaking wills, for that language links him with previous generations of
twice-born Protestants who also sought to ensure that their children had
no wills of their own.

Often a distinction is made between a child's will and his or her spirit.
Roy Lessin, for example, declares: "A correctly administered spanking
will break the rebellion and stubbornness in a child's will but will not
break his spirit."[44] James Dobson, a psychologist and the director of the
multimillion-dollar organization in California called Focus on the Family,
whose books on child-rearing (especially *Dare to Discipline*, which has
sold over a million copies) have been enormously popular among evangelical Christians, explores the issue of children's willfulness in *The
Strong-Willed Child: Birth Through Adolescence*, thus joining a long line
of corporal-punishment advocates obsessed with the wills of children.[45]
As a man who believes that "pain is a marvelous purifier," Dobson has
no hesitation in recommending that parents use "spankings" to control
and to suppress their children's willfulness and rebelliousness.[46]

The language of warfare is invoked at times in these treatises on will-
breaking and punishment. Dobson, for example, uses the imagery of
battles in his books such as *Dare to Discipline*, in which he notes:

> The child may be more strong-willed than the parent, and they both
> know it. If he can outlast a temporary onslaught, he has won a major
> battle, eliminating punishment as a tool in the parent[']s repertoire.
> Even though Mom spanks him, he wins the battle by defying her
> again. The solution to this situation is obvious: outlast him; win, even
> if it takes a repeated measure.[47]

Similarly, Fugate invokes the imagery of rebelliousness that arises from
the willfulness of children:

> If the child's rebellion has been the defiant resistance of his par-
> ents' authority, he should be chastised until he chooses to give in.

The child can decide on his own when he wants the chastisement to cease. Whenever he is willing to submit to the parent's will, he can profess his willingness to obey. He should be given the opportunity for an honorable, but *unconditional, surrender* [emphasis added].[48]

In his book *God, the Rod, and Your Child's Bod: The Art of Loving Correction for Christian Parents* (1982), Larry Tomczak (a charismatic from a Polish Catholic background) describes a battle of wills with his eighteen-month-old son which took place in a parking lot. When his small son refused to hold his father's hand, as he had previously been trained to do, Tomczak says that "He was defiantly challenging my authority." He adds, "What followed in the parking lot was a series of repeated spankings (with explanation and abundant display of affection between each one), until he finally realized that Daddy always wins and *wins decisively!*"[49] Apparently, only repeated acts of force could compel this small boy to submit to his father's authority and comply with his will. But the issue of winning clearly was paramount.

Win or lose: These are seemingly the only alternatives available to such parents. No choice is offered children except to surrender their wills to the wills and superior force of their parents. In the warfare between parents and children, the parents expect to win. If not, the war continues until such time as the children submit and obey. Only by giving in to the adults can children escape the pain and suffering brought about by the application of the rod or other implements in the name of Christian discipline.

Whether thought of in terms of breaking wills or shaping them, the obsession with authority, control, and obedience remains paramount. Evangelical writers have been preoccupied for centuries with authority and obedience, and the image of authoritarian family government often shapes their arguments in favor of harsh discipline for children. Early in the nineteenth century, one anonymous evangelical advocate of the rod offered this advice: "To insure, as far as may be, the proper behavior of his children, let every parent make it his inflexible determination, that he will be obeyed—*invariably* obeyed." He added, "The sum and substance of good government is to *be obeyed*; not now and then, when the humor suits; but always, and *invariably*." "The connexion between *your* command, and *his* obedience," this writer noted, "should be the unfailing consequent of the other."[50]

A woman writing in *The Mother's Magazine* in 1834 expressed similar

views: "God deals with his creatures as subjects of law. His will is their
rule of action: and he requires instant, unconditional, and unquestioning
obedience. Our views of the expediency of any of his commands, are
wholly immaterial. Our business is simply to obey." She added, "God has
required obedience to parental authority under tremendous sanctions of
the divine law." The child's welfare and ultimate fate thus become the
responsibility of parents, for salvation may depend upon the ability of the
child or young adult to obey the will of God.

> I do not say that conversion is to be the result of corporeal punishment;
> nor that a child, through fear of the rod, can be made to submit to
> the terms of the Gospel. But a habit of filial obedience, may go very
> far towards removing one obstacle in the way of the sinner's submis-
> sion to God, which is found to be almost universal. One principal
> reason why the sinner does not sooner yield to the influences of the
> Holy Spirit, is a fixed determination, on his part, not to be governed
> by the will of another. "Thy will be done," is a sentiment which we
> are all slow to adopt; and yet every sinner, if he would enter heaven,
> must come to this very point. . . . Conversions among that class of
> individuals, who have never been taught due subjection to the au-
> thority of their parents in early life, are believed to be of very rare
> occurrence. But let a child be taught uniformly to govern his con-
> duct by the will of his parents—let him form the habit of *instant,
> unconditional and unquestioning obedience* to parental law, and he
> will find less difficulty in submitting himself to God [emphasis
> added].

Parental punishments with a rod should be "a direct means of *coercing
obedience*" [emphasis added].[51]

Fundamentalist Protestants today often share a commitment to children's absolute obedience to parents, since injunctions to obedience permeate the literature they have written in recent decades. Most fundamentalists would agree with Jack Hyles, who asserts that

> Obedience is the foundation for all character. It is the foundation for
> the home. It is the foundation for a school. It is the foundation for a
> country. It is the foundation for a society. It is absolutely necessary
> for law and order to prevail.[52]

Hyles urges parents:

> *Require strict obedience.* This obedience should always be immediate,
> instant, without question or argument. What the father says do, the
> son does. He does it well, he does it immediately, and he does it without
> argument. The parents allow no exceptions to the rule. Hence, obe-
> dience is the law of the land and the child should not deem it necessary
> to have an explanation for the orders he has received from his
> parents.[53]

Similar advice is offered by Roy Lessin: "*Obedience from children should
be unquestioned*; it should not be based upon how reasonable a command
sounds to the child. A parent's directive does not have to be reasonable
to the child in order to be obeyed."[54]

Larry Christenson advises his readers (in words remarkably similar
to John Robinson's more than three centuries ago) that the command to
obey parents obligates children under every circumstance, including
those in which parents clearly are in error:

> The Bible . . . does not say, "Children obey your parents when they
> are right." It says: "Obey your parents in the Lord, for this *is* right"—
> even if they are wrong! (See Ephesians 6:1.) The child who obeys a
> "wrong" command will still bask in the light of God's approval. In the
> long run, he will be a happier and better adjusted child than one who
> is given the freedom to challenge and question the parents' authority.
> For the obedient child is living according to Divine Order, and there-
> fore participates in a deep sense of harmony and fitness.[55]

Thus Christenson describes the ideal "Christian" family, in which every
child obeys—without question, without thought, and without resistance—any order given by parents, no matter how mistaken or misguided.

Without force and violence, however, such automatic obedience
would surely be impossible to obtain. In *The Christian Family*, Christenson asserts that "If the punishment is of the right kind it not only
takes effect physically, but through *physical terror and pain*, it awakens
and sharpens the consciousness that there is a moral power over us, a
righteous judge, and a law which cannot be broken" [emphasis added].[56]
Such words and phrases may slip by quickly and without comment in
The Christian Family, but they can resonate ominously in a reader's

mind long afterward. If "physical terror and pain" are a normal part of Christian discipline, evidence of "moral power," "righteous" judgments, and unbreakable laws, it should come as no surprise to be informed by him that

> As Christians, we live under the discipline of Christ. He disciplines us severely as often as we need it. His object is not to spare us pain, but to surely slay the will of the flesh. Yet He disciplines us with moderation. He does not afflict us willingly. And as soon as He sees that we bow down and acknowledge our faults, He comes to us with consolation: He lets us feel how great is His kindness! So He deals with us, and so we ought to deal with our children.[57]

Thus Christenson, like so many others, rationalizes pain and suffering inflicted by adults upon their children. If God does it, so should we, and "physical terror and pain" will continue to be inflicted in the name of Jesus and Christianity. If the immense popularity of *The Christian Family* is any guide, the endless loop of punishments will continue, generation after generation, until such violent assaults and suffering are no longer rationalized and defended.

The rationales for physical punishments always mirror the theologies of those who advocate such practices. But knowing what to do and why is not the same as actually doing it. This is why the rationales for physical punishment so often include advice to parents on the methodology of discipline. The theories about punishment are enforced by real blows, real pain, real fear, real suffering. Most advocates are also practitioners.

Methodologies of Punishment

According to many Christian advocates of physical punishments, pain should begin to be felt early in life, often in infancy and the first years of childhood, and should continue to be inflicted, in many cases even through adolescence, until children learn obedience and submission to parental authority or until their wills have been broken. The lessons of discipline frequently start long before children have the ability to speak, remember, or resist. Nevertheless, unconscious memories of pain, fear, and anger remain encoded in the cells of the brain and body for the remainder of life.

Protestant advocates of physical punishment often advise parents to begin inflicting pain while their children are still infants. Larry Christenson recommends that "Discipline should begin when the child is in the cradle."[58] Roy Lessin agrees that children should be punished within the first two years, and that spankings can continue until children reach their teens, without ruling out the possibility of further spankings even in adolescence.[59] J. Richard Fugate believes six-month-old children should be switched for disobedience, observing that "The parents' controlled use of pain is not cruel and will not cause the child to fear his parents personally. . . . If he chooses willfully to ignore the commands, he chooses to receive pain."[60]

Similar advice is to be found in *Christian Child-Rearing and Personality Development* (1977), by an evangelical psychiatrist, Paul Meier, who has taught at the fundamentalist Dallas Theological Seminary and conducted seminars across the country on "Christian child-rearing and Christian counseling."[61] Meier considers corporal punishment indispensable for discipline: "Verbal reproofs are sometimes adequate," he observes, "but if the child is openly rebelling, spanking is the most effective form of discipline."[62] Meier's own experience as a parent confirms this principle: "My wife and I are both very loving and nurturing parents, and yet we remember spanking our older son or slapping his hand for open rebellion many times during those crucial twenty-one months (15th to 36th months)."[63] He believes that they fostered their son's "independence and exploration" at the same time, while "spanking him for willful disobedience." Meier comments, "I've heard a lot about the terrible threes, but I think we drove a lot of the terrible threes out of him when he was still two, because his third birthday brought on a new era of relative peace, although he still needed an occasional spanking."[64]

Rarely noted or acknowledged, but nevertheless obvious, is the fact that few children retain any conscious memories of their experiences prior to the age of three or four. Most children who are spanked, paddled, whipped, or beaten with hands, rods, belts, or anything else in infancy and early childhood have no direct access, in later years, to the painful memories that surround these encounters with adult discipline and punishment. This is why the breaking of children's wills usually takes place so early in life and has such enduring consequences.

One might imagine that successful will-breaking at an early age would preclude the necessity of further physical punishments and painful assaults as children grow up and reach adolescence, but the evidence, both from accounts of personal experiences and from prescripts, suggests that such punishments often continue throughout childhood and well into adolescence. Christenson tells readers that "In the first twelve years of life a child can learn through the seat of his pants what he must otherwise learn at great cost and suffering."[65] Lessin acknowledges that "Many people have come to believe that spankings should not be given once a child reaches the age of thirteen. Ideally, a child should not have to be spanked by the time the teenage years are reached. It would be unwise, however, to make a firm rule and say a teenager should never be spanked."[66] Fugate also agrees that teenagers can be punished with rods.[67] Meier writes, "When my children are eleven or twelve years old, I plan to do away with spankings and give them punishments that are related to the offense. I'll reason with them more, and try to communicate with them on an adult-to-adult level. "But," he adds threateningly, "I'll probably hang the paddle somewhere they can see it occasionally so they'll know it's available for special occasions. However, when they reach their teens, I will use other forms of discipline exclusively, punishments related to the offense."[68]

Dobson, too, discourages the use of physical punishments for adolescents. He notes in *Dare to Discipline* that "Spanking is the ultimate insult. Punishment for adolescents should involve lost privileges, financial deprivation, and related forms of non-physical retribution."[69] (Many parents find, however, that once children grow to be as large as themselves, the infliction of physical punishments becomes more difficult and dangerous, which probably accounts for the common assumption that childhood is the best time to inflict such pain.)

Given the belief that pain is necessary, what are the best methods for causing purposeful punitive pain in infants, children, and adolescents? For the past four centuries, the rod has been the overwhelming favorite among instruments recommended for corporal punishments, since it is the one most commonly prescribed in the Old Testament. Susanna Wesley's children were "taught to fear the rod" before the end of their first year. The Reverend John Witherspoon, the Scottish president of Princeton in the late eighteenth century, believed "that the rod itself is an evidence of love," although he recommended moderation in its application to children.[70] Modern fundamentalists have perpetuated this tradition and generally urge the use of the rod as well. *The Christian Family*'s long discussion of discipline includes a series of sections with such provocative titles as "The Rod: The Way of Love" and "The Rod: The First Response, Not the Last Resort."[71] In *God, the Rod, and Your Child's Bod*, Larry Tomczak notes that "The biblical definition of the rod is a small, flexible branch from a tree (a wooden stick)" and recommends that "a number of rods" should be kept "throughout the house, in your car, and in your purse" in order to be able to "apply loving correction immediately."[72] Fugate, citing biblical texts, says that "the rod is to be a thin wooden stick like a switch. Of course," he notes, "the size of the rod should vary with the size of the child. A willow or peach tree branch may be fine for a rebellious two-year-old, but a small hickory rod or dowel rod would be more fitting for a well-muscled teenage boy."[73]

The message is clear: Parents should use implements other than their bare hands when disciplining children with physical punishments. Roy Lessin points out that a "rod is a neutral object," and informs his readers that "A stick is the most effective instrument to spank with because its flexibility brings the greatest amount of stinging pain without the danger of physical injury. Stiff, hard objects like paddles or wooden spoons don't produce as much pain and also include the possibility of injuring a child. Belts, although flexible, are not as effective as a stick and also might cause injury."[74]

Despite the popularity of rods, other instruments can be used to inflict pain, depending upon the preferences of parents. Dobson, who was hit as a child with various things (including "a shoe," "a handy belt," and even "a girdle"), supports the use of rods as the biblical method but also recommends using belts and switches rather than hands.[75] The chart that he includes in *The Strong-Willed Child* suggests a preference for the more flexible leather strap so commonly used by parents.[76]

The timing of physical punishment—whether immediate or delayed— is often an issue. Lessin favors promptness, as does Dobson.[77] Fugate would agree, insisting upon instantaneous responses from children to parental commands.[78] However, at moments when extreme emotion, particularly anger, is felt by parents or other adults, discipline should be delayed. As Fugate notes:

> Chastisement is the **controlled** use of force. It should never be ad-
> ministered by an angry or emotional parent. If a parent cannot control
> himself, he should send the child to his room to wait for his whipping.

This action provides the parent time to "cool down," and it allows the child time to anticipate the coming consequences of his action.[79]

The whole procedure for inflicting pain and the degree of severity of the physical assault upon the child are matters that have received considerable attention from advocates of corporal punishment. Jack Hyles tells parents:

> *The spanking should be a ritual.* No mother or father should jerk the child up and in a fit of temper administer a spanking. In fact, no punishment should ever be given in a fit of temper. The ritual should be deliberate and last at least ten or fifteen minutes. (In the long run time will be saved using this method.) It should be a ritual dreaded by the child. He should not only dread the pain but the time consumed in the ordeal.[80]

This "ordeal" will last, presumably, until the child's will has been broken. Some children have very strong wills, and the spanking might therefore take even longer than Hyles assumes.

Among the recurrent issues in physical punishment are the proper methods for causing pain and the best ways to inflict the blows. Roy Lessin, for example, advises parents about the placement of children when being spanked: "A proper position also reflects an attitude of willingness to receive correction. Children who fight a spanking by kicking or twisting or blocking the spanking with their hands need to learn to submit to correction." He notes that "A child over a parent's knee may work fine when the child is young, but it is better to have older children simply bend over a chair or a bed." He cautions parents, "Spank the proper area," noting that "God has given parents the perfect area on which to administer a spanking—the child's bottom. It is a safe place because it is well cushioned, yet it is a highly sensitive area."[81] Fugate agrees: "The rod should be used on the bare back, preferably on the buttocks, especially on younger children (PROVERBS 10:13; 19:29; 26:3)."[82] Tomczak is convinced that "God, in His wisdom, prepared a strategic place on our children's anatomy which has enough cushiony, fatty tissue and sensitive nerve endings to respond to Spirit-led stimulation. This area is the base of the back, above the thighs, located directly on the backside of every child. All children come equipped with one!" he adds.[83]

The focal points of such painful assaults by parents generally are the child's buttocks—the anal zone of the body, which also happens to be intensely sensitive to erotic stimulations. Other parts of the body are often struck, of course, but the primary focus is usually upon the back of the body and the exposed naked buttocks of the child. After repeated experiences of being struck on the buttocks by hands, belts, switches, paddles, rods, or other implements, pain and love become inextricably associated with the hidden backside of the body.

Pain is the invariable immediate consequence of corporal punishments. Fugate provides his readers with explicit advice concerning both the application and the effects of the rod in discipline. He believes that

> The pain received from a rod is more humbling than harmful. There is no defense against it. The more a child braces himself, the more he tightens up and increases the sting. The most sensitive layer of skin is close to the surface where the nerve endings are located. The only way to stop the sting of a rod is to submit. That is exactly what a child will do—submit to his parents' will and thus end his rebellion.[84]

The infliction of pain requires a concerted effort by parents, and the severity of the punishment will depend upon the child's resistance, stubbornness, and willfulness. The systematic procedures set forth by Fugate address these issues, which many authors prefer to leave to the imaginations and experiences of their readers:

> The use of a rod enables a controlled administration of pain to obtain submission and future obedience. If a child's rebellion has been to disobey an instruction willfully, the parent can stop after a sufficient number of strokes and ask the child if he will obey instructions in the future. The parent is the best judge of the correct number and intensity of strokes needed for a particular child. However, if the child repeatedly disobeys, the chastisement has not been painful enough.[85]

Since the aftermath of punishment is often just as important to the advocates as the actual procedures themselves, the question of the immediate impact of punishment is addressed in a number of these books. Roy Lessin observes that "After correction, a parent needs to allow a child to cry for a reasonably short amount of time. Then a child should be told to stop crying and be brought under control."[86] But he offers no advice about how to accomplish this, apart from saying that "a period of reconciliation after a spanking provides a special time of love and intimacy to take place between a parent and a child."[87]

Larry Christenson believes that "More important even than the punishment itself is the succeeding quarter of an hour, and the transition of forgiveness." At that point, he observes, "The *terror and hatred of the punishment* are now past" [emphasis added]. Without pausing to consider the implications of "terror and hatred" as a normal part of "Christian" discipline, he comments that "Now gentle instruction finds its way, and brings healing with it, as honey assuages the sting of bees, and oil the pain of a wound."[88]

The important step after the punishment is "forgiveness." Christenson recommends that "After a child has been spanked, the father should kneel down with him and have the child ask God's forgiveness for the specific sin committed," while some fathers may want to "declare to him the forgiveness which God has given through Christ. And then your own forgiveness should also be expressed—most effectively with a hug and a kiss. For this is the goal of all discipline: forgiveness and reconciliation."[89] He never tells us how children who have experienced "terror and hatred" while being punished can actually *feel* forgiving of the adults who caused such anxiety, hostility, and fear.

What is to be done, however, when children persist in their tears and crying, and give voice to their own feelings of hurt, humiliation, or anger? Dobson believes that parents should set limits to the crying of children after punishment and spankings, observing that

> As long as tears represent a genuine release of emotion, they should be permitted to fall. But crying quickly changes from inner sobbing to an exterior weapon. It becomes a tool of protest to punish the enemy. Real crying usually lasts two minutes or less, but may continue for five. After that point, the child is merely complaining, and the change can be recognized in the tone and intensity of his voice. I would require him to stop the protest crying, usually by offering him a little more of whatever caused the original tears.[90]

Presumably this "whatever" was physical punishment inflicted by the child's parent. Dobson seems to be recommending further hitting to force children to stifle their feelings and to become silent, thus suppressing their protestations under the threat of further pain.

Beverly La Haye, who has given Family Life seminars with her husband, the Reverend Timothy La Haye (who once was a leader of Moral Majority), offers similar advice in her book *How to Develop Your Child's Temperament* (1977). She urges parents who have spanked their child once to repeat their spankings as often as necessary to teach the child who continues to cry after the initial punishment not to voice feelings of "anger" and "rage."[91] Her advice seems to be designed to train children to suppress their feelings of resentment and resistance, an emotional control brought about by parental blows, violence, coercion, and the purposeful hurting of the child. Given her general commitment to breaking children's wills and the use of rods in punishing children's bodies, such advice is not surprising.[92]

Given the intensity and duration of many punishments, the issues of both pain and physical marks indicative of the suffering of the child being assaulted by spankings, whippings, and beatings confront every advocate of corporal punishment. In *Dare to Discipline*, Dobson assures his readers that "It is not necessary to beat the child into submission; a little bit of pain goes a long way for a young child."[93] Lessin acknowledges that "there may be times when spanking with a rod can leave marks on a child's bottom, especially if several spankings are needed within a brief period of time. However," he adds, "these marks are temporary and should not become a source of discouragement to parents. It is better for children to carry a few temporary marks on the outside than to carry within them areas of disobedience and wrong attitudes that can leave permanent marks on their character."[94] Similarly, Tomczak cautions parents: "Keep in mind that 'posterior protoplasmic stimulation' can cause some redness on the skin. This is nothing to get upset about! These marks are only temporary," and they are preferable to keeping "improper attitudes inside that can leave permanent scars later in life."[95] Christenson acknowledges the pain of punishments—"the object being to cause the child enough pain to rouse wholesome fear"—but he is silent concerning the possibility of physical marks or wounds as a result of the application of rods to children's bodies.[96]

Fugate, however, directly acknowledges the virtual inevitability of

some physical marks on children's bodies as a result of corporal punishments. He observes:

> Children vary as to the number and intensity of strokes they require
> before they will submit. Some children are ready to give in when they
> first see the switch. . . . However, the child who has not yet learned
> to trust his parent's commitment to his obedience, or who is excep-
> tionally willful[,] will require more frequent and more intense whip-
> pings. Such a child is likely to require enough strokes to receive stripes
> or even welts. Some children have very sensitive skin that will welt
> or even bruise quite easily. Parents should not be overly concerned if
> *such minor injuries do result from their chastisement as it is perfectly
> normal* (2 SAMUEL 7:14; PSALMS 89:32; PROVERBS 20:30). However,
> parents should be careful that their use of the rod is not excessive
> and that the actual size of the rod is reasonable. Making stripes on a
> child is not the objective of chastisement, but parents *must realisti-
> cally expect them to be a necessary by-product* of the child's rebellion
> on some occasions [emphasis added].[97]

Children's bodies often bear silent witness to the marks left by the
rod or other implements: reddened skin; stripes; welts; bruises; broken
skin, cartilage, and sometimes bone; and bleeding. Fugate, at least, is
candid about the "minor injuries" that he finds "perfectly normal."
Most advocates hesitate to acknowledge in print the full extent of the
bodily harm that physical punishments can cause. Whether "minor"
or major, such injuries are common when adults inflict pain purposefully and intensely on the bodies of infants, children, or adolescents.

Given the infliction of pain, often repeated for subsequent offenses
against the authority and will of parents, and given the virtual inevitability
of some physical evidence of the force of the blows required to inflict this
pain, the question of potential abuse at times arises in the minds of
corporal-punishment advocates. Dobson, for example, is very sensitive to
the possibility of abuse arising from corporal punishments, as he notes
in *The Strong-Willed Child*.[98] However, he remains an advocate of painful
punishments, whether with belts or other things.

Roy Lessin, too, declares that "child abuse should be despised by
every parent." Nevertheless, he adds that

in rejecting even the thought of child abuse, parents must be careful not to reject God's way of providing loving correction through spanking. This is not to be confused with child abuse. Parents must guard against the fear that loving discipline is a form of child abuse. And they also must be careful not to become critical and wrongly judge parents who do provide this discipline.[99]

Lessin also contends that "The *failure* to provide loving discipline through spanking is also a form of child abuse" because "it affects eternal issues as well as temporal issues."[100] The fear of hell remains a central, if often implicit, justification for corporal punishments and pain in this present life, and makes the infliction of pain through spankings both necessary and nonabusive, in the opinion of those who share Lessin's convictions.

The limits of corporal punishment falling short of child abuse in the opinion of many advocates sometimes can extend very far, however. Paul Meier, writing as a Christian psychiatrist, replies to parents who say "that spanking simply doesn't work for their child" by insisting that "the spanking has to hurt; and it may need to be repeated a number of times for the same offense." He adds, "I am not advocating bruising the child; in fact I consider slapping his face or hitting him with a fist to be child abuse and provoking him to wrath. . . . But remember the words of Solomon," Meier cautions, invoking one of the direst of the proverbs: ["Withhold not correction from the child: for if thou beatest him with the rod, he shall not die"]. "God is almost mocking us here," he notes, "for being afraid to spank."[101]

Where, then, are parents to draw the line between discipline and child abuse? If spanking often needs to be repeated, while slapping and hitting with fists are unacceptable even though being beaten with rods is biblically approved, it is not surprising that Meier, like so many advocates of physical punishments, has difficulty setting forth a clear distinction between acceptable methods of punishment and unacceptable forms of abusive discipline. Since coercion and assault are inherent in physical discipline, is it any wonder that advocates of physical punishments have difficulty distinguishing abusive from nonabusive levels of pain and violence?

The Last Resort

Many Christians, especially "once-born" mainstream Protestants, have been and continue to be disturbed by the readiness of so many "twice-born" Christians to inflict suffering and pain in the name of discipline, and dismayed by the severity of many assaults associated with physical punishments, which often seem excessive, undesirable, and even deplorable. More moderate Protestants have always advocated gentleness, reasoning, and respect for the selfhood of children. Wishing to bend rather than to break children's wills, such moderates usually perceive themselves as being in the middle between the extremes of severity and indulgence. Nevertheless, the vast majority of parents have shared a deeply rooted conviction that physical punishments are necessary at some point if the goals of the parents or other adults are to be fulfilled and accomplished.

For Christian moderates, physical punishment often is justified as a "last resort." This argument has recurred with remarkable frequency during the past four centuries. From John Locke to young Benjamin Spock, some form of assault by adults has been justified as necessary in the disciplining of children. Despite their wish to appear to themselves and to others as kind, reasonable, and temperate people, many Christians have defended physical punishment as the ultimate tactic for accomplishing their goals of bending children's wills and teaching them to obey.

The most influential treatise written on child-rearing and discipline in the late seventeenth century was John Locke's *Some Thoughts Concerning Education* (1690), which was read and used by parents and educators on both sides of the Atlantic for many generations. Locke recognized the inherent violence in the use of the rod and physical punishments so common among his contemporaries. He believed that many parents "principle" their children "with violence, revenge, and cruelty. 'Give me a blow that I may beat him,' is a lesson which most children every day hear: and it is thought nothing, because their hands have not strength enough to do any mischief. But, I ask, does not this corrupt their minds? is not this the way of force and violence, that they are set in?"[102]

Locke sought to create self-discipline and self-governance in children, while also seeking to teach them obedience and submission early in life. But he was adamant that "Beating . . . and all other sorts of slavish and corporal punishments, are not the discipline fit to be used in the education of those who would have wise, good, and ingenuous men; and therefore very rarely to be applied, and that only on great occasions, and cases of extremity."[103] Note the qualifications: "very rarely," "on great occasions," "cases of extremity." Locke always preferred nonphysical punishments, since he was confident that "Esteem and disgrace are, of all others, the most powerful incentives to the mind, when once it is brought to relish them. If you can once get into children a love of credit, and an apprehension of shame and disgrace, you have put into them the true principle, which will constantly work, and incline them to the right."[104] He knew that

the pain of whipping will work but an imperfect cure. It only patches up for the present, and skins it over, but reaches not to the bottom of the sore. Ingenuous shame, and the apprehension of displeasure, are the only true restraints: these alone ought to hold the reins, and keep the child in order. But corporal punishments must necessarily lose that effect, and wear out the sense of shame, where they frequently return.[105]

Locke's intention was clear: to discourage the use of physical punishment and encourage other less violent and abusive methods of discipline to create the self-disciplining, self-governing, and reasonable adult whom he admired. But even he knew that the rod remained a last resort for many parents, and thus he was not prepared to denounce categorically any form of physical force or pain used for the purposes of punishment.

Locke's desire to create self-disciplining and self-denying children required parents to begin teaching self-governance very early in the lives of their infants and children. Children's wills had to be bent but not broken:

A compliance, and suppleness of their wills, being by a steady hand introduced by parents, before children have memories to retain the beginnings of it, will seem natural to them, and work afterwards in them, as if it were so; preventing all occasions of struggling, or repining. The only care is, that it be begun early, and inflexibly kept to, till awe and respect be grown familiar, and there appears not the least reluctancy in the submission, and ready obedience of their minds.[106]

Locke did not need Freud to inform him that the unconscious exists and continues to shape character long after the formative experiences in life have been forgotten. Obedience and submission remained vitally important, but Locke's presumption was that such obedience should seem to be voluntary, chosen rather than coerced.

On the other side of the Atlantic, the Reverend Cotton Mather shared many of Locke's views, including a reluctance to employ physical punishments except in extreme situations. He described his personal methods of child-rearing and discipline in his observations on the education of his children (1706):

I first begett in them an high Opinion of their Father's Love to them, and of his being best able to judge, what shall be good for them.

Then I make them sensible, tis a Folly for them to pretend unto any Witt and Will of their own; they must resign all to me, who will be sure to do what is best; my word must be their Law.

I cause them to understand, that it is an *hurtful* and a *shameful* thing to do amiss. I aggravate this, on all Occasions; and lett them see how *amiable* they will render themselves by well doing.

The *first Chastisement*, which I inflict for an ordinary Fault, is, to lett the Child see and hear me in an Astonishment, and hardly able to beleeve that the child could do so *base* a Thing, but beleeving that they will never do it again.

I would never come, to give a child a *Blow*; except in Case of *Obstinacy*; or some gross Enormity.

To be chased for a while out of *my Presence*, I would make to be look'd upon, as the sorest Punishment in the Family.[107]

Unlike many of his contemporaries, Mather preferred alternatives to corporal punishments whenever possible, although blows nevertheless remained part of his domestic methods of discipline.

The cult of domesticity and motherhood that shaped the consciousness of so many middle-class families in the first half of the nineteenth century mirrored many of the precepts articulated long before by Locke and others. Many Americans felt ambivalent about physical punishment and pain yet were unable to bring themselves to oppose all forms of physical punishments. In 1831 Lydia Maria Child, one of the most prolific and influential of the women writers of the antebellum era, published *The Mother's Book*, one of the earliest manuals for motherhood. Hers is a subtle and insightful book, which recognizes the importance of infancy and early childhood for the development of character and morality, and contains various alternatives for discipline besides corporal punishments. Child writes:

> I have said much in praise of gentleness. I cannot say too much. Its effects are beyond calculation. . . . The victims of oppression and abuse are generally stupid, as well as selfish and hard-hearted. How can we wonder at it? They are all the time excited to evil passions, and nobody encourages what is good in them. We might as well expect flowers to grow amid the cold and storms of winter.

But then she adds a crucial qualification, characteristic of moderates:

> But gentleness, important as it is, is not all that is required in education. There should be united with it firmness—great firmness. Commands should be reasonable, and given in perfect kindness; but once given, it should be known that they must be obeyed.[108]

Although she believes reasoning can be used much of the time, Child is convinced that parents nevertheless might need to resort to physical punishments in order to achieve their goals. She notes that

> I shall very naturally be asked if I approve of whipping. I certainly do not approve of its very frequent use; still I am not prepared to say that it is not the best punishment for some dispositions, and in some particular cases. I do not believe that most children, properly brought up from the very cradle, would need whipping; but children are not often thus brought up; and you may have those placed under your care in whom evil feelings have become very strong. I think whipping should be resorted to only when the same wrong thing has been done over and over again, and when gentler punishments have failed. A few

smart slaps sometimes do good when nothing else will; but particular
care should be taken not to correct in anger.[109]

Assault in the form of slaps and whippings thus remained Child's last
resort, as it does for many otherwise kind and gentle Christians who far
prefer reasoning to physical violence and pain. Even though her image
of God was that of a loving Father, not a wrathful or fearful one, she was
prepared to use violence and suffering when other means seemed insufficient to achieve her parental goals. Corporal punishments remained
part of the parent's repertoire of discipline. Not even the gentleness advocated by Mrs. Child could forestall entirely the pain that had marked
Christian child-rearing for centuries.

The most illuminating and influential example of the enduring tension
between persuasion and coercion is to be found in the Reverend Horace
Bushnell's *Christian Nurture*, published in 1861, which epitomizes many
moderate assumptions about parenting and discipline.[110] Bushnell wrote
in opposition to the views of many evangelicals, who insisted upon defining Christianity exclusively in terms of the experience of new birth
and conversion. His goal—the central goal of all those Christians whom
William James would later identify as the once-born—was to rear children
who would be Christians without ever undergoing a visible or traumatic
personal and spiritual transformation. Bushnell's Christianity, consciously nonevangelical, was a form of mainstream or liberal theology
which rested upon a view of human nature and divinity far more benign
and loving than the views characteristic of most evangelicals of his day.
Unlike many of his contemporaries, particularly the Millerites and ad-
ventists of the 1830s and 40s, Bushnell was not an apocalyptic, being
always confident that human history would extend far into the future
rather than ending in the sudden all-engulfing catastrophe anticipated
by so many Americans then and now.

Bushnell was convinced that "it is the only true idea of Christian
education that the child is to grow up in the life of the parent and be a
Christian in principle from his earliest years."[111] This process of education
begins in infancy, he believed, since "the most important age of Christian
nurture is the first," which he "called the age of impressions."[112] He
presumed that, during this period, character was being shaped and unconscious impressions were being formed that would continue to influence both personality and piety for the rest of life.

Long before Freud, Bushnell recognized the enduring power of the unconscious. He noted, for instance, that

> it may be true, in multitudes of Christian conversions, that what appear to be such to others, and also to the subjects themselves, are only the restored activity and more fully developed results of some predispositional state, or initially sanctified property, in the tempers and subtle affinities of their childhood. They are now born into that by the assent of their own will, which they were in before, without their will. *What they do not remember still remembers them, and now claims a right in them.* What was before *unconscious*, flames out into consciousness, and they break forth into praise and thanksgiving, in that which, long ago, took them initially, and touched them softly without thanks. For there is such a thing as a seed of character in religion, preceding all religious development [emphasis added].[113]

This was remarkably prescient. Bushnell added his "solemn conviction, that more, as a general fact, is done, or lost, by neglect of doing, on a child's immortality, in the first three years of his life, than in all his years of discipline afterwards."[114]

For Bushnell, as for so many Christians, the crucial issues in early childhood were the will, obedience, and submission to parental authority. Bushnell opposed breaking children's wills and advocated bending them instead. When a child begins "to lift his will in mutiny, and swell in self-asserting obstinacy, refusing to go or come, or stand, or withhold in this or that, let there be no fight begun, or issue made with him, as if it were the true thing now to break his will, or drive him out of it by mere terrors and pains. This willfulness, or obstinacy, is not so purely bad, or evil, as it seems." Bushnell noted that "nothing in fact is more dreadful to thought than this breaking of a will, when it breaks, as it often does, the personality itself, and all highest, noblest firmness of manhood. The true problem," he asserts, "is different; it is not to break, but to bend rather, to draw the will down, or away from self-assertion toward self-devotion, to teach it the way of submitting to wise limitations, and raise it into the great and glorious liberties of a state of loyalty to God."

Bushnell's method was nonviolent but firm. He described the process in detail:

See then how it is to be done. The child has no force, however
stout he is in his will. Take him up then, when the fit is upon him,
carry him, stand him on his feet, set him here or there, do just that
in him which he refused to do in himself—all this gently and kindly,
as if he were capable of maintaining no issue at all. Do it again and
again, as often as may be necessary. By and by, he will begin to
perceive that his obstinacy is but the bluster of his weakness; till
finally, as the sense of limitation comes up into a sense of law and
duty, he will be found to have learned, even beforehand, the folly of
mere self-assertion. And when he has reached this point of felt obli-
gation to obedience, it will no longer break him down to enforce his
compliance, but it will even exalt into greater dignity and capacity,
that sublime power of self-government, by which his manhood is to
be most distinguished.[115]

Bushnell thus advocated a seemingly benign and kindly form of control,
to bend rather than break a child's will. But his method was unlikely to
create a genuine sense of autonomy in the child, or a sense of choice
and responsibility. The child still had to accept the parent's will as the
child's own.

However, Bushnell was adamant that children are not to be treated
harshly by parents, or made afraid of them. He observed that

it is a great discouragement to piety in children, when they are governed in a hard, unfeeling way, or in a manner of force and overbearing
absolutism. Any thing which puts the child aloof from the parent or
takes away the confidence of love and sympathy will as certainly be
a wall to shut him away from God. If his Christian father is felt only
as a tyrant, he will seem to have a tyrant in God's name to bear; and
that will be enough to create a sullen prejudice against all sacred
things. Nor is the case at all better when the child is cowed under
fear of such a parent, and reduced to a feeling of dread or abject
submission.[116]

Bushnell was fully conscious of the analogies between earthly fathers
and the Father in heaven, and his sense of the authoritarianism of such
punitive and harsh parenting is evident throughout this passage.

Bushnell made his opposition to abusive and severe parenting utterly
clear in an eloquent denunciation of corporal punishment and domestic
violence:

I would not undervalue a strong and decided government in families. No family can be rightly trained without it. But there is a kind of virtue, my brethren, which is not in the rod—the virtue, I mean, of a truly good and sanctified life. And a reign of brute force is much more easily maintained than a reign whose power is righteousness and love. There are, too, I must warn you, *many who talk of the rod as the orthodox symbol of parental duty*, but who might really as well be heathens as Christians; who only storm about their house with heathenish ferocity, who lecture, and threaten, and castigate, and bruise, and call this family government. *They even dare to speak of this as the nurture of the Lord.* So much easier is it *to be violent than to be holy*, that they *substitute force for goodness and grace*, and are wholly unconscious of the imposture. It is frightful to think how they *batter and bruise* the delicate, tender souls of their children, extinguishing in them what they ought to cultivate, crushing that sensibility which is the hope of their being, and *all in the sacred name of Christ Jesus.* By no such summary process can you dispatch your duties to your children. You are not to be a savage to them, but a father and a Christian [emphasis added].[117]

No one has said this better: Force, battering, bruising, and using the rod are not truly Christian.

Still, this is not all of it. Even Bushnell—despite the clarity and power of his testimony against physical punishment and domestic violence in Christian parenting, and despite his vocal opposition to force and brutality—was prepared to accept some form of physical punishment in certain circumstances.* Not even he could renounce physical pain and coercion entirely, nor was he prepared to forgo fear as part of parenting. He wrote:

There is, then, to be such a thing as penalty, or punishment, in the government of the house. . . . First of all, it should be threatened as seldom as possible, and next as seldom executed as possible. It is a most wretched and coarse barbarity that turns the house into a

---

* This may be because he felt the need to justify what had been done to himself as a child. Bushnell "once told one of his own children that his father 'never whipped him but once, and then he *flogged* him;' and also said to a friend that he remembered this tremendous discipline as one of the best things that ever happened to him." *Life and Letters of Horace Bushnell* (London: Sampson Low, Marston, Searle & Rivington, 1880), p. 7.

penitentiary, or house of correction. When the management is right
in other respects, punishment will be very seldom needed. And those
parents who make it a point of fidelity, that they keep the flail of
chastisement always a going, have a better title to the bastinado themselves than to any Christian congratulations. The punishments dis-
pensed should never be such as have a character of ignominy; and
therefore, except in cases of really ignominious wickedness, it would
be *better to avoid, as far as may be, the infliction of pain upon the
person* [emphasis added].[118]

Always seeking a middle ground, Bushnell added that "Punishments
should be *severe enough* to serve their purpose; and *gentle enough* to
show, if possible, a tenderness that is averse from the infliction. There
is *no abuse more shocking*," he added, "than when they are administered
by sheer impatience, or in a fit of passion" [emphasis added].[119] Severity
and gentleness, the constant polarities of the middle way, inconsistent
and opposed as they always are, form the tangled threads of his argument
favoring occasional physical punishment.[120] Even for a man who recognized how "much easier is it to be violent than to be holy," pain and
suffering remained part of Christian nurture and discipline.

Obedience remains Bushnell's central goal, and pain is sometimes an
integral part of achieving it. Bushnell thus advises parents that "it should
be a law never to cease from the discipline begun, whatever it be, till the
child is seen to be in a feeling that justifies the discipline. He is never
to be let go, or sent away, sulking, in a look of willfulness unsubdued.
Indeed," he adds, "he should even be required always to put on a pleasant,
tender look. . . . No reproof, or discipline, is rightly administered till this
point is reached. Nothing short of this changed look gives any hope of a
changed will." Only then, Bushnell believes, will there be evidence "that
there is entered into the heart some real beginning of right, some spirit
of really Christian obedience."[121]

Even for Bushnell, the nature of obedience requires "a changed will,"
and he, like the evangelicals whom he opposed and deplored, was prepared to use physical force, coercion, and pain to obtain the "changed
look" that would signal a "changed will." At this point, Bushnell clearly
betrays his affinity to the advocates of the rod whom he most ardently
and eloquently denounced earlier. Violence and force remain a part of
his repertoire of discipline despite his stated wish "to avoid, as far as may
be, the infliction of pain upon the person."

The long-standing tradition of ambivalence among Christian moderates such as Bushnell, who both oppose and advocate physical punishments and painful discipline, is evident today throughout D. Ross Campbell's *How to Really Love Your Child* (1977), written from the perspective of a mainstream, nonfundamentalist Christian psychiatrist. Campbell's viewpoint reflects a self-conscious alternative to the ardent advocacy of the rod found in so many books by fundamentalists and evangelicals.

Campbell's argument is grounded in his conviction that "Real love is unconditional, and should be evident in all love relationships (see I Corinthians 13:4–7)." He believes that "Unconditional love can be viewed as a guiding light in child rearing."[122] He recommends several methods of conveying such love, including "eye contact, physical contact, focused attention, and discipline." But he also adds that

> The area most overemphasized today, to the exclusion of the rest, is discipline. I see many children of Christian parents who are well-disciplined but feel unloved. In many of these cases the parents have unfortunately confused discipline with punishment, as though the two are synonymous. This is understandable when one reads books and articles and attends seminars on the subject. I frequently read or hear authorities tell parents to use the rod and physically punish their child with no mention of loving him. . . .
>
> Every day I see the results of this approach to childrearing. These children are well-behaved when they are quite young, although usually overly quiet, somewhat sullen, and withdrawn. They lack the spontaneity, curiosity, and childish exuberance of a love-nurtured child. And these children usually become behavior problems as they approach and enter adolescence because they lack a strong emotional bond with their parents.[123]

From a statement like this, readers might assume that Campbell strongly opposes physical punishments and pain. He provides some cogent arguments in opposition to the use of the rod:

> Anyone can beat a child with a rod as the primary way of controlling his behavior. That takes no sensitivity, no judgment, no understanding, and no talent. To depend on corporal punishment as the principal method of discipline is to make that critical error in assuming that

discipline equals punishment. Discipline is *training* the child in the way he should go. Punishment is only one part of this, and the less the better. Please remember this statement: *the better disciplined a child is, the less punishment will be required.*[124]

Campbell takes note of the "punishment trap" so many parents encounter, which arises in part because of the writing, speaking, preaching, and teaching of advocates of physical punishments. He observes:

Few plead for a child and his real needs. Too many today are dogmatically calling for children to be punished, calling it discipline, and recommending the harshest, most extreme form of human treatment. Most perplexing of all, many of these advocates call this a biblical approach. They quote three verses from the book of Proverbs (Prov. 23:13; 29:15; 13:24) to totally justify beating a child. They neglect to mention the hundreds of Scripture verses dealing with love, compassion, sensitivity, understanding, forgiveness, nurturing, guidance, kindness, affection, and giving, as though the child has little or no right to these expressions of love.[125]

Campbell's reading of the Bible, which implicitly opposes the use of the rod, provides a scriptural context for his declaration that "Corporal punishment degrades, dehumanizes, and humiliates a child." He also notes that "using corporal punishment as a principal means of behavioral control is dangerous" because "it drastically alleviates guilt." It also affects the formation of conscience. "If you want to prevent your child from developing a normal responsible conscience which will enable him to *control himself*, build your relationship with him on a punitive basis. Control his behavior primarily by spanking and scolding, especially spanking."[126]

Campbell is disturbed by the "frightening advent of violence in all modes of mass communication, especially television"; he asks, "is it any wonder child abuse and all other forms of violence have become a national disgrace?" He is convinced that

Until we parents begin to proclaim the indispensable needs of a child, namely, unconditional love and loving discipline, the situation will continue to become worse. We parents must stand up against the

avalanche of demanding critics who insist that beating a child (confusing punishment with discipline) should be the primary way of
relating to him.[127]

Despite the detrimental effects that he has outlined so cogently and
persuasively, Campbell, like most moderates, is a reluctant advocate of
physical punishments. Perceiving himself as part of the middle ground,
he takes note of parental confusion when caught between "disciplinarians
(actually punishment-oriented) on one side and advocates of vague,
difficult-to-follow programs on the other," polarities that enable him to
argue for a more moderate form of discipline, which yet relies at some
point on force, coercion, and pain. "Yes, punishment and techniques are
at times necessary, quite helpful, and often good, but let's face it, they
are not the best; appropriate love and guidance are."[128]

Campbell recommends that "Punishment is occasionally necessary
but because of its negative effects from overuse, punishment should be
used *only as a last resort*."[129] Thus he joins the long tradition of people
who are willing, under pressure, to resort to "physical force" despite their
preference for controlling "a child's behavior in the most gentle, most
considerate, and most loving way possible."[130]

For Campbell, as for most moderates, the crucial issue that ultimately
justifies the infliction of pain and the use of physical punishments involves obedience and willfulness. "Defiance," he believes,

> is one of the few indications for punishment. Defiance is openly re-
> sisting and challenging authority—parental authority. It is stubbornly
> refusing to obey. Of course defiance, as well as any misbehavior,
> cannot be permitted. At these times, punishment is often indicated,
> and such times occasionally occur no matter what we do.[131]

Centering as it does upon resistance to authority and the refusal of a
child to obey, this statement is virtually indistinguishable from countless others by fundamentalist and evangelical advocates of harsh
punishments.

However, Campbell tries to provide alternatives, much as Bushnell
had done long before. He notes, for instance, that "Loving parents of a
two-year-old will, of course, be firm, but firm in *limit setting*, not in
punishment. These parents will control the child's behavior by gently

maneuvering the child physically, for example, picking him up, turning him around, guiding him, or placing him in the correct place or position."[132] This sounds remarkably similar to Bushnell's method of bending a child's will rather than breaking it.

Parental authority still remains the central issue, however, especially as children grow older. Campbell recommends that parents use his techniques of "eye contact, physical contact, focused attention, *and* discipline *simultaneously*. A child must have our love and firmness together." But then he adds the threat, characteristic of moderates, of further force and coercion when such methods fail:

> When parents have conscientiously provided all the preceding means of loving and disciplining a child, and he remains belligerently defiant, the parents must punish him. This type of defiance *must be broken.* The punishment *must be severe enough to break* the belligerent defiance, but it must also be *as mild as possible* to prevent the problems we have already discussed. If a command or explanation to a child is sufficient to break the defiance, why be more punitive? If sending a child to his room for a period is required and will suffice, fine. If taking a privilege away from a child is necessary to crush the defiance, proceed to do so. *Let's face it, corporal punishment is sometimes necessary* to break a pronounced belligerent defiance, *but only as a last resort* [emphasis added].[133]

The tradition of severity combined with gentleness thus continues, a child's defiance and a parent's desperation being sufficient reasons to resort to force, violence, and pain. All the earlier arguments are put aside, especially those acknowledging the degradation, dehumanization, and humiliation experienced by children who are corporally punished. Physical punishment thus remains at the core of Christian discipline even for a psychiatrist who is not an advocate of the rod.

The use of physical punishment is still the "last resort" today for most moderates and mainstream Protestants, just as it always has been. Religious rationales for physical punishments have been, and remain, among the most powerful and influential theoretical justifications for violence known in the Western world. For generations, they have woven the threads of pain and suffering into the complex fabric of our characters and our cultures.

Secularized versions of these religious rationales have had a profound impact on American character and culture throughout the latter part of the twentieth century through the various guides to child-rearing and discipline written by doctors, pediatricians, and others. The most important and influential work surely has been Dr. Benjamin Spock's *Baby and Child Care*, which has gone through many editions since 1945 and has sold more than thirty million copies throughout the world. Spock has shaped the child-rearing practices and the lives of people around the world.

Spock's views on discipline reflect the moderation characteristic of so many mainstream Protestants. Spock's sense of being located in the middle of the spectrum between the extremes of authoritarianism and permissiveness is apparent throughout his writings, especially those from earlier in his life. In the 1957 edition of his book, Spock confronted the question "Is punishment necessary?" by acknowledging that "The only sensible answer is that a great majority of good parents feel that they have to punish once in a while. On the other hand," he added, "a few parents find that they can successfully manage their children without ever having to punish. A lot depends on how the parents were brought up."[134] He cautions readers: "we ought to realize" that punishment "is **never** the main element in discipline—it's only a vigorous additional reminder that the parent feels strongly about what he says." He notes that "The main source of good discipline is growing up in a loving family— being loved and learning to love in return."[135]

Spock's cautious support of physical punishment is evident in early editions of his book. "I'm not particularly advocating spanking but I think it is less poisonous than lengthy disapproval, because it clears the air, for parent and child."[136] Subsequently, in the 1985 edition, revised in conjunction with Michael B. Rothenberg, Spock retains much of his previous viewpoint but de-emphasizes physical punishment. The authors observe:

> The best test of a punishment is whether it accomplishes what you are after, without having other serious effects. If it makes a child furious, defiant, and worse behaved than before, then it certainly is missing fire. If it seems to break the child's heart, then it's probably too strong for him. Every child reacts somewhat differently.[137]

Readers might infer from this that Spock and Rothenberg still find moderate physical punishment acceptable. But the 1985 edition adds new words of caution:

There are several reasons to try to avoid physical punishment, I feel. It teaches children that the larger, stronger person has the power to get his way, whether or not he is in the right, and they may resent this in their parent—for life. Some spanked children feel quite justified in beating up on smaller ones. The American tradition of spanking may be one cause of the fact that there is **much** more violence in our country than in any other comparable nation—murder, armed robbery, wife abuse, child abuse.[138]

Avoiding punishment, however, is not quite the same as rejecting physical punishments entirely. Although Spock seems to be moving toward a position of outright opposition to physical punishment, the 1985 edition of *Baby and Child Care* is not yet explicitly against all forms of physical punishment.

In recent years, however, Benjamin Spock has at last taken a clear public stand against the practice of corporal punishments. "I hope," he wrote in 1988, "American parents can outgrow the conviction, which a majority have, that physical punishment is necessary to bring up well-behaved children."[139] In *Dr. Spock on Parenting* (1988), Spock acknowledges that

> In earlier decades—and in earlier editions of *Baby and Child Care*—I avoided a flat statement of disapproval of physical punishment. I contented myself with the statement that I didn't think it was necessary. This was because of my belief that it's disturbing to parents when a professional person appears to imply that he knows better than they. What made me go against my own rule was my growing concern over the sky-high and ever-rising figures for murders within the family, wife abuse, and child abuse in America, and our government's enthusiasm for the nuclear arms race and for an aggressive foreign policy. It's not that physical punishment creates these alarming conditions by itself, but it certainly plays a role in our acceptance of violence. If we are ever to turn toward a kindlier society and a safer world, a revulsion against the physical punishment of children would be a good place to start.[140]*

---

* For further discussion of alternatives to physical punishment, see the conclusion to this book: "Choices," pp. 215–22.

SECULAR RATIONALES

The transformation of Dr. Benjamin Spock from hesitant advocate to ardent opponent of physical punishment suggests the complex and powerful ways in which both religious and secular motivations, experiences, beliefs, and practices can shape and alter our consciousness. In the late twentieth century, it is often easy to forget just how profoundly influential the Judeo-Christian heritage has been and continues to be in our lives and our society. The values and viewpoints shaped by centuries of tradition and practice imprint even areas that we believe to be most remote from religious convictions and traditions. Issues of morality and conscience infuse education, the law, politics, and even the behavioral sciences.

Most secular issues involving punishment cannot escape the enduring assumptions and perspectives generated over the centuries by American and European religious rationales. So embedded are these assumptions in our minds and culture, and so familiar are they to most of us, that it is often almost impossible to discern their actual influence on us.

Even when they seem most remote from anything religious, secular rationales for punishment are often rooted in the religious rationales that we have explored so far. We now turn our attention to some of these secular rationales, first in the context of education and the law, and then in the context of the empirical behavioral sciences, which might seem to be the most remote from religiosity, hellfire, and eternal damnation. But the biblical roots of punishment are so central to American character and culture that even those areas we label secular commonly reflect underlying assumptions shaped by centuries of writers, preachers, and parents who have advocated and practiced painful coercion and punishments. The law has never been an exception, since tradition and experience have always been guides to present decisions. Justifying punishment has been as much a part of our legal as of our religious heritage.

Judicial Justifications

The physical punishment that occurs within private households also takes place in schools across the nation. As of March 1990, twenty states have prohibited the infliction of corporal punishments in public schools.* This is a significant increase over the two states—Massachusetts and New Jersey—that had prohibited corporal punishments in public schools prior to 1977, when the Supreme Court, by a bare majority of five votes to four, decided the case of *Ingraham* v. *Wright*. This remains a landmark decision, shaping the legal rationales for permitting physical assaults, characterized as discipline, against children and adolescents by teachers and administrators in public schools. As a result of *Ingraham* v. *Wright*, American schoolchildren lack any protection against physical punishment on the basis of either the Eighth or the Fourteenth Amendment to the Constitution.[141]

In 1974, at an earlier stage of *Ingraham*'s progress toward the Supreme Court, a panel of the United States Court of Appeals for the Fifth Circuit took careful note of the evidence in the original trial of school officials at Drew Junior High School in Dade County, Florida. The ma-

---

* These states are Alaska, California, Connecticut, Hawaii, Iowa, Massachusetts, Maine, Michigan, Minnesota, Nebraska, New Hampshire, New Jersey, New York, North Dakota, Oregon, Rhode Island, South Dakota, Vermont, Virginia, and Wisconsin. Other states are considering banning corporal punishment (*Ohio Center for More Effective School Discipline Newsletter*, vol. III [June 1989 and Spring 1990], p. 1). The states that physically punish the most students each year include, in descending order, Texas, Florida, Georgia, Alabama, Tennessee, Arkansas, Mississippi, Oklahoma, Ohio, and Louisiana (National Coalition to Abolish Corporal Punishment in Schools [Westerville, Ohio 43081], "Corporal Punishment Factsheet"). From this it can be seen that the traditional Bible Belt remains the region where the most belting and physical punishment of schoolchildren is still being done today.

For a general overview of corporal punishment in our public schools, see the important analysis by Irwin A. Hyman, the Director of the National Center for the Study of Corporal Punishment and Alternatives in Schools, which is located at Temple University in Philadelphia, Pa.: *Reading, Writing, and the Hickory Stick: The Appalling Story of Physical and Psychological Abuse in American Schools* (Lexington, Mass.: Lexington Books, 1990).

jority, in an opinion by Judge Richard T. Rives, noted: "The evidence shows that corporal punishment in Dade County during the relevant period consisted primarily, if not entirely, of 'paddling.' Paddling involves striking the student with a flat wooden instrument usually on the buttocks."[142] In the county schools using physical punishment (only 16 of 231, a small but noteworthy minority, did not), "the punishment was normally limited to one or two licks, or sometimes as many as five, with no apparent physical injury to the children who were punished."[143]

In Drew Junior High School, however, students were struck many more times and with far more severe injuries, according to the testimony cited by the court. In one such instance, James Ingraham, then fourteen, was one of a number of students who "were slow in leaving the stage of the school auditorium when asked to do so by a teacher," and was one of those "taken to the principal's office and paddled. James protested, claiming he was innocent, and refused to be paddled." Nevertheless, he was held by two school administrators "by his arms and legs" and was "placed . . . struggling, face down across a table." The principal "administered at least twenty licks." Young Ingraham then left school and went home, where he found "his backside was 'black and purple and it was tight and hot.'" Later, "The examining doctor diagnosed the cause of James's pain to be a 'hematoma,'" and told him to remain home for one week. During the trial, "James testified that it was painful even to lie on his back in the days following the paddling, and that he could not sit comfortably for about three weeks."[144] Other students told similar stories; some experienced up to fifty blows from paddles at various times. One student, after wiping something off a seat in the school auditorium, had his number placed on a board and was then summoned to the office of the assistant to the principal. "Because he thought he was innocent," the student "refused to 'hook up,'" that is, "To assume a position standing in back of a chair, with hands on the seat of the chair, in preparation to being paddled." The school administrator "then hit him five or ten times on his head and back with a paddle, and then hit him with a belt. The side of . . . [his] head swelled, and an operation proved necessary to remove a lump of some sort which had developed" after being "struck." On another occasion, the same student had been given "ten licks," after which his "chest hurt and he threw up 'blood and everything.'" The opinion explains: "Perhaps because he had asthma and heart trouble of some sort," the student "also reacted to this paddling by 'shaking all over' and 'trembling,' and required treatment at a local hospital." Perhaps there were other reasons as well, such as anxiety or even rage, but that remains unclear. What is evident is that such incidents were commonplace at this particular school. The court was called upon to decide whether the Eighth Amendment to the United States Constitution, which prohibits "cruel and unusual punishment," would protect students from such assaultive and painful school discipline.[145]

In considering the relevance of the Eighth Amendment, the Court of Appeals panel noted that "A number of federal courts have held that corporal punishment of school children is not *per se* a violation of the constitutional prohibition against cruel and unusual punishment." The court then stated:

> We agree that at the present time corporal punishment *per se* cannot be ruled violative of the Eighth Amendment. Mild or moderate use of corporal punishment as a disciplinary measure in an elementary or secondary school normally will involve only transitory pain of a non-intense nature and will not cause intense or sustained suffering or permanent injury. For this reason, although many might object to corporal punishment for a variety of reasons, such punishment *per se* cannot presently be held to be "excessive" in a constitutional sense, or so "degrading" to the "dignity" of school children as to violate the Eighth Amendment.

The court then noted the continued "use of moderate corporal punishment" in many states and schools and acknowledged, "Faced with this evidence of what is apparently considered appropriate by the American people, we would be loath to suggest that at this time corporal punishment is 'unacceptable to contemporary society.' " This suggests the possibility that such punishment might become unacceptable to the courts at a later time.

However, the judges declared, "the regime at Drew Junior High School was in fact a system of punishment established and imposed by those in authority." They observed that "The injuries sustained by various students at Drew demonstrate that the punishment meted out at this school was often severe, and of a nature likely to cause serious physical and psychological damage." Furthermore, "The frequency of the use of corporal punishment suggests real oppressiveness." They also noted that such punishments were "degrading to the children at that institution." The court concluded that "the system of punishment at Drew not only violated the constitutional prohibition against cruel and unusual punishment, but also violated due process."[146]

The judges' key assumption, which they made explicit, was that some forms of corporal punishment are acceptable while others are not: "We are unwilling to say that *mild or moderate corporal punishment* is unrelated to the achievement of any legitimate educational purpose. However, in this case the *severe punishment* meted out at Drew went *beyond legitimate bounds*" [emphasis added].[147] Thus the court assumes a range of punishments, from mild to moderate to severe, and draws the boundary of legitimacy between "moderate" and "severe." But the opinion does not state the court's assumptions about what constitutes each degree of pain, suffering, and physical harm, although the decision makes clear the court's belief that the punishments meted out at Drew did go too far, amounting to "cruel and unusual punishment" that violated the Eighth Amendment.

The conclusions reached by the panel were rejected in 1976 by the full Court of Appeals for the Fifth Circuit, which denied the applicability of both the Eighth and Fourteenth amendments to this case. Five of the fifteen Court of Appeals judges dissented, including Judge Rives, who had written the opinion for the panel that earlier had considered the case. The majority opinion declared, without qualification, that "the Eighth Amendment does not apply to the administration of discipline, through corporal punishment, to public school children by public school teachers and administrators."[148] However, the court stated, "We do not mean to imply by our holding that we condone child abuse, either in the home or the schools. We abhor any exercise of discipline which could result in serious or permanent injury to the child." The federal Appeals Court insisted that recourse for "severe" discipline was to be found in the Florida state courts. "The basis of such actions is, however, tort and criminal law, *not* federal constitutional law." The majority argued that "the administration of corporal punishment in public schools, *whether or not excessively administered*, does not come within the scope of the Eighth Amendment protection" [emphasis added].[149] In a footnote, the court refused to accept the logic of the *Jackson* case concerning physical punishments of prisoners: "While whipping an adult prisoner is sufficiently degrading to offend 'contemporary concepts of decency,' we cannot believe paddling a child, *a long-accepted means* of disciplining and *inculcating concepts of obedience and responsibility,* offends current notions of decency and human dignity" [emphasis added].[150] The court also observed that "Paddling of recalcitrant children has long been an accepted method of promoting good behavior and instilling notions of responsibility and decorum into the mischievous heads of school children."[151]

The fundamental values and assumptions held by the Court of Appeals majority about physical punishments are evident from the decision's language: "obedience," "responsibility," "good behavior," and "decorum" for "recalcitrant" and "mischievous" children in schools. There is no question, therefore, about the approval of physical discipline by these judges or their unwillingness to set any judicial limits on the severity of such punishments. Perhaps this is why the majority drew a distinction between "a suspension" and "a paddling, which involves no deprivation of a property interest or denial of a claim to education [despite evidence that several students were out of school for at least a week as a result of the paddlings they had received at school] and which is certainly a *much less serious event* in the life of a child than is a suspension or an expulsion" [emphasis added]. The court also found that "no substantial interest in reputation" was "violated by a paddling. . . . for while a recorded suspension can indeed have a permanent adverse impact on a person's reputation and could conceivably harm that person's chance to obtain employment or higher education, we find it difficult to contend that a paddling, *a commonplace and trivial event in the lives of most children,* involves any such damage to reputation" [emphasis added].[152]

Surely this is the key to the court's rationale for assault, pain, and bodily injury: that it is a "commonplace and trivial event," and therefore, presumably, without enduring consequences of any significance either for the child or for our society. Such views persisted when the case reached the Supreme Court for a final determination.

In 1976, the Supreme Court considered *Ingraham* v. *Wright,* reaching a split decision in 1977 (five votes to four) concerning the constitutional issues the case raised. The majority (in an opinion written by Justice Lewis Powell and concurred in by Associate Justice William Rehnquist, now the Chief Justice of the Supreme Court) skipped quickly over the evidence generated in the original trial, although they acknowledged that this evidence "suggests that the regime at Drew was exceptionally harsh."[153] In one compact paragraph, they referred briefly to the experiences of two students, but the rest of the testimony concerning the pain and injury caused by the paddlings was passed over in silence, without any visible empathy or compassion for the students victimized by these beatings.

The majority advanced several rationales in defense of their harsh conclusion that (in the words of dissenting Justice Byron White) "corporal punishment in public schools, no matter how severe, can never be the subject of the protections afforded by the Eighth Amendment" and that public-school students "are not constitutionally entitled to a hearing of any sort before beatings can be inflicted on them."[154] They based their reasoning on history, tradition, and the common law (reaching back for precedents to England and the eighteenth-century *Commentaries* of William Blackstone), and they stressed the distinction between criminal and civil constitutional law.

The first rationale offered by the majority in their defense of violence against children is tradition: "The use of corporal punishment in this country as a means of disciplining school children dates back to the colonial period."[155] The fact that many other practices, including slavery and the denial of the vote to women, also dated back to the colonial era does not appear to be recognized. The majority did take cognizance of the petitioners' observation that "the Framers of the Eighth Amendment could not have envisioned our present system of public and compulsory education, with its opportunities for noncriminal punishments" (the majority being convinced that it applied *only and exclusively* to criminal cases) but insisted that "Whatever force this logic may have in other settings, we find it an inadequate basis for wrenching the Eighth Amendment from its historical context and extending it to traditional disciplinary practices in the public schools."[156] The majority thus refused to acknowledge that the America of the 1970s was far different from that of the 1780s.

The majority of the Supreme Court justices also rooted their arguments concerning punishment in English and American common-law precedents reaching back to the eighteenth century. In their consideration of the Fourteenth Amendment's applicability to this case, the majority acknowledged that

Were it not for the common-law privilege permitting teachers, to inflict reasonable corporal punishment on children in their care, and the availability of the traditional remedies for abuse, the case for requiring advance procedural safeguards would be strong indeed. But here we deal with a punishment—paddling—within that tradition, and the question is whether the common-law remedies are adequate to afford due process.[157]

The key assumption concerning the applicability of common-law traditions to punishment is set forth in the majority's statement, citing Blackstone's views, that "a single principle has governed the use of corporal punishment since before the American Revolution: Teachers may impose reasonable but not excessive force to discipline a child."[158] Given this traditional distinction between reasonable and excessive force, we might have expected the majority to argue along the lines taken by the Court of Appeals panel that decided in favor of Ingraham, but they did not do so.

Having observed that twenty-one states permitted "the moderate use of corporal punishment in public schools," the justices concluded their introductory statement by noting the "background of historical and contemporary approval of reasonable corporal punishment" prior to considering the constitutional issues.[159] Before turning to other considerations, however, they had acknowledged that

Despite the general abandonment of corporal punishment as a means of punishing criminal offenders, the practice continues to play a role in the public education of school children in most parts of the country. Professional and public opinion is sharply divided on the practice, and has been for more than a century. Yet we can discern no trend toward its elimination.[160]

This is the only recognition by the majority of alternative views respecting corporal punishments.*

* Given the fact that, as of March 1990, an additional eighteen states have voted to ban corporal punishment in public schools, the "trend" that the Supreme Court failed to discern in 1977 is readily apparent now. Perhaps the time will come when the issues dealt with in Ingraham v. Wright will be reconsidered by the Supreme Court and the decision itself reversed.

The majority clearly wished to defend the continued use of corporal punishments in schools. They provided the nation with no guidelines concerning the limits of physical assaults—in the guise of discipline—against children in public schools. Despite the majority's contention that "The prisoner and the schoolchild stand in wholly different circumstances, separated by the harsh facts of criminal conviction and incarceration," prisoners are now protected against physical punishments with straps while schoolchildren are not.[161] The Supreme Court's unwillingness to set any limits to punishments in schools and its refusal to apply the Eighth Amendment to noncriminal cases have left students of all ages at risk for severe injury and acute pain caused by blows from paddles, belts, and other implements wielded in public schools. This is to say nothing of the religious schools, both Protestant and Catholic, in which corporal punishments are still used frequently.

Underlying the arguments of both the majority and the minority in *Ingraham* v. *Wright*, however, is one assumption that rationalizes the continuation of such punishment in schools: the belief that some form of physical punishment is necessary, desirable, and legitimate. Even the dissenting opinion by Justice Byron White does not oppose all forms of corporal punishments:

> I am therefore not suggesting that spanking in the public schools is in every instance prohibited by the Eighth Amendment. My own view is that it is not. I only take issue with the extreme view of the majority that corporal punishment in public schools, no matter how barbaric, inhumane, or severe, is never limited by the Eighth Amendment. Where corporal punishment becomes so severe as to be unacceptable in a civilized society, I can see no reason that it should become any more acceptable just because it is inflicted on children in the public schools.[162]

But it is the degree of severity, not the punishment *per se*, that offends Justice White, and he thus joins in the other justices' commitment to perpetuating physical punishments in a "civilized society" such as ours for the foreseeable future. Admirable as this dissent is in many respects, it does not go far enough, in my opinion, to protect children and adolescents from being hit and injured by teachers and administrators in public schools.

Unfortunately, Judge Rives's eloquent and compellingly argued dissent from the decision of the full Court of Appeals did not weigh heavily enough in the determinations by the Supreme Court. Richard T. Rives, and his colleagues Irving L. Goldberg and Robert A. Ainsworth, Jr., who joined in the dissent, are among the very few judges who seem to have been moved deeply by the suffering that initiated this case. Their dissent is remarkable for its compassion and empathy, and for its direct and urgent recognition of the need to address the problem of violence against children and adolescents in the context of official public-school policies at the state and local levels. Their voices must be heeded by those who believe that physical punishments have no place in education or in the public schools of this land.

Judge Rives addressed the historical background and context of the Eighth Amendment and the applicability of this amendment to the states. He wrote: "In approaching this problem, we cannot turn the clock back to 1791," when the first ten amendments to the Constitution were ratified.[163] He insisted that the Eighth Amendment could apply to the states and hence to the public schools. "The presence of alternative remedies in state courts should not deter federal judges from their primary duty of defending and supporting the Constitution," he observed. He then acknowledged: "I cannot escape the conclusion that these school children have a constitutional right to freedom from cruel and unusual punishment when applied under color of state law, and that it is our duty as federal judges to enforce that right."[164]

Judge Rives boldly declared: "The administration of cruel and severe corporal punishment can never be justified. The circumstances and severity of the beatings disclosed by the presently undisputed evidence amounted to arbitrary and capricious conduct unrelated to the achievement of any legitimate educational purpose."[165] He subsequently noted that "the undisputed evidence" in *Ingraham* "shows deprivations of liberty, probability of severe psychological and physical injury, punishment of persons who were protesting their innocence, punishment for no offense whatever, punishment far more severe than warranted by the gravity of the offense, and all without the slightest notice or opportunity for any kind of hearing."[166] He emphasized that "The brutal facts of this case should not be swept under the rug," something that the Supreme Court majority clearly did in minimizing the amount of testimony presented in their opinion. Judge Rives concluded his dissent by observing that "The precedent to be set by the en banc majority [and subsequently affirmed by the Supreme Court majority] is that school children have no federal constitutional rights which protect them from cruel and severe beatings administered under color of state law, without any kind of hearing, for the slightest offense or for no offense whatsoever. I strongly disagree," he declared.[167]

Reading these opinions sequentially and observing the judges rationalize their refusal to provide constitutional protections to American school children should lead us to wonder what experiences shaped such judicial indifference to so much suffering. One could imagine, as the dissents by Justice White and Judge Rives make clear, that alternative rationales could have led the Supreme Court to an entirely different conclusion in *Ingraham* v. *Wright*, a conclusion that would have extended the protections of the Eighth and Fourteenth amendments to the bodies and spirits of school children for generations to come. It is easy to forget that the men and women who become Court of Appeals judges and Supreme Court justices once were children, and that they, too, must have had some experiences with discipline. Given their commitment to the perpetuation of corporal punishments in public schools, it seems plausible to assume that they may have had some personal encounters with physical punishments when they were small. Judges rarely discuss such matters in print, yet childhood experiences with discipline and punishment must resonate on at least some occasions when judges are called upon to determine cases like *Ingraham.*

Too often, we forget that experience, which so commonly is cited in legal cases as historical precedents and traditions, has a human and personal dimension as well as a public and collective dimension. This suggests that every judge called upon to make a decision regarding the infliction of pain on children or adolescents, whether in homes or schools, should remember and acknowledge what was done to him or her early in life. When judges were assaulted in childhood in the name of love, it is often as difficult for them as for others to oppose violence against children in the form of physical punishments.

Perhaps in the future many judges will be able to share the conviction, articulated so powerfully by Judge Rives in his dissent, that "the brutal facts of this case should not be swept under the rug." So long as *Ingraham* v. *Wright* constitutes the precedent that binds United States courts, children will remain at serious risk of suffering and injury from physical punishments in public schools in many states. Secular, legal rationales for violence against children are no less consequential than the rationales rooted in the Bible and in religious convictions, nor are they any less deplorable.

Behaviorist Arguments

Modern behaviorism has made punishment into a science. Punishment has been embedded in the behavioral sciences just as it has been in schools and the law, and arguments for pain and suffering are as much a part of behavioral psychologists' language as of educators', lawyers', and judges'. The language of empiricism and scientific rationality, abstract and often intentionally remote from human emotions and experiences, obscures and disguises the religious and personal roots of the concern with physical punishment and pain that many behaviorist psychologists and educators share.

B. F. Skinner, one of the founders and leading theoreticians of behaviorism, was acutely conscious of the religious roots of his scientific convictions and practices. He acknowledged in the third volume of his autobiography that "Much of my scientific position seems to have begun as Presbyterian theology, not too far removed from the Congregational of Jonathan Edwards."[168] Skinner was fully aware of the parallels between Edwards's Calvinist theology and his own most basic scientific convictions concerning free will, determinacy, predestination, and responsibility. He was conscious, even if many of us are not, of the religious roots of much modern behaviorism and science. The preoccupation with inflicting punishment and avoiding it is one of the most enduring of the tangled and painful legacies of the Judeo-Christian heritage among secular behaviorists.

Hell has cast its shadow over the behavioral sciences just as it has over the religious convictions of fundamentalists and other Christians who ardently advocate physical punishments. Punishment haunted Skinner throughout his life, since he was first threatened with the fires of hell as a small child:

> The first religious teaching I can remember was at my grand-
> mother Skinner's. It was her desire that I should never tell a lie, and
> she attempted to fortify me against it by vividly describing the pun-
> ishment for it. I remember being shown the coal fire in the heating
> stove and told that little children who told lies were thrown in a place
> like that after they died.

Subsequently, he inadvertently told a false story about a man whom he
identified as his uncle and felt "suddenly overwhelmed with the reali-
zation that I had told a lie. It may seem horribly absurd but I actually
suffered torments over that incident." On another occasion, young Skinner "went to a magician's show," which involved "the appearance of a
devil. I was terrified," he recalled. "I questioned my father as to whether
a devil just like that threw little boys to Hell and he assured me it was
so. I suppose I have never recovered from that spiritual torture."[169] In a
subsequent volume of his autobiography, Skinner added parenthetically
that "When I was very young, hellfire was the great punishment, and I
escaped to agnosticism."[170] Even for a child who was never physically
punished (except once by having his mouth washed out with soap),
hellfire and the threat of punishment—"that spiritual torture"—remained
an enduring legacy of childhood, shaping his adult preoccupations as a
behaviorist far more profoundly than most of us have recognized.

   Although never physically assaulted or struck by his parents, Skinner
knew other forms of punishment, which remained powerful sources of
his scientific and intellectual obsessions. He remarked: "I must have
been punished in other ways because my parents' disapproval was something I carefully avoided." He remembered that "My mother was always
quick to take alarm if I showed any deviation from what she called 'right,'
but she needed only to say 'Tut tut,' or to ask 'What will people think?' "[171]
In another context, he observed: "I have reacted to punitive contingencies
in other ways. I have escaped from the punishers. I concealed unacceptable behavior from my parents," and he noted that "To free myself
from these emotional effects of punishment, I have practiced a kind of
self-management."[172] Surely his own experiences as a child resonate in
his observations concerning control and punishment: "The literature of
freedom has never taken into account the dangers inherent in control
that 'works through volition' rather than through punishment."[173] Skinner's adult fascination with punishments and other forms of inducements

to alter behavior mirrored his childhood experiences. However, Skinner was not an advocate of physical punishments, preferring other behavior-modification methods such as positive reinforcements.[174] But issues of punishment have always been central to the behaviorist psychology to which he committed his entire adult life.

The rationales for physical punishment in the behaviorist essays collected by Saul Axelrod and Jack Apsche in *The Effects of Punishment on Human Behavior* (1983) speak the language of empirical science to describe, to justify, and to distance the reader from pain caused by punishments of "organisms" such as rats, monkeys, pigeons, and humans. Much of the research and experimentation which these essays draw upon has focused on the behavior of animals and birds, yet the writers' presumption clearly is that such studies can be applied, often directly, to the behavior and emotions of human beings. Research on humans, however, has been limited in many instances to children and adults, many of whom have been hospitalized or institutionalized, who suffer from disabilities such as autism, mental retardation or brain damage, and psychoses or schizophrenia. Far less experimentation has been done with "normal" children and adults, it would appear, despite the readiness of some behaviorists to extrapolate from animal and abnormal human behavior to ordinary childhood and adult experience and behavior in schools, homes, and other social settings. It is not surprising, therefore, that Ron Van Houten concludes his essay on "Punishment: From the Animal Laboratory to the Applied Setting" with this observation: "Although much has been learned about punishment through carefully controlled laboratory studies carried out with infrahuman subjects, more remains to be learned about how punishment influences the behavior of humans in natural social settings."[175] Despite this warning, many of the essays in the collection merge the findings from lab experiments with ordinary childhood and adult experiences in the "real world" outside, extrapolations with painful consequences for many individuals and groups.

Pain, so common in the experimental research conducted by behaviorists in this century, can be induced by many methods in animals, birds, and human beings. Many experiments have used electric shock as an aversive agent to "teach" or "train" or "modify behavior"—shocks that Edward Carr and O. Ivar Lovaas insist "can be an effective intervention for serious behavior problems that have proven refractory to other forms of treatment." Carr and Lovaas remark: "Subjectively, the pain has been described as being similar to that experienced when one is hit with a leather strap or a willow switch. However, shock is not as dangerous as either of these events nor does it leave a durable, radiating pain. In fact, the pain is localized and stops as soon as the shock is terminated."[176] In terms of punishment, Van Houten includes "all punishers that involve the application of intense physical stimuli," as well as "all forms of corporal punishment, such as spanking or slapping a child's hand, as well as electric shock, loud noises, unpleasant tasting substances, and aromatic ammonia. The most popular form of physical punishment employed in laboratory work has been electric shock."[177] Van Houten adds: "Other commonly employed forms of physical punishment that have proved effective in the natural environment are spanking . . . and slaps."[178]

In their essay, "The Side Effects of Punishment," Crighton Newsom, Judith E. Favell, and Arnold Rincover confront the issue of pain directly:

> The *physical* effect of a punisher refers to the immediate, unavoidable physiological effects inherent in the administration of some punishers—for example, pain and reddening of the skin with slapping or spanking, pain and startle with electric shock, and muscle fatigue with most kinds of overcorrection. These effects are sometimes viewed as tangential to treatment and unfortunate side effects, analogous to the pain that accompanies most surgical and dental procedures. But this analogy is erroneous. For surgery and dentistry, pain is the result of an inadequate technology of anesthesiology, which can be expected to improve with advancing knowledge, and is not essential to the effectiveness of the particular procedure. In the use of some punishment procedures, pain *is* necessary if the procedures are to be effective, and reducing the pain involved would reduce their efficacy. That is, pain functions as an intervening variable for some punishers, serving as a necessary mediator between the observed independent variable (e.g., applying a live shock device to the arm) and the observed dependent variable (e.g., cessation of face hitting). It is hard to imagine a painless shock or a painless slap functioning as an effective punisher. The necessity for pain to be present as an intervening variable is probably the greatest hindrance to the use of certain punishers. No one responsible for the treatment or education of others prefers to use a procedure whose effectiveness depends on the induction of pain. But that is *the hard reality that must be chosen in some cases* [em-

phasis added] if the client's welfare rather than personal or societal preference is to be served.[179]

This viewpoint is remarkably similar to the advice offered parents by many Christian advocates of physical punishments, though their purposes in applying such punishments are very different. Both groups, however, share a concern with changing behavior. They also share a concern with the methodologies and implications of punishment.

Given the necessity of pain, it is not surprising to discover that many experiments have concluded that "when punishment is sufficiently intense, the targeted behavior can be completely suppressed." Van Houten adds that "if the intensity of punishment is high enough, the degree of suppression may be so complete that the punished behavior may not occur again without specific efforts to shape it."[180] He cautions that "it is unwise to begin with mild punishment and gradually make punishment more intense" since "far more intense punishment [is then required] to suppress unwanted behavior than if punishment is originally introduced at a reasonably intense level." Van Houten does not specify what might constitute "reasonable" levels of pain, but he does add parenthetically: "This is an important point because human rights committees sometimes insist that punishment be introduced at a low intensity and increased until it is effective."[181]

Behaviorist experimentation thus might seem to provide a "scientific" confirmation of the advice offered by so many Christian advocates of physical punishment. As Van Houten observes: "Punishment offers several advantages over alternative methods of suppressing unwanted behavior."[182] But he also acknowledges that "In past years, many psychologists have recommended that punishment not be employed or else be employed with great caution because of the existence of various drawbacks or side effects," a perspective that Van Houten does not share. He believes that "a close examination of recent work in the area of punishment suggests that punishment can be safely employed in a wide range of settings provided basic rules of sound practice are followed."[183]

Similar views are articulated by Newsom, Favell, and Rincover, who note that

punishment procedures have *social* effects, producing reactions in persons other than the recipient of punishment. More appropriately,

it is the *use* of punishment procedures, themselves socially and eth-
ically neutral, which has social effects. The use of punishment as a
therapeutic intervention commonly arouses fear over its possible effects and often provokes criticism from professional and lay groups,
including media reporters. Legislative and regulatory bodies pass laws
and issue policies regulating certain controversial punishers, such as
paddling in schools and electric shocks in institutions.

Their assumption that "punishment procedures" are "socially and ethi-
cally neutral" still appears to be widely shared among behaviorists.[184]

One crucial and recurrent issue confronting advocates of such punishments, therefore, involves the long-term consequences of such punishments. Newsom, Favell, and Rincover note:

> The reason for considering side effects as response-class phenom-
> ena is that, at a theoretical level, this approach provides a conceptual
> scheme which encourages a search for order in experimental results.
> The hope is that in time the multiple effects of a given punisher with
> a given behavior in a certain type of subject might become predictable
> to a clinically significant degree. This cannot be done at present be-
> cause most of our information on side effects is anecdotal and because
> too few attempts at replication of reported side effects have been
> made.[185]

This observation ought to give pause to anyone advocating physical pain
and punishment. Yet the authors insist that

> Conspicuously absent from these studies [of side effects] is convincing
> evidence of serious, lasting harm to the recipients of punishment,
> despite warnings of numerous authorities of various theoretical per-
> suasions. Most of the undesirable side effects described lasted only
> for a few minutes or days, were quickly responsive to treatment if they
> did not disappear spontaneously, and constituted a *relatively small
> and ethically justified price* to pay in return for the elimination of
> much more detrimental behaviors [emphasis added].[186]

Among the most commonly observed side effects, however, is aggression, an issue that arises in both of these essays. Van Houten says ex-

perimenters have observed that "eliminating a response by punishing it may produce aggression by the organism whose behavior is being punished directed at either the punishing agent or some nearby individual who had nothing to do with delivering the punishment. They further point out that this side effect of punishment could have serious implications, since the survival of humanity appears to be related to the maintenance of harmonious social relationships."[187] Despite such a possibility, Van Houten immediately adds: "Fortunately, subsequent work has suggested that the problem of elicited aggression is not really serious in most situations, because aggression can easily be suppressed through the use of contingent punishment." He then extrapolates to the socialization of humans, after first discussing evidence from studies of monkeys and rats:

> It is interesting to note that most socialized individuals have already learned not to attack those who may use punishment legitimately, because they have been punished for such attacks in the past. Indeed, if such socialization were not the rule but were rather the exception, we might expect that every person given a speeding ticket would kick, punch, or bite the police officer or that an employee docked for tardiness would attack his or her supervisor. Indeed, such attacks are fortunately rare. Similarly, most children do not attack their parents when they are punished for some wrongdoing. We can speculate that those who do, have probably never been effectively punished for such behavior.[188]

Echoes of original sin and human depravity are audible even here; secularized Calvinism is hidden in the language of a behaviorist. Van Houten seems certain that human beings are naturally violent and aggressive, prone to kicking, punching, and biting policemen as a matter of course if they have not first been taught, by being assaulted themselves in childhood, to avoid such aggressive behavior. The physical punishment of children would seem to be as inevitable and necessary from this perspective as it is from that of punishment advocates among Protestants, past and present.

Experimental studies of the effects of punishments by behaviorists—studies vital for an understanding of the short- and long-term consequences of physical punishments—raise the crucial issue of what impact pain and coercion have on the emotions of the "infrahumans" and humans receiving such aversive stimuli. Behaviorists have had a profound suspicion of feelings and emotions. Skinner, for instance, consciously distanced himself from his own emotions both in his work and in his life. In his autobiography, he stated bluntly: "I also do not think feelings are important. Freud is probably responsible for the current extent to which they are taken seriously."[189]

Other behaviorists appear to share this antipathy to feelings, despite the strong and uncontrollable emotions that inevitably arise during encounters with painful punishments in the laboratory or elsewhere. Van Houten observes, for example, that "It is fortunate that punishment does not produce strong lasting emotional effects under most circumstances since it would be impossible to eliminate punishment from the natural environment. Although it is true that emotional behaviors are frequently observed following punishment, it is also true that *these effects are usually short lived* [emphasis added]."[190] Similarly, Newsom, Favell, and Rincover observe that "Punishment is experienced subjectively as pain, startle, discomfort, loss, or external control. Therefore, it is not surprising to find that it can have some immediate, emotionally charged effects in addition to its intended suppressive effects." However, they add that "*emotional* is at best a slippery term," before proceeding to examine the evidence from the experimental literature.[191]

Despite evidence of "Facial expressions and bodily movements suggesting fear" that is "frequently reported in studies employing intense electric shock as a punisher," and despite other evidence of responses that include "whining," screaming, and "trembling," Newsom and his coauthors observe that "When treatment progresses successfully, most of the more expressive emotional responses disappear, leaving a brief display of fear and an unconditioned startle reaction as the major emotional reactions to receiving shock."[192]

Newsom, Favell, and Rincover are concerned about "the emotional effects of shock punishment . . . because of its uniquely controversial nature."[193] More generally, however, they observe that "concern focuses on the possibility of highly generalized, severe, and enduring pathological effects collectively described as 'emotional disturbance.' " Noting succinctly that "Evidence for such claims, except in the case of aggression, is nonexistent," they insist that

At the present time, there is simply insufficient evidence to conclude that punishment, as commonly used in homes, schools, and
clinical settings, produces maladaptive behavior patterns that might
be considered to indicate emotional disturbance. Note the qualification, "as commonly used." Those attributing the most damaging effects to punishment often confuse punishment as used contingently
by parents, teachers, and therapists with child abuse, the excessive
use of painful stimuli in a generally noncontingent manner. Little
progress in resolving the question of a possible connection between
emotional disturbance and punishment is likely until this distinction
is widely understood.[194]

Here behaviorists seem to join fundamentalists and other religious
advocates of physical punishments in insisting that "punishment, as *commonly used* in *normal homes, schools, and clinical settings*" cannot be
associated with "maladaptive behavior patterns" or "emotional disturbance." Yet even here, the issue of "child abuse" arises, since many
behaviorists, like so many Christians, use physical punishment and pain
in their quest for altered states of being and behavior.

But most important, this study of the short-term and long-term side
effects of physical punishment concludes by recognizing how little is
actually known about such effects. Newsom, Favell, and Rincover
acknowledge:

Although numerous positive and negative side effects of punishment have been identified, as yet they have little clinical utility. It is
difficult to make an informed decision on the use of punishment when
(*a*) we know very little about the conditions under which various
punishers will have given effects; and (*b*) we still know so little about
the social effects of punishment.[195]

Their candor ought to give anyone who advocates the use of physical
punishment reason to reconsider the issue before inflicting pain on another person in the name of science, education, or therapy. As Newsom,
Favell, and Rincover observe:

The consumers of punishment include the parents, colleagues, administrators, and legislators who ultimately determine whether a pun-

ishment procedure may or may not be used. They control the long-term viability of every recognized punishment technique through their opinions, policies, regulations, and laws. Most of the time, their decisions seem to reflect very inadequate information about the nature and efficacy of punishment procedures and their side effects.[196]

Given the dearth of published studies—whether by behaviorists, historians, educators, sociologists, anthropologists, political scientists, or psychoanalysts and other kinds of psychologists—of the long-term effects of punishments, it is impossible to disagree with these authors' comment that "Punishment is a great deal more than just another behavioral technique, and the society which allows its use deserves as complete an account of its effects as possible."[197]

During the 1980s, a sustained controversy over the use and efficacy of physical punishment and other forms of aversive methods of behavior modification and therapy has arisen among behaviorists. In 1987, in an essay reviewing Gary Lavigna and Anne Donnellan's book, *Alternatives to Punishment: Solving Behavior Problems with Non-Aversive Strategies* (1986), Saul Axelrod addressed these controversies in the field and concluded that "one group of humane behavioral scientists has evaluated the research and concluded that punishment is unnecessary. Another group of humane behavioral scientists has concluded that selective use of punishment procedures, combined with reinforcement techniques, *is* necessary to solve some problems."[198] The division, it thus appears, is now between those behaviorists who still adhere to the use of some forms of painful punishments and those who prefer nonpunitive methods, with the balance apparently shifting increasingly in the direction of those who oppose painful punishments.

Edward Carr, for instance, is a behaviorist whose views on the issue of punishment have changed dramatically over the past decade.[199] Having once favored at least some occasional use of physical punishments, he now is opposed to them on theoretical as well as practical grounds. Carr and his colleague V. Mark Durand are among the behaviorists who have sought to decode the communications of children who suffer from autism or mental retardation and have concluded that aversive methods of training and treatment are unnecessary. As Carr and Durand note, "For many years psychologists considered the bizarre behavior of disturbed children to be either meaningless or the expression of mysterious unconscious conflicts. We believe instead that such behavior is often a primitive way of communicating needs."[200] Many other behaviorists have become convinced that older methods of physical punishments and aversive methods of behavior modification are inappropriate and unwarranted under any circumstances.

Other behaviorist psychologists and researchers, such as Crighton Newsom, remain convinced that at least some forms of physical punishment may be used when other methods of treatment fail or prove to be unsatisfactory.[201] The range of opinions in the field thus seems to be increasingly narrowed to those who support moderate levels of pain and occasional use of physical punishments and those who no longer support any use of physical punishments. Put in the religious context discussed earlier, perhaps we could see those behaviorists who favor aversive methods as being "a last resort" as occupying the center of the spectrum, while increasing numbers apparently have moved to the outer edge of opposition to all forms of physical punishments. If this proves to be the case, perhaps even the behavioral sciences will become increasingly opposed to the infliction of pain in the guise of education and the modification of behavior in both children and adults in the decades to come. Certainly the intense controversy currently raging in the profession suggests that behaviorists, unlike many others, take the issue of physical punishment seriously, and seek to fathom the implications—theoretical, practical, and moral—of the use of pain and punishment. Perhaps the day will come when most behaviorists, too, will recognize the negative long-term consequences of physical punishments and find better alternatives than pain and shocking and hurting.

With so little still known about the long-term consequences of punishment even by empiricists who examine behavior while remaining skeptical of feelings and the existence of the unconscious mind, the time has come to turn our attention to the emotional and psychological implications of corporal punishment and physical abuse—those experiential, cognitive, and social dimensions of human emotions, thought, and behavior that have borne the scars from suffering early in life. By exploring a wide range of issues associated with our psyches and our selves, our families and our society, perhaps we can expand our understanding of the long-term impact of painful punishments, the templates for so much that follows.

PART IV

Consequences

Only recently have we begun to recognize the profound dangers posed by the destruction of ozone high in the atmosphere above the poles. Only recently have we begun to perceive the deadly long-term consequences of the increasing acidity of the clouds, the rains, and even the fogs that flow across the land and water of North America and Europe. Only recently, too, have some of us begun to recognize the personal and collective dangers that physical punishments of children pose for us as individuals, for us as a people, and for all of humanity.

As the end of the twentieth century approaches, we need to begin exploring the realms of feeling, experience, and thought, associated with physical discipline, that have been hidden from our view through much of our history. Recognition of the enduring consequences of corporal punishments will be the psychological and intellectual equivalent of the discovery of the Rosetta stone. Suddenly feelings, thoughts, and behaviors that were indecipherable before the realities of childhood punishments and pain were seen and acknowledged will begin to make sense.

We have an urgent task: to explore and try to understand some of the consequences of painful assaults done in the name of discipline. The task is not simple and this essay is only a beginning. Given the endless ripples from the impact of the physical blows in childhood, from our innermost beings to the outermost edges of our consciousnesses, our communities, and our world, it is clear that the consequences flowing from physical punishments early in life wash over every aspect of our lives and soak through nearly every part of our society and culture. Punishment is so incorporated into our bodies, our minds, and our characters that its impact and ramifications extend far beyond the scope of any single effort to grasp them.

Nevertheless, we must ask ourselves how the pain of punishment in childhood affects our innermost selves, our feelings and personalities. Then we must seek some understanding of how these childhood punishments continue to affect our beliefs and our actions in the public realms of life. We must also ask how punishment shapes our consciousness and our convictions about authority and power, about the ways in which the coercive domination so many children experience becomes the authoritarianism that pervades American life and politics. Finally, we must reckon with the enduring impulse to annihilate life on this earth which is embodied in the apocalyptic feelings, fantasies, and beliefs that have been present in Christianity—and especially in certain forms of evangelical and fundamentalist Protestantism—from the beginning. For many Americans, past and present, the end of the world seems always at hand, and their eagerness both to witness the destruction of life on earth and to be rescued by their God from the tribulations that they expect to befall sinners at the end of history merit our close attention. Punishment is always at the center of such convictions and beliefs. We must begin, however, with the anxiety and fear and anger that physical punishments generate in children.

Anxiety and Fear

For two millennia, Christians have spent much of their lives anticipating punishments and worrying about how to escape the pains, terrors, and tortures of hell. "Heaven" has always meant the absence of punishment as well as eternal life.[1] But these anticipations begin in childhood, when the reality of pain from punishment begins to be familiar. Once a child is struck, the memory remains encoded in the brain and the body for life. Even those who were struck only once or twice can often remember the pain and shock years afterward. For those children who are punished more frequently, however, the anticipation of pain itself becomes a part of the punishment, and the anxiety and even dread generated by experiential knowledge of the burning sting of a hand, or a belt, or a rod, or any other implement, cannot easily be quelled. Fear thus becomes a central component of the process of physical discipline, for no child welcomes the pain, at least not initially. If children do welcome the pain, it is only because—like the children from Island Pond—they have come to associate pain with love. The fear remains, to haunt and distort their lives for years to come.

Fear is an inevitable and appropriate feeling when faced with the probability of pain. No child can expect to avoid the pain of punishment when adults are intent upon inflicting it. The longer the delay, the greater the tension and fear. "Go to your room and wait" is one of the most terrifying things a child who is about to be punished can hear. The persistent anxieties over the approach of doom that haunt the lives of apocalyptics mirror the childhood experience of awaiting pain to be inflicted upon the body and self by adults who are loved and depended upon for life itself.

Children cry when they are hurt and when they are frightened, and corporal punishments entail both pain and fear. Tears of anticipation, which are ineffectual efforts to ward off or delay the pains to come, are usually followed by tears of suffering, as Christenson, Dobson, Fugate, Lessin, and others have noted. Children who resist are often hurt the most, since adults who intend to inflict corporal punishments usually do not allow children to retaliate or to resist. The big and powerful always find ways of intimidating and dominating the small and powerless, and pain is the most compelling method of all for forcing children to submit their wills and selves to the wills and commands of adults. The pain generates fear, as so many corporal-punishment advocates readily acknowledge, and the fear never disappears entirely. As centuries of writings by Protestants and other Christians in both America and Europe demonstrate, many adults want children to experience fear, considering it necessary and desirable. But fear usually gives way to anger and hate.

Anger and Hate

Love is natural; hate is created. All children initially love their parents, but some learn to hate them, and for good reason. Being assaulted violently in the name of discipline invariably produces anger and often rage in children, just as it does in most adults. Anger is the key to an understanding of the long-term consequences of corporal punishment, for it is the central emotion that shapes our psyches long after the original pain has subsided and been forgotten or denied.[2]

Anger is a child's best (and often only) defense, for it arises out of a powerful sense of self, a self being violated and abused by painful blows and hurtful words. The child has been hurt on purpose by an adult in order to teach a lesson in discipline, but the child experiences this pain and reproach as an assault upon the self as well as upon the body. Often the result is not only anger but also hatred and a powerful desire for revenge, which often takes the form of imagined mutilation or murder of the person who inflicted the pain. These powerful emotions are permanently stored in unconscious memories, but sometimes people also remember them quite consciously, years after the events that provoked the feelings. These ancient angers resonate in our psyches throughout our lives; they are more powerful and dangerous when ignored or forgotten than when felt and acknowledged—and, ultimately, healed through understanding and forgiveness.[3]

When in his early fifties, Edmund Gosse recalled in his famous autobiography, *Father and Son* (1907), his one encounter with corporal punishment as vividly as if it had just happened. Gosse was the only child of two intensely apocalyptic parents, English members of the sect of Plymouth Brethren. He recollected: "It was about the date of my sixth birthday that I did something very naughty, some act of direct disobedience, for which my Father, after a solemn sermon, chastised me, sacrificially, by giving me several cuts with a cane. This action was justified, as everything he did was justified, by reference to Scripture." Gosse also had vivid memories of his own reactions and feelings to this encounter with corporal punishment. He recollected "being made, not contrite or humble, but furiously angry by this caning. I cannot account for the flame of rage which it awakened in my bosom," he wrote, but added that "I have to confess with shame that I went about the house for some days with a murderous hatred of my Father locked within my bosom." Although he says that he soon "forgot and thus forgave" the caning, Gosse's ability to remember his feelings of "rage" and of "murderous hatred" nearly half a century later indicates that the memory never vanished.[4]

The rage that finally erupted from Allen Wheelis (a psychoanalyst) as a boy smoldered an entire summer. He obediently submitted to his father's orders to cut the vast yard filled with tall grass—with a straight-razor blade. Wheelis's bedridden and very ill father used whippings to discipline his reluctant son and to enforce his command, which he continually oversaw with intense concern. Wheelis's memoir of his summer cutting grass is one of the most astonishing recollections of child abuse yet written. Wheelis recalls that he "became inured to the work but not reconciled to it, and throughout the summer continued to resist. Whippings—which had been rare before—were now common, and after each I would, in the evening, be required to apologize." He felt afterward that he was "innately lazy, unworthy, and impulsive," and soon "would become sullen or rebellious and again would be punished." During this interminable summer, he was forbidden to play with his friends until the work was entirely completed; his resentment, however suppressed, grew ever more powerful. One day it rained, yet the boy still was not allowed to play with his friends, and the flood of imprisoned feelings gushed forth:

> A feeling of strangeness swept over me. I had never cursed, was not used to such words. Something violent was stirring in me, something long stifled was rankling for expression.
>
> "If you think you can kick me around all the time you're wrong . . . you damned old bastard!"
>
> At any moment I expected to be called. I would go inside then and receive a whipping worse than I had known possible.

But nothing happened. His father did not respond, although he certainly had heard his son's epithets and curses.

> "You're the meanest man in the world. You lie up there in bed and are mean to everybody. I hate you!"
>
> I began to feel astonished at myself. How incredible that I should be saying such things—I who had never dared a word of disrespect!

Yet the silence from his father continued, and the boy's puzzlement increased.

> I became frantic, poured out a tirade of abuse, searched my memory for every dirty word I knew, and when the store of profanity was exhausted and I stopped, breathless, to listen . . . there was no response.

"You goddamn dirty son of a bitch!" I screamed, "I wish you was dead! I wish you was dead, do you hear? Do you hear me?"

I had finished. Now something would happen. I cowered and waited for it, but there was no word from the porch. Not a sound. Not even the stir of bedclothes.

The rage passed and I became miserable.[5]

Wheelis thus reveals the overwhelming sense of murderous rage evoked in the boy whose father not only punished him repeatedly but enforced a regime so harsh that it resembled a prison's. Not surprisingly, his father justified this discipline—of both work and pain—by telling him: " 'Remember, son . . . whenever it seems I'm being hard on you . . . it's because I love you.' " Little wonder, then, that the boy awoke "in terror from a nightmare" that night, and worried obsessively about the whereabouts of his razor. He searched for it and then discovered that it was "in its usual place, properly closed." The weapon that might have been used to wound someone unnamed was safe still. But Wheelis, as his memoir subsequently makes clear, was not; the momentary rage resonated for years to come.[6]

Often rage is repressed, however, and the feelings that punishment provokes in the child are blanked out of conscious memory. Such repression of rage is normal and commonplace. It explains why so few adults recall the anger they experienced as children when being punished and hurt by their parents. To remember is to recognize the ambivalent feelings of love *and* hate.

Alice Miller has recognized the centrality of ambivalence and the inevitability of anger in children who are corporally punished. Miller notes, for instance, that "It is inconceivable that they were able to express and develop their true feelings as children, for anger and helpless rage, which they were forbidden to display, would have been among these feelings—particularly if these children were beaten, humiliated, lied to, and deceived." She asks the crucial question—"What becomes of this forbidden and therefore unexpressed anger?"—and answers: "Unfortunately, it does not disappear, but is transformed with time into a more or less conscious hatred directed against either the self or substitute persons, a hatred that will seek to discharge itself in various ways permissible and suitable for an adult."[7] This answer is one of the central themes of Miller's analysis of the implications of corporal punishment. Yet, as she knows all too well, it is the very thing most people, century after century, have been unable to acknowledge and to accept. The violation of the child's body and soul by painful punishments generates the anger and the rage that later foster violence against the self and others. That rage is the most common and continuous source for the destructive and aggressive impulses felt, imagined, and acted on throughout our collective histories and present experiences.

Empathy and Apathy

One of the most enduring consequences of corporal punishments—and yet one of the least appreciated and studied—is the stifling of empathy and compassion for oneself and others. The ability to put oneself in the place of others and to understand how they feel and experience life, and the ability to grasp sympathetically both their suffering and their joy is one of the greatest human achievements. As we have seen, however, the books written by many advocates of corporal punishments are notably deficient in empathy for the suffering of children whose bodies bear the impact of painful assaults justified as discipline. The ability to put oneself in another's place often might seem sufficient to curb the aggressive impulses to inflict physical and emotional suffering on children, but most people hurt in childhood by their parents develop immunities to empathy that often persist for a lifetime. Much pain is inflicted in the name of morality and conscience when empathy, compassion, and respect for others are absent.[8]

The parent who hurts a child while imposing discipline is teaching a lesson in indifference to suffering as well as one in obedience. J. Richard Fugate, an advocate of the rod, recognizes the impulse toward empathy and compassion in some parents, especially mothers: "A mother naturally cringes at the thought of switching her own child. The reality of intentionally inflicting pain, especially in using a rod that can make a mark (which will quickly go away), goes against the natural tendency to protect, comfort, and nurture her child. Uninformed mothers may even try to interfere with the father's proper use of a rod."[9] His advice is for mothers to think of the long-term consequences of their use of the rod in obtaining the obedience of their children, however much they may feel the need "to protect, comfort, and nurture" their children.

Far too little has been done as yet to probe and understand the roots of empathy among adults, but it is clear that physical punishments, especially severe ones, inhibit the development of empathy in later life.[10] Nonphysical modes of discipline generally foster the ability to empathize with others in adulthood. The reason is that adults who use nonviolent forms of discipline usually respect the body, the feelings, and the selfhood of the child even when experiencing and expressing disapproval of particular actions or ways of expressing the will or the self. Compassion, as Jessica Benjamin recognizes, is grounded in a sense of mutuality, "the ability to share feelings and intentions without demanding control, to experience sameness without obliterating difference."[11] By its very dependence upon assault and pain, coercive physical discipline makes such a sense of mutuality and respect impossible.

Altruism, for example, reflects a particular pattern of child-rearing, as remarked by Ervin Staub:

> The parents who transmit altruism most effectively . . . exert a firm control over their children. Although they are nurturant, they are not permissive. They use a combination of firmness, warmth and reasoning. They point out to children the consequences to others of misbehavior—and good behavior. And they actively guide the child to do good, to share, to be helpful.[12]

Other studies confirm the significance of non–physically punitive methods of child-rearing for the fostering of empathy and compassion in later life.[13] Nonviolent discipline, especially that which emphasizes reasoning with children, fosters an awareness of and sensitivity to the viewpoints and feelings of other people that sustain the empathy of later years.[14]

Equally enduring are the apathy and passivity so often experienced by children who are physically punished and abused. Ruth and Henry Kempe point out:

> Another outstanding characteristic of young abused children is their compliance and acceptance of whatever happens. They are passive and obedient, even when in the hospital they are required to

submit to painful procedures, or when in the process of an evaluation
they are taken away from their parents by a stranger. They will remain
in uncomfortable positions for a long time if asked to do so, or sit
quietly while their mothers talk for a long time. That this truly is
compliance is proved by their gradual growth of assertiveness and
resistance, if they are removed to a more permissive environment.[15]

Other observers have noted similar behavior in children who have been
abused, but the long-term effect—a more generalized apathy and passivity, including the choice of passive modes of aggression—too often is not
fully appreciated.

Apathy and passivity, which often persist throughout adulthood in
many different forms and degrees, are the counterparts, the mirror opposites, of the anger and aggression also caused by painful punishments
in childhood. Acting out aggression is far more visible and potentially
dangerous both to individuals and to societies, but passivity has its dangers as well, both to individuals and to the world as a whole. Recent
studies confirm that violence depicted on television fosters aggression
among children while simultaneously fostering apathy toward others'
sufferings from violence and aggression. Ross Parke and Ronald Slaby
note that "Research has demonstrated that television must be considered
one of the major socializers of children's aggressive behavior. Two major
behavioral effects of heavy viewing of televised violence are: (1) an increase in children's level of aggression; and (2) an increase in children's
passive acceptance of the use of aggression by others."[16] Both aggression
and apathy thus are intensified by an immersion in television violence
although the roots of both undoubtedly are to be found in the life histories
of punishment and abuse of those who view such violence with either
indifference or enthusiasm.

Children learn early in life to distance themselves from the actual
suffering they witness—or experience. Television augments the apathy
both through the frequency of the violence depicted hourly and daily in
cartoons for children and the physical violence and murder continually
depicted on the screen for juveniles and adults alike to witness. The
culture of violence—rooted in physical assaults upon children—is reenacted daily on television for anyone to see.

Melancholy and Depression

For many people, buried anger becomes the basic source of aggression against the self. The most common form this self-aggression takes in America, past and present, is the emotional experience of depression. Although the illness itself has been present since ancient times, we still lack an adequate understanding of the experiential roots of this persistent phenomenon.

The etiology of depression remains unclear despite the substantial literature on depression written mostly from psychoanalytic and clinical psychological perspectives. Although a primary focus of research has been the infant and early childhood origins resulting from separation and loss (which John Bowlby and others have explored in detail), there has been almost no recognition of the enduring impact of ordinary experiences with punishment in childhood.[17] Despite all that has been written about depression, the literature seems to be remarkably barren of an awareness of the role that childhood discipline and pain and anger have played in the psyches of many individuals who subsequently suffer from various forms of depression. While the etiology undoubtedly is complex, punishment in childhood always has been one of the most powerful generators of depression in adulthood.

One of the least recognized tragedies of the twentieth century was the failure of Sigmund Freud, the most daring investigator of the unconscious mind in this or any other century, to explore the enduring psychological impact of painful corporal punishments and physical abuse upon individuals and upon culture as a whole. Sigmund Freud's incisive and insightful essay "Mourning and Melancholia" (1917), which continues to shape our perceptions of adult depression, overlooks experiences with punishment in childhood. His description of the symptoms of depression is revealing: "a profoundly painful dejection, abrogation of interest in the outside world, loss of the capacity to love, inhibition of all activity, and a lowering of the self-regarding feelings to a degree that finds utterance in self-reproaches and self-revilings, and culminates in a delusional expectation of punishment."[18] The crucial word here is "delusional." Freud never took the reality of punishment seriously. He never connected the feelings and self-destructive impulses of his melancholy adults with the feelings generated by corporal punishments in childhood. Even in his famous essay " 'A Child Is Being Beaten': A Contribution to the Study of the Origin of Sexual Perversions" (1919) he focused upon fantasies of being beaten, denying the significance of actual beatings in the individual lives he analyzed.[19]

Freud never explored the psychological implications of corporal punishment. He apparently could not bring himself to acknowledge the legitimate experiential basis in childhood for the accusations his depressed adult patients characteristically directed against themselves. Freud noted, however, that

> If one listens patiently to the many and various self-accusations of the melancholiac, one cannot in the end avoid the impression that often the most violent of them are hardly at all applicable to the patient himself, but that with insignificant modifications they do fit someone else, some person whom the patient loves, has loved or ought to love. This conjecture is confirmed every time one examines the facts. So we get the key to the clinical picture—by perceiving that the self-reproaches are reproaches against a loved object which have been shifted on to the patient's own ego.[20]

Presumably, the "loved object" was once a parent or another adult responsible for the rearing and discipline of the child. Yet Freud recognized from his careful observations that his patient's "complaints are really 'plaints' in the legal sense of the word," and "the reactions in their behaviour still proceed from an attitude of revolt, a mental constellation which by a certain process has become transformed into melancholic contrition."[21] Freud recognized that "The self-torments of melancholiacs, which are without doubt pleasurable," along with the experiences of obsessives, constitute "a gratification of sadistic tendencies and of hate, both of which relate to an object and in this way have both been turned round upon the self." Thus hate and sadism are connected, somehow, to depression. He then added that "In both disorders the sufferers usually succeed in the end in taking revenge, by the circuitous path of self-punishment, on the original objects and in tormenting them by means of the illness, having developed the latter so as to avoid the necessity of openly expressing their hostility against the loved ones."[22] Freud never once says explicitly that this hostility and wish for revenge might initially have arisen because of painful, assaultive punishments inflicted in childhood. Freud could not bring himself to admit the obvious implication of his analysis: depression often is a delayed response to the suppression of childhood anger that usually results from being physically hit and hurt in the act of discipline by adults whom the child loves and on whom he or she depends for nurturance and life itself.

Freud did recognize, though, the ultimate danger of depression: the possibility of literally murdering the self. Suicide is too often the ultimate outcome of the varying degrees of assault, aggression, and revenge against oneself that stem from childhood anger. Freud recognized that "we have long known that no neurotic harbours thoughts of suicide which are not murderous impulses against others re-directed upon himself."[23] Murder of the self, through suicide, remains the most deadly individual consequence of corporal punishment, and depression is commonly the central antecedent and propulsion toward self-destruction.

Melancholy and depression have been persistent themes in the family history, religious experience, and emotional lives of Puritans, evangelicals, fundamentalists and Pentecostals for centuries.[24] Assaults on the self and on self-will are the central obsession of vast numbers of men and women from the early seventeenth century to the present. Suicidal impulses frequently appear in these Protestants' self-portraits as well, although those who write memoirs and autobiographies are usually survivors, not suicides. They may have successfully thwarted their inner impulses toward self-destruction, but the experience of conversion and the new birth rarely relieved them fully of their depressive symptoms. Michael Wigglesworth, whose apocalyptic "Day of Doom" was one of the best-selling publications in early New England, suffered from profound melancholy from his early twenties through at least his early fifties. Punishment was central to both his psyche and his theology.[25] Many evangelicals, generation after generation, voiced their anxiety and depression in their diaries, letters, and autobiographies. In some families, such as the Mathers, melancholy afflicted fathers and sons for at least three successive generations. The persistence and, indeed, the centrality of melancholy and depression for an understanding of religious and secular experience in America, from early-seventeenth-century Puritans to late-nineteenth-century Victorians, has been explored brilliantly by John

Owen King in his illuminating book, *The Iron of Melancholy*.[26] Some of the most compelling historical evidence we possess concerning the nature and history of depression comes from the religious tradition associated most directly with Calvinism and evangelical Protestantism over the past four centuries.

Closely linked to the recurrent depression evident in so many individuals is the theme of buried and smoldering anger—more often suppressed and denied, disguised and obscured, than openly acknowledged and expressed—visible in many of the most subtle studies of the life histories of Puritan, Calvinist, and evangelical individuals. The depression that manifests itself consistently throughout their lives is nearly always associated with the suppression of anger throughout their adulthood. Cotton Mather, for example, was one of the angriest men living in New England during the colonial period. His words and actions betrayed his inner rage however much he sought to deny it and obscure it from himself and others. Kenneth Silverman has noted that the preacher's early stuttering was rooted in anger; Silverman observes the continuous impact of the "muffled rage" that Mather simultaneously vented and denied. Throughout his life, this rage underpinned his apocalyptic fantasies of the end of time. Mather "projected personal anger into visions of a world consumed, and hopes for personal vindication into sights of Christ returned to punish the wicked and avenge the virtuous." The violence suffusing his language and his religious experience, including his intense apocalypticism, is exceptionally clear.[27]

At about the same time, across the Atlantic, the brilliant mathematician, philosopher, and scientist, Isaac Newton, was also obsessed with apocalyptic fantasies brewed by an intense and inescapable, though obscured, rage. As a Puritan's son, young Newton suffered a "generally depressive state" throughout his adolescence, with a "general mood of anxiety" prevailing. Frank Manuel, in his luminous psychological analysis, notes that "Newton was aware of the mighty anger that smoldered within him all his life, eternally seeking objects, and he made heroic attempts to repress it." Nevertheless, "many were the times" when his inner "censor" was "overwhelmed and the rage could not be contained." Although Manuel does not entertain the possibility that at least some of this lifelong rage could have arisen from childhood discipline and punishment—Puritan parents were among the most abusive in using the rod upon their children's bodies and wills—the rage itself clearly shaped

Newton's character and life. Manuel speculates that Newton's rage "accumulated in personal historical situations, that it was the onerous heritage of childhood traumas, beginning with the infant's anxiety after separation from the person who nurtured him—his mother [who remarried and moved away, leaving him with his grandmother]. . . . So deep is the hurt and so boundless the anger, however, that he cannot be appeased as long as he lives."[28] Newton, like Cotton Mather and countless others, paid a high personal price for the emotions generated in childhood, chief among them depression, anxiety, and rage.

The long-sustained persistence of melancholy and depression among twice-born Protestants is clearly no accident, since it has consistently been paralleled by the tradition of assault, coercion, and violence against children committed with the rod, the belt, the hand, and other such instruments of parental discipline. What remains to be done is to connect these disparate realms of experience, something Freud and most of his followers to date have been reluctant to do. From all this historical evidence, it ought to be clear that depression is often the central mood characteristic of adults whose bodies were assaulted, whose wills were broken in childhood, and whose anger was forcibly suppressed. The rage and resentment never disappear; they just take more covert and dangerous forms, dangerous to the self and, potentially, to others.

Depression rooted in anger remains so potent because it often begins so early—in the first three years of life, precisely the period corporal-punishment advocates have always stressed as critical for the start of physical punishments and the suppression of children's wills and self-assertion. The first assaults upon children's bodies and spirits generally commence before conscious memory can recall them later. The unconscious thus becomes the repository for the rage, resistance, and desire for revenge that small children feel when being struck by the adults they love. The impact of pain and physical violence is most severe because the children are unable to protect themselves from the blows. Though they cannot remember consciously what happened to them during the first three or four years of life, the ancient angers persist while the adult conscience directs rage inward upon the self. The psyches of so many Puritans, evangelicals, and others who have suffered from adult depressions bear witness to this process.

If we are willing to learn from past experience, the painful life stories of individuals long deceased have much to teach us about the nature and origins of melancholy and depression. Once we connect the pains of early childhood and the experience of violent physical assault with the feelings of anger and resentment, the subsequent moods of self-assault and self-deprecation characteristic of depression will make far better sense than has been the case hitherto. The long-term persistence of melancholy among twice-born Protestants in previous centuries, as in the present, was and is rooted in the consciously forgotten but unconsciously persistent traumas of physical abuse from punishments in early childhood.[29]

Obsessiveness and Rigidity

Physical assaults upon children through corporal punishments often result in the formation of obsessive-compulsive characters, which become defenses against the rage and revengefulness arising from the hurts experienced from infancy through adolescence. Rituals, rules, rigid self-regulations and controls are always evident, along with persistent anxieties and doubts generated by contrary impulses and thoughts. Issues of control and autonomy are usually paramount, precisely because of the presence of impulses and desires opposed to control. But obsessives lack a sense of freedom in much of their lives, since they feel compelled by inner impulses and needs to think certain things and to act and feel only certain ways. Fundamentalist Protestants, of course, often epitomize such obsessive traits, both in their adamant insistence upon the doctrine of biblical inerrancy and in many aspects of their characters and their behavior.[30]

David Shapiro has described the rigid characters of obsessive-compulsives in terms of their conflicts over autonomy and will: "It happens regularly that, in their purposiveness and determination, rigid individuals misidentify what they want, what they intend, and even what they believe. They mistake what they think they should want for what they actually do want, what they think should be their intentions for actual intentions, ideas that they think they should believe for convictions."[31] In other words, such individuals are alienated from their own sense of self and of self-will. More extreme obsessive compulsives experience constant compulsions to say or do things that appear to be independent of their own wills or desires. As Shapiro notes, "the compulsive person's identification of himself with the regime of dutiful work and purpose transforms the subjective meaning of autonomy from being free to follow one's own wishes and live according to one's own lights to self-discipline, self-control, the subordination of one's wishes to one's will. Such a person lives," he adds, "in a state of continuous tension between will and underlying inclination."[32]

In adults, the symptoms of obsessive-compulsive modes of being and behavior have been observed and described many times and are readily recognizable. The Reverend George Whitefield, for instance, a great evangelist of the eighteenth century both in England and America and an ardent advocate of breaking children's wills early in childhood, was described by an acquaintance as being "very exact to the time appointed for his stated meals; a few minutes delay would be considered a great fault. He was irritable, but soon appeased. . . . Not a paper must have been out of place, or put up irregularly. Each part of the furniture must have been likewise in its place" before Whitefield could sleep. Jonathan Edwards was described by one of his students, who had lived in his household, as being "very strict and exact" in his diet, living by rule and practicing "great self-denial." "In his conduct in his family, he practised that conscientious exactness which was perspicuous in all his ways."[33] Such examples could be multiplied, as the portraits of Puritans, Calvinists, and evangelicals limned in my book *The Protestant Temperament*, in David Leverenz's *The Language of Puritan Feeling*, and in John Owen King's *The Iron of Melancholy* demonstrate in abundant detail.

All three studies confirm the presence of an obsessive character among many of the people labeled Puritans and evangelicals in the seventeenth, eighteenth, and nineteenth centuries. Leverenz argues that "Puritans sought, with varying degrees of success, to remold themselves into what we would now call an 'obsessive-compulsive' personality, and their religion into obsessive ordering."[34] He remarks: "Obsessives tend to suppress anger against parents or displace it, often against the self." He also notes, very perceptively, that "Feelings are split into exaggerated love for an authority figure and repressed hate, repressed because of the enormous fear of aggressive feelings toward those whose love is all-important." Leverenz recognizes, too, that "Because the hate side of ambivalence is so fearful, the hate becomes terrifyingly magnified into omnipotent, apocalyptic destructiveness that must be caged at all costs."[35] Leverenz recognizes that such feelings are rooted in familial experiences, but he insists that "Puritanism was not the product of strong patriarchs breaking the child's will, at least at the start."[36] He fails, however, to reckon with the enduring impact of the rod and other corporal punishments in the shaping of the obsessive ideation and behavior that he describes so perceptively.

Like studies of depression, studies of the etiology of obsessive-compulsive character often have failed to provide a persuasive analysis of the early childhood origins of this emotional disorder.[37] Most analysts and observers have overlooked the most obvious, most common possibility for the origins of these repetitive traits: corporal punishments and the physical and emotional traumas associated with this kind of early discipline. Perhaps, though, the case is one of seeing but not recognizing what is in front of our eyes. Most analysts and psychologists, from Freud to the present, have been blind to the implications of physical punishments of children.

Sigmund Freud's famous study of the "Rat Man" in his "Notes Upon a Case of Obsessional Neurosis" (1909) has rarely been appreciated for its contributions toward an understanding of the psychological impact of corporal punishment.[38] Freud had blinders where the impact of physical discipline and punishment of children was concerned, even though he encountered ample evidence in his daily life and psychoanalytic practice. *Postcards from the End of the World*, Larry Wolff's exploration of child abuse in Freud's Vienna, makes clear the extent to which Freud evaded the realities of physical abuse, both corporal punishments and sexual assaults. For Freud, fantasy, not reality, was to become the key to his response to evidence from adults of early childhood abuse.[39] Yet Freud was also intent upon demonstrating the early sexual origins of subsequent neurosis, even while describing vividly the actual nonsexual childhood experiences that accompanied the formation of the symptoms he associated with obsessive-compulsive disorder.

Freud's patient's obsession began when he heard a fellow army officer in Vienna defending "the introduction of corporal punishment," which "obliged" him "to disagree . . . very sharply." The officer then told a story of "a specially horrible punishment used in the East": a rat placed in a pot against a person's "buttocks" would bore into the "anus." The patient had thought that similar punishments might be inflicted on both a woman whom he admired and his long-dead father, obsessions that haunted him for a long while.[40]

Ultimately, Freud hypothesized that when his patient "was a child of under six he had been guilty of some sexual misdemeanour connected with onanism and had been soundly castigated for it by his father. This punishment . . . had put an end to his onanism, but . . . it had left behind it an ineradicable grudge against his father and had established him for all time in his role as an interferer with the patient's sexual enjoyment." The patient, however, "had no recollection of it whatever," but had been told by his mother of an incident that occurred when he was between three and four:

> he had done something naughty, for which his father had given him a beating. The little boy had flown into a terrible rage and had hurled abuse at his father even when he was under his blows. But as he knew no bad language, he had called him all the names of common objects that he could think of, and had screamed: "You lamp! You towel! You plate!" and so on. His father, shaken by such an outburst of elemental fury, had stopped beating him, and had declared: "The child will be either a great man or a great criminal!"

Freud added that the patient said his father "never beat him again," although the patient "attributed to this experience a part of the change which came over his own character. From that time forward he was a coward—*out of fear of the violence of his own rage* [emphasis added]." In addition, even if he himself was never struck another blow, which is unlikely but possible, his siblings were beaten and he observed their painful assaults with powerful feelings: "His whole life long, moreover, he was terribly afraid of blows, and used to creep away and hide, filled with terror and indignation, when one of his brothers or sisters was beaten." The punishment, the mother reported, had been due to the boy's biting someone. Freud, however, clearly wanted to believe that she misrepresented the occasion and that it had had sexual roots, but he could not help acknowledging "its objective reality." Later, the patient would often get up from the analyst's sofa and "roam about the room," clearly agitated, finally explaining to his analyst "that he was avoiding my proximity for fear of *my giving him a beating* [emphasis added]." Freud then observed that

If he stayed on the sofa he behaved like someone in desperate terror trying to save himself from castigations of boundless dimensions; he would bury his head in his hands, cover his face with his arm, jump up suddenly and rush away, his features distorted with pain, and so on. He recalled that his father had had a passionate temper, and *sometimes in his violence had not known where to stop* [emphasis added].[41]

This was corporal punishment of the severest kind, which might have seemed potentially murderous to the small boy being beaten. Freud reported the violence but did not comment upon it as being anything unusual or significant. His patient, however, through his obsessional neurosis, had betrayed the presence within of unconscious feelings generated in childhood, feelings that oscillated around the axis of love and hate, particularly for his own father.

The key to obsessiveness, Freud noted earlier, is the "battle between love and hate," for compulsive acts reflect "a conflict between two opposing impulses of approximately equal strength: and hitherto I have invariably found that this opposition has been one between love and hate."[42] Earlier in the essay, Freud noted his patient's intense suicidal and homicidal fantasies, remarking that "they both arose as reactions to a tremendous feeling of rage, which was inaccessible to the patient's consciousness and was directed against some one who had cropped up as an interference with the course of his love."[43] He does not say that such murderous and suicidal impulses could equally have arisen from being beaten by the father, despite the rage generated by the beatings. Freud was so intent upon exploring more deeply his theories of infantile sexuality and the unconscious origins of adult neurosis that he saw but did not grasp the full implications of the physical pain, terror, and rage experienced by the little boy being beaten. Without this paternal violence and physical abuse, however, this case of obsessional neurosis makes no sense. Freud failed to recognize the traumatic nature and enduring emotional consequences of such beatings.

Erik Erikson achieved what Freud had not: the acknowledgment and appreciation of the enduring consequences of physically violent discipline in the shaping of an obsessional and depressive character. Writing about *Young Man Luther*, Erikson asserted that "there is no doubt that in his depressed moods he displayed at times what we would call the clinical picture of a melancholia." Later in his life, though, Luther "abandoned this melancholic mood altogether for occasional violent mood swings between depression and elation, between self-accusation and the abuse of others." But "Sadness . . . was primarily the over-all symptom of his youth, and was a symptom couched in a traditional attitude provided by his time."[44]

Depression often precedes or accompanies an obsessive mode of being, which in Luther's case remained central to his character throughout his life. As Erikson observes: "According to the characterology established in psychoanalysis, suspiciousness, obsessive scrupulosity, moral sadism, and a preoccupation with dirtying and infectious thoughts and substances go together. Luther had them all. One of Martin's earliest reported remarks (from his student days) was a classical obsessive statement: 'the more you cleanse yourself, the dirtier you get.' "[45] Erikson explored Luther's early experiences in the closely regulated world of the monastery as a welcome relief from anxieties, tensions, and doubts. "It makes psychiatric sense," Erikson noted, "that under such conditions a young man with Martin's smoldering problems, but also with an honest wish to avoid rebellion against an environment which took care of so many of his needs, would subdue his rebellious nature by gradually developing compulsive-obsessive states characterized by high ambivalence."[46] This theme would subsequently resonate through the lives of countless Puritans, evangelicals, and fundamentalists in the New World as well as in Europe. What underlay all of this rebelliousness and anxiety, however, is clear from Erikson's analysis of the role of discipline in the shaping of Luther's character.

Erikson first deals with the universality of corporal punishments in Luther's period and culture, insisting that "the assertion that the cause was too common to have an uncommon effect on one individual—is neither clinically nor biographically valid. We must try to ascertain the relationship of caner and caned, and see if a unique element may have given the common event a specific meaning."[47] He then quotes two comments by Luther himself concerning his experiences with corporal punishments as a child: " 'My father once whipped me so that I ran away and felt ugly toward him until he was at pains to win me back.' 'My mother caned me for stealing a nut until the blood came. Such strict discipline drove me to a monastery although she meant it well.' "[48] Erikson notes that "Martin, even when mortally afraid, *could not really hate his father*, he could only be sad," and his father, "while he could not let the boy come close, and was murderously angry at times, *could not let him go for long.*" Erikson's clear presumption is that Martin "did hate" his father "underneath," the proof being found "in action delayed, and delayed so long that the final explosion hits nonparticipants."[49]

Erikson recognizes and understands the powerful long-term consequences of the beatings that Martin Luther experienced as a boy, for they resonated throughout his life in the religious beliefs and experiences that ultimately led to the transformation of the religious world and the emergence of one particular form of Protestantism. For Luther himself, however, one of the most enduring consequences was the shaping of an obsessive-compulsive personality, the imposition of self-control to contain the enduring rages generated by the pains of childhood punishments. The buried impulses of love and hate, reconciliation and rage, surely were among the major reasons why "Luther all his life felt like some sort of criminal, and had to keep on justifying himself even after his revelation of the universal justification through faith had led him to strength, peace, and leadership."[50]

Ambivalence: Protect and Destroy

The ambivalence at the heart of obsessive-compulsive feelings, thoughts, and behavior is rooted in the contradictory feelings of love and hate experienced by children who are being struck and abused by parents who profess to love them. Ambivalence is the key to David Leverenz's analysis of Puritanism, but it is visible also in the lives of most people who suffered pain from the hands and voices of loved adults during their childhoods. Alice Miller has recognized the centrality of these ambivalent feelings and explored them throughout her book *For Your Own Good.* But what often passes unnoticed are the contradictory impulses, which arise from the simultaneous presence of love and hate, both to protect and to destroy the person or persons who have been the source of suffering and pain, hurt and rage. Often assaults against the self are necessary to protect those against whom the original impulses were properly directed (initially parents, but often other adults as well). The early rage that assaults by adults generated leaves permanent impulses to aggression and destruction. The paradox is that *both impulses are always present*: The impulse to protect is mirrored by the impulse to destroy.

Cotton Mather and Isaac Newton epitomize the contradictory impulses generated by love and hate, which left both men with an inner ambivalence throughout their lives. Kenneth Silverman sees ambivalence at the core of Cotton Mather's character and life, producing "a disturbing discrepancy between act and intent," a persistent tendency "of simultaneously saying and unsaying." He observes:

> Mather also felt intensely guilty about his anger: in "my Hatred and Malice towards other Men," he wrote, "I have been a Degree of a Murderer." Thus in provoking others to condemn and revile him, he evidently also sought to thrash his own hated murderousness. More than any other characteristic of Mather's, it is this impossibly provocative fusion of the conciliator and the troublemaker, of his goodwill and his rage, that has always made him seem at once splendid and contemptible.[51]

To protect and to destroy remained the keys to Mather's life, thought, and actions, responses to the murderous rage and suppressed aggression that he never was able to escape despite his massive efforts, both intellectual and emotional, to deny and control them.

Newton, too, had the same dangerous and inadmissible impulses, rooted in his early childhood experiences. As Frank Manuel observes, "The dark deeds drowned in the welter of minor sins were the threats of parricide and matricide and the thoughts of self-slaughter and death to others that dominated him," thoughts and impulses from which Newton "was never wholly released."[52] Later, he too would experience the contradiction that marked Cotton Mather: "To love and to destroy—an ambivalent commandment."[53]

In some extraordinary mid-seventeenth-century poems, Michael Wigglesworth captured the impulse to protect fathers who inflict dire pain upon helpless children. Wigglesworth knew how some children felt when being beaten, as he observed in one poem, "God doth in Mercy scourge His own. / In Wrath he others lets alone." In a dialogue between the Flesh and the Spirit, the Flesh says:

OH but I greatly fear,
My sufferings are not such
As Childrens Nurture use to be
But that they differ much.
They are too great and long
(I fear) to stand with love:
Such overwhelming strokes methinks
Do rather hatred prove.[54]

Such thoughts, provoked by the repeated blows inflicted by a beloved parent, are inevitable, however much they may be feared or denied. Judith A. Martin and Alfred Kadushin interviewed parents who, after having physically abused their children through harsh punishments, speak directly to the experience of hate in the children being beaten. One mother said, "If I had to put myself in her place in her age, I'd be totally afraid of me. Probably even hate me. I mean a total hatred feeling for a while. Because what happened is I broke a certain relationship between us." Kadushin and Martin document such feelings with a series of comments from parents who were "asked what they imagine the child was feeling and thinking at the end of the incident," and who "perceive the child as responding negatively to them." Parents said:

She wanted me dead.
He probably didn't like me.
She carried on for an hour afterward, crying and saying that she
    doesn't like me and I hurt her.
She thinks I am bigger than she is and I am mean and I always hurt
    her.

·   ·   ·   ·

She probably hated me.
Total defeat and probably being unwanted and unloved, that she was
    unjustly pushed around, probably. She has even mentioned not
    being loved.
She was feeling that maybe I don't love her because if I did, how
    could I treat her this way?[55]

Some children, it should be noted, are fortunate in being able to articulate their feelings of being unloved, even hated, by the parents who had beaten them. They do not protect their parents from their hostility, anger, and sense of hurt and outrage; they put into words what Michael Wigglesworth's Flesh was able to acknowledge very briefly. Very often, though, children are too afraid to speak out either openly or inwardly. They deny and repress the hostility and hate they feel when assaulted by those whom they most love, and by this denial protect them.

The ability of a child to absorb the blows and pain and to suppress his own feelings and sense of outrage is made absolutely clear in Wigglesworth's poem "The Carriage of a Child of God / Under his Fathers smarting Rod," first published in 1669. God the Father afflicts all his children, Wigglesworth knew, even when it might appear that other individuals or circumstances were immediately responsible for the pain being suffered.

> *He sees a hand of God in his Afflictions all,*
> *And owns it for to be his Rod, Whatever Cross befall.*
> *For whosoever be th'immediate instrument*
> [including earthly fathers or mothers],
> *He knows right well that God himself was the Efficient.*

Wigglesworth (himself the only son of intensely pious Puritan parents, and a man who harbored an intense sense of guilt for his own inability to love his father) believed, nonetheless, that corporal punishments, great or small, were necessary and justified.

> *If that the Grief be small or the Chastisement light:*
> *Yet since God finds it not in vain, light strokes he dare not slight.*
> *If greater be the Blow, it doth not him dismay:*
> *Because he knows a Fathers hand such stripes may on him lay. . . .*

The child thus accepts the inevitability of punishment, no matter how painful or harsh.

> *Himself he humbleth under the mighty hand of God:*
> *And for the sake of that sweet hand doth kiss the sharpest Rod.*
> *He taketh up his Cross, denieth his own will,*
> *Advanceth God's above his own, and yieldeth to him still.*

Clearly, the point of this chastisement is to break the child's will and force him to submit to the commands of the father. There is no choice but to submit.

But what does the child actually experience when being beaten with his father's rod? What are his feelings under the blows and pain?

> *Unto the yoke of Christ he doth his neck submit:*
> *He turns his cheek to him that smites, and meekly taketh it.*
> *Yea when his grief is most, and sorest is his pain:*
> *He still endeavoureth good thoughts of God for to retain.*

This is where the protective impulse arises, for the child cannot allow himself to express the feelings he has as a result of the pain his father is inflicting on his body and spirit.

> *His earnest care and prayer when greatest is his smart,*
> *Is that he never may blaspheme God with his mouth or heart.*
> *He beggeth Patience in his extremities*
> *To bear Gods hand, that so his heart may not against him rise.*

But Wigglesworth knew, no doubt from his own experience, that such rebellious thoughts and feelings were hard to suppress.

> *If murmuring thoughts do rise (or hearts begin to swell)*
> *He strives to beat them down again; he hates such thoughts like Hell.*

The anxiety generated by the child's feelings is intense, and his impulse is to repress such thoughts completely.

The child will protect the father no matter what is being done to him, even at the risk of life itself. In an astonishing passage, Wigglesworth puts into words the impulse of an abused child to protect the abuser even under the threat of death:

> *God he resolves to love, deal with him as he will:*
> *And in his mercy to confide although he should him kill.*[56]

Anne Sexton reckoned with the same impulses in her powerful poem "Red Roses":

> *Tommy is three and when he's bad*
> *his mother dances with him.*
> *She puts on the record,*
> *"Red Roses for a Blue Lady"*
> *and throws him across the room.*

When Tommy, battered and bruised, is taken to the hospital, his mother says to him:

> *You fell, she said, just remember you fell.*
> *I fell, is all he told the doctors*
> *in the big hospital. A nice lady came*
> *and asked him questions but because*
> *he didn't want to be sent away he said, I fell.*
> *He never said anything else although he could talk fine.*

Tommy, like Michael Wigglesworth's child of God, learns to absorb any pain or punishment out of love for the mother who causes it.

> *He pretends he is her ball.*
> *He tries to fold up and bounce*
> *but he squashes like fruit.*
> *For he loves Blue Lady and the spots*
> *of red red roses he gives her.*[57]

What Tommy does not voice, however, are the other feelings he had when being tossed about and violated: terror, panic, and rage, the feelings that arise out of the need to protect ourselves. He protected his mother by denying himself.

Alice Miller has recognized the centrality of children's impulses to protect their parents from the emotional consequences of the outrage and hatred felt in the context of corporal punishments and physical abuse. Her sensitive and moving portrait of Christiane F.—a young drug addict and prostitute, whose father beat her regularly yet whom she was unable to hate or denounce, protecting him at her own expense for most of her adolescence and young adulthood—epitomizes the long-term consequences of this kind of childhood protection. Miller observes:

Her tolerance has no limits; she is always faithful and even proud that her father, who beats *her* brutally, never would do anything to hurt an animal; she is prepared to forgive him everything, always to take all the blame herself, not to hate him, to forget quickly everything that happens, not to bear a grudge, not to tell anyone about it, to try by her behavior to prevent another beating, to find out why her father is dissatisfied, to understand him, etc. . . . And what happens to all this repressed affect? It cannot simply disappear from the face of the earth. It must be directed toward substitute objects in order to spare the father.[58]

Christiane F.'s impulse to protect her battering and abusive father is shared by most, if not all, children, who often go to immense lengths to protect their mothers and fathers from the feelings that arise when they are being hit and hurt.

Adults' physical assaults on children produce both rage and outrage; they cause injuries to the body and the spirit that have long-lasting consequences. But the powerful impulse to love and the anxieties generated by the helplessness of the child, who cannot survive without the nurture and support of the adults who are abusing him or her, often makes repression of the rage and hate inevitable. Some children are able to tolerate the presence of both feelings, love and hate, sufficiently to permit them to remain in some sort of balance, precarious and difficult as it may be, intolerable as it might seem, but a balance that is manifested in a persistent ambivalence that later can take the form of an obsessive-compulsive character or neurosis. The original circumstances that generate such ambivalence are usually forgotten or repressed, but they are present still.

For some children, however, the conflicts generated by feelings of both love and hate are too painful to tolerate, and they respond by dissociating and splitting, amnesia serving to protect both the child and the adult from the unbearable knowledge. This process of dissociation has always proven to be one of the most common outcomes of the traumas generated by physical abuse—whether in the form of corporal punishments or that of sexual assaults—in early childhood.

Dissociation

The ability to disconnect feelings from their contexts and to disconnect one's sense of self from the external world are at the heart of the process of dissociation that underlies so many psychological phenomena. Dissociation is one of the most basic means of survival for many children, who learn early in life to distance themselves, or parts of themselves, from experiences too painful or frightening to bear. Traumas, both physical and emotional, are often coped with by denial and repression of the feelings they generate. The dissociative process is rooted, it appears, in the ability of so many children and adults to hypnotize themselves, to render unconscious aspects of their feelings and experiences that, for whatever reasons, they find unbearable or unacceptable.[59]

Dissociation takes many shapes in subsequent life. Classically, hysterical personalities and behaviors are rooted in dissociative processes; "borderline" personalities, too, often make use of dissociative means for coping with rage and aggression; and, in the most extreme cases, multiple personalities are created to cope with the emotions generated by intolerable abuses early in life.[60] Since pain felt and experienced takes many forms and comes in many degrees, from mild to severe to unbearable, children often discover ways to survive their pain through disconnecting and splitting, in the most extreme cases creating alternate selves and personalities, which bear and express feelings that otherwise would have been overwhelming to a small child. Dissociation, therefore, must be seen as one of the central means by which children and adults cope with the suffering and traumas that have afflicted them both earlier and later in life.

The crucial thing to recognize is that we are dealing with a complex spectrum of experiences, which, being associated with varying degrees and forms of pain, result in an equally complicated spectrum of psychological consequences in adults. Such consequences range from mild dissociative states, to hysterical trances, to multiple personalities.[61] At the root of these dissociative phenomena is usually a history of suffering, pain, and abuse early in life. The most common source of such suffering has always been corporal punishment.*

The power of the unconscious lies in the fact that the experiences of infancy and childhood are encoded in our memories permanently, in visual, tactile, and verbal forms. We too often fail to acknowledge that these memories persist throughout our lives, for most of them are buried and inaccessible to us despite our utmost efforts at recovery. What is most remarkable, though, is that these ancient memories survive intact, whole, complete in all details, as the evidence from both hypnosis and the study of post–traumatic stress victims consistently confirms. The studies of hysteria done in the late nineteenth century by Pierre Janet, Josef Breuer, Sigmund Freud, and others made the persistence of such memories clear for the first time. Breuer noted that "Hysterics suffer mainly from reminiscences."[62] Eugene Bliss, a psychiatrist who has used hypnosis in his treatment of patients suffering from multiple personalities, observes that when "reactivated in hypnosis, a memory is not a bare recollection. It seems to contain every element of the experience—the emotions, physical sensations, the auditory and visual components, the tastes and smells. When the patient returns to consciousness, all elements are still present as if the experience has just occurred."[63] When the memories of trauma victims are recovered and become accessible to the

---

* Dissociative behavior in religious experiences and contexts has yet to be explored adequately, but the ability to speak in tongues, characteristic of Pentecostalism, is rooted in dissociative states of mind. The extraordinary scenes described in Helen Kooiman Hosier's *Kathryn Kuhlman: The Life She Led, the Legacy She Left* (Old Tappan, N.J.: Fleming H. Revell, 1976), Chapter 6, "Detachment," fit the depictions of dissociative states by others. Given the childhood encounters with her mother's whippings, Kuhlman's ability to disconnect and disembody herself when preaching ought not to be overly surprising. Other biographies and autobiographies of Pentecostals reflect similar dissociative experiences and states in the context of their religious worship and lives.

Robert Anderson's cogent description of charismatic and Pentecostal worship notes that "Belief in spirit possession often leads to altered states of consciousness that produce unusual psychological and physical effects. Since these effects are dissociated from full consciousness, they are perceived as coming from some external, supernatural force." He also observes that "many experienced tongue-speakers are able to enter a state of dissociation with such little effort that neither they nor others are aware of the change. Yet the underlying alteration of consciousness is normally there, as it is in the case of all automatic behavior." Robert Mapes Anderson, *Vision of the Disinherited: The Making of American Pentecostalism* (New York: Oxford University Press, 1979), pp. 11, 13.

patients who have blocked them from consciousness, they too display this totality.[64] As Frank Putnam, Jr., a psychiatrist as well as a physiologist, noted with respect to multiple personalities, "They have amnesia, but they forget nothing."[65]

The ability to *appear* to forget, through repression or amnesia, is crucial to the dissociative process, for inability to connect parts with the whole underlies the protective measures that sustain so many varied responses to early traumas and pain. Dissociation allows many people to keep unacceptable feelings at a distance and to disconnect from parts of the self that seem intolerable and unacceptable. Dissociation allows individuals to survive otherwise intolerable pain and anguish and anxiety in childhood, but the memories of these sufferings survive, even when buried in the innermost recesses of their bodies and brains.

These abstractions take astonishingly vivid visual form in the imagery created by Ingmar Bergman in his last film. *Fanny and Alexander* centers on the calm, deliberate, and harsh beating of a ten-year-old boy by his stepfather, a Protestant bishop. The film is one of the most remarkable depictions yet of the dissociative process arising from the rage, hatred, and murderous impulses created by corporal punishment. The film clearly has roots in Bergman's own experiences with punishments as the son of a Swedish Protestant minister.* He often watched his mother mop blood from his brother's back after particularly brutal beatings by their father.[66] The film invites the entire world to witness a beating that draws blood from a boy's buttocks, a sight Bergman often had to see although he apparently never experienced it himself. *Fanny and Alexander* is a case study in the emotional consequences of corporal punishment; dissociation becomes the primary means by which the victim of the beating copes with the feelings that haunt him long afterward.

Bergman designed his film around two archetypal families. The Ekdahls, who clearly represent his fantasy of the ideal family, are a large,

---

* See Bergman's vivid description of childhood punishments in *The Magic Lantern: An Autobiography*, trans. by Joan Tate (New York: Viking, 1988), especially pp. 7–10. When reflecting on the outcomes of such punishments for his brother and sister, Bergman notes (p. 10) that "I think I came off best by turning myself into a liar. I created an external person who had very little to do with the real me. As I didn't know how to keep my creation and my person apart, the damage had consequences for my life and creativity far into adulthood. Sometimes I have to console myself with the fact that he who has lived a lie loves the truth."

theatrical extended family, full of vitality and energy and love, in which sexuality is not hidden and denied; "children are drawn into the Ekdahl lovingness; they live as it were in a protective incubator of physical affection."[67] The Vergéruses, Bergman's own family distilled to its puritanical essence of cruelty, control, domination, and hostility to life and love, live isolated in the Protestant bishop's fifteenth-century palace, where "punctuality, cleanliness, and order are the rule."[68]

When Bishop Edvard Vergérus marries Alexander's beautiful young actress mother after Alexander's father's death, he requires the entire family to come to live in his house without any prior possessions whatsoever, not even playthings. All previous connections are severed and the children become virtual prisoners in their stepfather's house. They are forced to eat all the food on their plates, their bedroom door is locked at night, and they clearly feel as though they are being held hostage by hostile people. One day Alexander, who has always had a very creative and active imagination, tells the maid a story about the bishop's first wife and children, who, he says, had been locked in the room, escaped, and drowned. When the bishop is told, he summons Alexander to his study to confront him with the story, which implies that he had murdered his wife and children. Before the bishop's mother and sisters and other female members of the household (his own mother is absent at the time), Alexander denies that he has told any such story. The bishop tells him that he must be punished for telling the story and for perjuring himself by his denial. Alexander, who clearly has never been struck a punitive blow in his entire life, cannot quite comprehend what is about to happen to him. He thinks that the bishop hates him, and says so. The bishop replies:

> I don't hate you. I love you. But the love I feel for you and your mother and your sisters is not blind and is not sloppy. It is strong and harsh, Alexander. If I must punish you, I suffer more than you know. But my love for you compels me to be truthful. It compels me to chasten and form you even if it hurts me.

He tells Alexander of the harsh methods of punishment common in his own boyhood. "Naughty boys were punished in an exemplary but loving manner. With the cane. The motto was: 'Spare the rod and spoil the child.'" The bishop offers a choice of methods, including taking castor oil and being locked in a cellar hole. Alexander chooses to be caned. He takes his pants down, bends over, and is struck ten blows. *"He bites his hand, tears fill his eyes, his nose runs, he is dark red in the face, and blood oozes from the weals in his skin."* Afterward, the bishop demands that he ask for forgiveness, which Alexander refuses to do, whereupon he is threatened with further beatings. This is more than he can bear, and he succumbs, begging "forgiveness." The bishop then says to him: "You understand that I have punished you out of love," to which Alexander replies "Yes," and the bishop then commands: "Kiss my hand, Alexander!" The boy's humiliation is complete, and his submission symbolically acknowledged. But the punishment is not over; Alexander, who is terrified of the dark, is locked for the night in an attic. He is found there and rescued the next day by his mother, who returns to find her precious son still in pain from the beating during her absence. This sequence, the pivot of the movie, embodies Bergman's long-delayed response to the childhood beatings his father inflicted on him and forced him to witness. The adult Bergman has ensured that anyone who watches *Fanny and Alexander* can see what it looks like and imagine what it feels like to be beaten bloody with a cane in the name of paternal love.[69]

Subsequently, Alexander and his sister are rescued by his grandmother's former lover, Isak Jacobi, a Jewish shopkeeper, who takes them to his own house for safekeeping till they can be returned to the Ekdahls. During the night, Alexander gets up to urinate, and wanders through the densely packed house. He sees his father's ghost once again and says, "Papa, why can't you go to God and tell him to kill the bishop? That is his department." The murderous thought had formed in his mind, however much he might resist it on other occasions. Soon thereafter, Aron, Jacobi's young nephew, takes Alexander to meet Aron's brother, Ismael, who is kept locked in a room for his own and others' safety. Ismael is male yet very feminine, about sixteen, and "considered dangerous." When they meet, Ismael asks Alexander to write his own name on a piece of paper. Having done so, Alexander reads the name and finds that he has written "Ismael Retzinsky." "Perhaps we are the same person," Ismael says. "Perhaps we have no limits; perhaps we flow into each other, stream through each other, boundlessly and magnificently." He immediately adds, however, that "You bear terrible thoughts; it is almost painful to be near you." Alexander grows very uncomfortable with this conversation, and declines to talk about such matters. Ismael observes: "You don't want to talk about what you are thinking of every moment." But Alexander refuses to say what he is thinking. Ismael, though, can read his mind; he puts into audible words what Alexander is thinking, and Bergman proceeds to display it on the screen.

The two boys merge, Ismael standing directly behind Alexander, their bodies touching, their minds in synchrony, their fantasies joined. Alexander has found his alter ego, his other self, dangerous and potentially violent, the murderous self incarnate. The dissociated self thus becomes embodied in the two boys, and the screen reveals the buried impulses and wishes that flow from the brutal beating Alexander suffered. "You have in mind a man's death," Ismael says to Alexander. Alexander asks him not to "talk like that." But Ismael says, "It is not I talking. It is yourself. I am saying your mental pictures aloud. I am repeating your thoughts." Ismael describes the bishop and the bishop's house, which the screen faithfully portrays in ghastly detail. Alexander protests, "I don't want to! I don't want to!" but Ismael says, "It is too late. I know your wish. . . . A little boy like you nursing such hatred, such horrible wishes!" He then articulates the fantasies, which are being enacted as reality on the screen. The bishop's elderly, sickly, bedridden aunt catches fire from the oil lamp beside her bed and rushes into the bishop's bedroom, where he has been drugged asleep by Alexander's pregnant mother, who has just escaped herself. Both the aunt and the bishop are engulfed in flames. It is the apocalyptic end of this puritanical and brutal man, just as Alexander had wished. The bishop dies a horrible death, prolonged sufficiently for him to say that "his agony was unendurable." The tortures of hell thus are foreshadowed in the flames of his own death. Alexander is suddenly free. His wish has been fulfilled. He is reunited with his mother and the entire Ekdahl family. In the film, however, although not in the printed script, the bishop's ghost returns at the very end, knocking Alexander to the floor and telling him that he has not seen the last of him yet.[70]

Bergman has captured on film the experience of dissociation arising from unacceptable murderous impulses and hatred that emerge from the pain and terror of corporal punishments. The splitting of the psyche into two (or more) parts—the good boy and the bad boy, the loving self and the murderous self—is enacted for everyone to see. These themes resonate deeply within Bergman's own psyche, since abuse—physical, sexual, and emotional—has played a crucial role in his creative life and films from the outset.

Corporal punishment, however, is the critical factor shaping the action in *Fanny and Alexander*, for Bergman's fantasy enacts the wishes of the boy victimized by the man—the bishop—of whom his wife once said: "His rage is terrible. I don't know how a man can live with so much hate."[71] Yet the bishop, too, had been victimized as a child by harsh corporal punishments, which clearly shaped his character into the tyrannical, brutal, and unloving man he has become. His ancient rage, vented calmly upon the body of the boy, and the hate that imprisons him and all who surround him, are the residues of the pains and terrors of his own childhood. He, too, was divided inwardly. It was no accident that he kept over his desk a picture of Abraham sacrificing Isaac!

Alexander, though, was able to recover his own equilibrium in the safe web of the loving family in which he had been reared, the family Bergman himself never had. Bergman's film is an imaginative creation, but no one who sees the bishop inflict pain by caning Alexander could doubt that this particular scene also describes the reality of Bergman's childhood. The depiction of the dissociative experience that follows is truly remarkable.

The splitting of the self into two or more parts, often experienced in mild forms through dissociative processes, can also be observed in Edmund Gosse's childhood, following the caning he experienced at the hands of his father. The murderous rage was suppressed, but during the same year, his sixth, he discovered that he "had found a companion and a confidant in myself. There was a secret in this world and it belonged to me and to a somebody who lived in the same body with me. There were two of us, and we could talk with one another." Gosse adds: "It is difficult to define impressions so rudimentary, but it is certain that it was in this dual form that the sense of my individuality now suddenly descended upon me, and it is equally certain that it was a great solace to me to find a sympathizer in my own breast." He began to injure himself secretly, putting pins into his flesh and hitting his "joints with books." He grew pale and ill, knowing that his parents believed any illness "showed that 'the Lord's hand was extended in chastisement.' " He "became very pale and nervous, and slept badly at nights, with visions and loud screams in my sleep," all of which

> culminated in a sort of fit of hysterics, when I lost all self-control, and sobbed with tears, and banged my head on the table. While this was proceeding, I was conscious of that dual individuality of which I have

already spoken, since while one part of me gave way, and could not resist, the other part in some extraordinary sense seemed standing aloof, much impressed. I was alone with my Father when this crisis suddenly occurred, and I was interested to see that he was greatly alarmed.[72]

Gosse thus became a dual personality, one having an hysterical attack, the other observing, distant, calm, disengaged. Like many others, he experienced what Ernest Hilgard has identified as the "hidden observer" phenomenon, which occurs in dissociative states.[73]

Both Alexander Ekdahl and Edmund Gosse experienced dissociative states after being beaten only once, which suggests that such states can arise quite readily in some individuals. They thus can be considered examples of the mildest forms of dissociation, and the mildest forms of physical punishments, one end of a long and very complicated spectrum. But most people who experience corporal punishments have repeated encounters with pain, each of which is imprinted upon the memory and stored for future reference, providing a kind of psychic warehouse of assaults, fears, and pains from which future experiences, actions, fantasies, and thoughts will draw, shaping the character and life of those who have suffered these forms of abuse early in life.

In the past decade, the childhood roots of hysteria and dissociation have begun to be reassociated with abuse and trauma. The pioneering work on hypnosis and hysteria done by Breuer and Freud in the 1880s resulted in Freud's brilliant analysis "The Etiology of Hysteria," first published in 1896 and subsequently repudiated after his development of the Oedipal theory of sexuality. Jeffrey Masson's illuminating analysis of the process by which Freud came to deny his original insights into the abusive and traumatic origins of hysteria leaves no doubt that the 1896 essay was essentially correct in its insights into hysteria's etiology.[74] Freud declared that "at the bottom of every case of hysteria will be found one or more experiences of premature sexual experience, belonging to the first years of childhood, experiences which may be reproduced by analytic work though whole decades have intervened." He also noted that "Sexual experiences in childhood consisting of stimulation of the genitals, coitus-like activities, etc., are therefore in the final analysis to be recognized as the traumata from which proceed hysterical reactions against experiences at puberty and hysterical symptoms themselves." Freud as-

sumed that "without previous seduction children cannot find the way to
acts of sexual aggression. The foundation of the neurosis would accordingly have been laid in childhood by adults." Freud later repudiated this
argument, insisting that most, if not all, hysterical disorders were the
result of fantasies, not actual sexual assaults or seductions in childhood.[75]

It has taken nearly a century for us to return to Freud's original
insights concerning the abusive roots of the dissociative disorder known
as hysteria. He saw only the sexual roots, however, always missing the
more common roots in physical pain and fear arising from corporal punishments. But at least, as Masson makes clear, Freud did acknowledge
briefly that children suffered real pain and terror from being sexually
abused and assaulted by adults, most often members of their own families.
Freud also recognized the problem inherent in his analysis of the etiology
of hysteria: Not all those who suffered from such abuses became hysterics. He remarked: "It makes no difference that many people go through
infantile sexual experiences without developing hysteria, so long as all
those who do become hysterics have had such experiences." The same
applies to the victims of corporal punishments: Although many suffer
from the pains of punishment, only some develop dissociative responses.[76]

Freud also noted that the roots of hysterical personalities and symptoms in adolescence and adulthood reach back to childhood before the
age of eight, lodged in the realm of the unconscious. "These scenes must
exist as *unconscious memories*; only so long and in so far as they are
unconscious can they produce and maintain hysterical symptoms." Subsequently, he added an important and often overlooked observation:
"Every one of my cases of obsessional neurosis revealed a substratum of
hysterical symptoms, mainly sensations and pains, which were traced to
those earliest experiences of childhood. What then," he asked, "deter-
mines whether the subsequent developments of the infantile sexual
scenes shall take the form of hysteria or obsessional neurosis, or even
paranoia, when the other pathogenic factors supervene?" He himself had
no answer to this question in 1896.[77]

The connections Freud makes among these three distinctive emotional disorders remain vitally important, however, even if his assumptions about their specific origins in the form of sexual abuse in early
childhood are actually only a relatively small part of a far greater con-
catenation of circumstances that foster the emergence of these seemingly
different forms of symptomatology and character. Corporal punishments

have equal, if not greater, claim to being the formative traumas shaping these varied forms of neurosis, in varying combinations and degrees, in many adults. Freud's excessive concern with the sexual origins of psychological disorders, followed faithfully by many of his adherents within both the psychoanalytic and nonpsychoanalytic schools of psychology during this century, has been a major factor in the common failure to acknowledge the damaging effects of even the most ordinary forms of corporal punishments.

What Freud and most of his followers did not recognize is that sexual assaults and punitive physical assaults and abuses *have the same damaging consequences* for children and adults, since they involve the same feelings of anger and rage, fear and terror, humiliation, and shame. The dissociations that shape hysterical personalities emerge from experiences that, as Freud realized, also formed the basis for both obsessive and paranoid defenses and character traits. We have seen the obsessional consequences of corporal punishments, and we will explore the paranoid dimensions shortly. But it is from the radical splitting of the self that occurs in multiple personalities—an extreme form of hysterical personality and the outermost edge of the dissociative continuum—that we gain the most insights into the abusive origins of adult suffering.

Multiple personalities provide an invaluable set of clues to the processes of survival through amnesia and dissociation, which are common in less dangerous and dramatic forms. The splitting of the self into many parts, which is the hallmark of multiple-personality disorder, merits our closest scrutiny, since it confirms that the dissociations have originated to protect and sustain the psyches and the souls, and often the bodies, of those who learned to survive terrible pain, anxiety, and trauma by inventing alternate selves.

Although Freud never recognized the devastating consequences of corporal punishments in fostering dissociation and splitting, Sándor Ferenczi—his student, analysand, friend, and colleague—certainly did. Jeffrey Masson has drawn attention to Ferenczi's brilliant contribution to our understanding of the abusive roots of dissociation. "Confusion of Tongues Between Adults and the Child" was Ferenczi's last paper; he wrote it shortly before his death in 1933, having been shunned by both Freud and his psychoanalytic peers, who subsequently refused to publish his paper in English and sought to deny and repress the implications of Ferenczi's insights and arguments. In this paper, given in Wiesbaden,

Germany, in 1932, Ferenczi shared his hard-won insights into the early traumas that had scarred his patients for life, traumas that originated in sexual and physical abuses, not fantasies and fabrications.[78] He took up where Freud had left off in 1896, but went far beyond Freud's formulations in the profound insights he offered into the origins of dissociation and splitting. "Confusion of Tongues" remains an unsurpassed analysis, meriting the closest attention for its clues to the consequences of harsh corporal punishments as well as sexual assaults.[79]

Ferenczi noted that "trauma, specifically sexual trauma, cannot be stressed enough as a pathogenic agent," adding that "Even children of respected, high-minded puritanical families fall victim to real rape much more frequently than one had dared to suspect." He acknowledged:

> It is difficult to fathom the behavior and the feelings of children following such acts of violence. Their first impulse would be: rejection, hatred, disgust, forceful resistance. "No, no, I don't want this, it is too strong for me, that hurts me. Leave me be." This or something like it would be the immediate reaction, were it not paralyzed by tremendous fear. The children feel physically and morally helpless, their personality is still too insufficiently consolidated for them to be able to protest even if only in thought.[80]

Ferenczi then explored the crucial issue that underlies all such violence: the domination, control, and power being asserted by the adult doing the assaulting. Ferenczi was the first to identify such adults in terms of the symbiotic connections created by the very act of assault:

> The overwhelming power and authority of the adults renders them [the children] silent. Often they are deprived of their senses. *Yet that very fear, when it reaches its zenith, forces them automatically to surrender to the will of the aggressor, to anticipate each of his wishes and to submit to them; forgetting themselves entirely, to identify totally with the aggressor.*

What Ferenczi assumed, without explicitly stating, is that such assaults can take several forms, one sexual, the other punitive. Every time an adult physically hits a child in the name of discipline, an act of painful aggression against the body and spirit of the child takes place. Punitive

assaults and sexual aggressions equally violate children, equally trau-
matize them, and often are equally painful to experience.[81]

Ferenczi set forth the emotional consequences to the victimized children of aggressive assaults by adults. The child, he said, identifies with
and internalizes the aggressor, creating a "dreamlike state" and a "traumatic trance" during which the child identifies with the adult. Ferenczi
noted that "the most important transformation in the emotional life of
the child," which rests upon "an identification based on fear," is *the
introjection of the guilt feeling of the adult*, which gives hitherto innocent
play the appearance of a punishable act." The crucial fact is that "When
the child recovers from such an attack, he feels extremely confused, in
fact already split, innocent and guilty at the same time; indeed his confidence in the testimony of his own senses has been destroyed."[82]

One example of the phenomenon that Ferenczi described—the identification with the aggressor and the dissociation from the self in the face
of overwhelming trauma and pain—is to be found in the diary of the
Reverend Cotton Mather in the early eighteenth century in New England.
Mather described his own experience as a child of God under his Father's
punishing blows:

> I find in my soul a strange Experience. I meet with very breaking and
> killing Things, which are the Chastisements of the holy GOD upon
> me, for my manifold Miscarriages. In the sad Things that befall me,
> the glorious GOD is gratified: it pleases Him, to behold His Justice
> thus Inflicting Strokes upon me. Now such is my Love unto my God;
> and so united is my Soul unto Him, that I have a secret Pleasure in
> my Thoughts of the Gratification which is done unto Him, in the sad
> Things which tear me to Pieces before Him. I fly away from even my
> very self into Him, and I take part with Him against myself: and it
> pleases me, that He is pleased, tho' I myself am dreadfully torn to
> Peeces in what is done unto me.[83]

Mather's experience is precisely analogous to Ferenczi's description of
the identification with the aggressor, which involves the child's introjection of the punitive adult: Mather flies "away from even my very self *into
Him*," thus becoming one with the Father who is assaulting him in the
name of love and duty. Such examples could be multiplied many times
over; Mather knew from experience centuries earlier what Ferenczi later
described from observation.

Ferenczi recognized from his clinical work as an analyst (noted in the privacy of his diary as well as in this public lecture) that "there can be no shock, no fright, without traces of a personality split." With exceptional insight, he comprehended the psychological process that culminates in the splitting of the self into various alternative personae: "If traumatic events accumulate during the life of the growing person, the number and variety of personality splits increase, and soon it will be rather difficult to maintain contact without confusion with all the fragments, which all act as separate personalities but mostly do not know each other." Ferenczi saw clearly the phenomenon of multiple personalities, something that neither Freud nor his psychoanalytic colleagues ever apparently noted or heeded.[84]

Ferenczi also knew that such splitting can result not only from sexual traumas but from traumas of all kinds, including those arising from the pain of corporal punishments: "We have known for the longest time that *not only forced love but also unbearable punishments* can have a fixating effect [emphasis added]." Unfortunately, this remarkably prescient insight was lost on Freud and his other psychoanalytic colleagues, as it was lost on the psychological profession as a whole from Ferenczi's day to ours. Yet the impact of traumas, both sexual and punitive in origin, remains one of the most powerful instigators of the dissociative process known, a process that leads, in its most extreme forms, to the creation of multiple personalities.[85]

Until very recently, multiple personalities were assumed to be extremely rare, if they existed at all. Recent evidence, however, has shown that the phenomenon is actually far more prevalent than anyone thought possible. Many, if not most, multiples have been repeatedly misdiagnosed, their symptoms taking the forms of virtually every known psychological disorder.

Most psychoanalysts and psychologists have been disinclined to acknowledge and deal with evidence of serious child abuse. As Jean Goodwin, a physician, observes, "Despite evidence that half of psychiatric patients were abused in childhood, psychiatrists have yet to implement standard interview schedules that would make questioning in this area routine."[86] Many therapists, including some who deal regularly with patients suffering from multiple personalities, fail to recognize the splitting and dissociation that accompany the fragmentation of self characteristic of multiples.

Virtually every known case of multiple personality results from severe abuse or trauma in childhood. The experiences of pain, suffering, fear, and rage always underlie emergence of alternative selves. Richard Kluft, a professor of psychiatry, believes that "the aggregate of available data supports the view of multiple personality disorder as a form of childhood post–traumatic stress disorder," a perspective shared by Bessel van der Kolk (the director of a trauma center in Boston) and others who have explored the psychological impact of trauma.[87] Van der Kolk notes that "Multiple personality is probably the most extreme example of how severe traumatization can lead to dissociation and subsequent reexperiencing or reenactment of the trauma."[88] Van der Kolk and William Kadish, both psychiatrists, observe:

> Except when related to brain injury, dissociation always seems to be a response to traumatic life events. Memories and feelings connected with the trauma are forgotten and return as intrusive recollections, feeling states (such as overwhelming anxiety and panic unwarranted by current experience), fugues, delusions, states of depersonalization, and finally in behavioral reenactments.[89]

Eugene Bliss, in his remarkable study of multiple personality and hypnosis—which confirms Ferenczi's earlier observations and hypotheses—argues that the key to an understanding of the phenomena is "spontaneous self-hypnosis," which, he notes, "is a rapid, unpremeditated withdrawal into a trance, a dissociation, untaught and instinctive, a primitive defensive reflex that people experience usually when anxious or fearful—often in response to some psychological or physical threat."[90] The response to trauma, however, depends upon a process of forgetting, or repression, so that amnesias provide children protection from pain and terror and permit the proliferation of selves characteristic of multiple-personality disorder. Bliss believes that "the key to hypnotic amnesia lies in the retrieval mechanism. The information has been recorded and coded, but it can't be retrieved."[91]

The result, in the extreme cases of individuals who develop multiple personalities, is the splitting of the emotions into separate selves, whose internal role is to embody or personify some particular aspect of the individual's feelings and impulses that were present at the time of the initial experience of abuse or trauma. These feelings include, among others, anxiety, terror, and rage, which arise out of assaults or other situations of intense pain and fear. As Bliss observes, "Most often delegated to personalities are depression, suicidal despair, anger, rage, and fear. Personalities who cry for patients, are dedicated to suicide, become angry, or carry homicidal rage are common. All have been created because such feelings were forbidden, punished, immoral, or terrifying."[92] In every known instance, these dissociative splits originally were necessary for the survival of the child's psyche and self. They were means of protection for an otherwise helpless child.

Although sexual abuse frequently figures in the etiology of multiple personalities, other forms of assault, particularly those associated with severe punishments, often supply the traumas and pain that generate the dissociative process. The childhood experiences of "Eve," who developed twenty-two personalities, focused upon her need to escape from the pains of punishment. Her dissociations began at an early age, partly from the trauma of seeing a man sawed in two in an accident, and partly from repeated encounters with corporal punishments. She recalled: "When the pain grew unbearable, something happened, something changed, and then I felt nothing, nothing. I couldn't feel, I couldn't see, I couldn't hear! I just seemed to go away, far away; everything seemed to be so very far away." She was certain that another little girl had done the naughty deeds for which she was being punished. "Was that somebody else? Was that somebody who came and took away the pain and hurt?" Many years later, in her psychiatrist's office, her parents witnessed the successive appearance of her various personalities:

> They remembered all the times they had punished her as she tearfully protested her innocence. They first watched a shallow caricature of their daughter smile carelessly and admit to hating her twin sisters and to biting their toes as babies. They then watched their now familiar, sad, browbeaten daughter discuss the whipping she had received for biting her loved sisters—still protesting, after twenty years, her innocence of the despicable act, still describing the "other child" whom she had seen biting the tender baby toes.[93]

Her dissociations and splitting were often associated with the harsh punishments her parents and others meted out to her.

Dr. Cornelia Wilbur (the analyst of the multiple-personality "Sybil") observed that "Several multiple personality disorder patients have com-

plained bitterly that child abuse starts with society's approval of the spanking of children. They report that they were frequently spanked so hard,
they were left covered with bruises."[94] Harsh corporal punishments are
often factors in the early dissociative experiences of individuals who subsequently develop multiple personalities. Wilbur comments on the complex processes whereby children create alternative personalities to deal
with emotions that are unacceptable, particularly "rage, anger, and
hostility":

> This is quite a common finding in female multiple personality disorder
> patients who, as youngsters, were punished severely when they be-
> came angry, and were informed that their expression of anger proved
> that they were sinful, and would go to hell. In the several cases known
> to me, the young girls came to the conclusion that they must not
> express anger or rage. Consequently, these patients suppressed their
> feelings, although they knew these feelings were present. In making
> the effort to suppress the affect, they appeared to be "clouding up,"
> or to be in a trance. They were then punished physically for looking
> distracted, and told that this behavior was not acceptable. They then
> completely repressed the hostile affects, no longer consciously coping
> with the pressure to control them.[95]

These patients were typical in their dissociative responses to intense
anger, which was forbidden by the adults who controlled their lives.

The suppression of pain, of terror, and of rage is the primary ac-
complishment of the splitting that results in multiple personalities.
Children who have no other recourse sometimes are able to protect
themselves and to survive the assaults upon their bodies and spirits by
escaping their intolerable and unbearable feelings through the creation
of alternative selves, parts of the whole whose specific purpose is to
contain and to express the feelings and impulses and thoughts that the
child otherwise cannot tolerate. What appears over and over again in
multiple personalities is evidence for the centrality of pain, fear, and
rage. When these powerful feelings are stifled and suppressed in childhood, when children are not protected from intense pain inflicted by
adults, the dissociations and amnesias associated with the development
of multiple personalities permit children to survive by curbing the rage
and the aggression that erupt from the abuse suffered throughout childhood.

Very commonly (some would argue consistently), multiple personalities contain at least one persona who is suicidal, who turns the rage
and aggression inward against the body and at least one of the selves,
and another persona who is murderous, whose rage and aggression are
turned outward against other individuals, usually not the ones who per-
petrated the original abuse and pain. Murderous rage contained within
one or more of the separate personalities is extremely common, as many
therapists who have treated multiple personalities report. The murderous
rage that Edmund Gosse remembered feeling at the age of six persists
undiluted in the split-off part of the self in many multiples, causing these
persons to act out and to express their rage, hatred, and aggression in
many different ways over the course of their lives.

The powerful and enduring effects of ancient angers are visible in
the complex psyche of "Sybil," who developed sixteen distinctive personalities. Sybil was born into an intensely apocalyptic, fundamentalist
Protestant family; both her grandfather and her father lived continually
in the shadow of the catastrophic end of the world. Her father left college
early because he thought the world was about to end. "Armageddon was
table talk, and the end of the world was a threatening reality." The apocalyptic violence anticipated eagerly by the adult men was enacted within
the family by Sybil's schizophrenic mother, whose assaults, cruelties, and
tortures were the repeated traumas that caused the little girl to split into
many selves. Sybil, as her biographer, Flora Rheta Schreiber, notes, "was
a battered child four decades before the battered child syndrome was
medically identified." Her father, who only spanked her once in her life,
pretended to notice nothing, and did nothing to intervene or to protect
his child from his wife's abuses. Sybil was forced to rescue and protect
herself through the dissociations and amnesias that shaped her development of sixteen alternate selves. She was the victim of "a drama of
cruelty, secret rituals, punishments, and atrocities inflicted" by her
mother, part of "a large, complicated capture-control-imprisonment-
torture theme that pervaded the drama." Her mother gave "cold water"
enemas to the helplessly tied-up child, who dangled from a ceiling fixture;
beat her brutally; burned her; punished her severely; and subjected her
to other horrendous experiences that could be survived only by silence
and splitting. What remains most remarkable is that the child being
tortured never blamed the mother who was hurting her. She blamed the
"instruments" of her "torture" instead.[96] But what she felt throughout

all these assaults remained intact, safely buried through amnesias and dissociations.

"Rage" was the primary feeling that Sybil was forced to repress for so long.[97] She protected herself from the consequences of her powerful rage by splitting and forgetting. She protected her mother until many years later, when she was finally able to get in touch with the original feelings she had hidden from herself, with only partial success, for so long. Her murderous rage expressed the hatred that Sybil was never allowed to feel as a child. But neither the hatred nor the rage was possible until years of therapy had freed her to tolerate her own feelings and impulses.

In the climactic moment of Sybil's work with Dr. Wilbur, the psychic dam burst, releasing the emotions that had been repressed and hidden for so many years:

> Silence. A low moan of suffering. Dr. Wilbur held her breath. She knew that Sybil, like a surgeon pointing a knife at the crucial lesion, was poised on the threshold of traumatic revelation. Sybil's voice rose. "I told myself I loved mother and only pretended that I hated her. But it was no pretense." Sybil's voice broke. The crisis had passed. Sybil went on: "I really hated her—ever since I can remember."
>
> Overpowering feelings of hatred flooded Sybil. "I hate her," she gasped. "Whenever she hurt me, I saw myself put my hands around her throat. Other ways, too. Stab her. Lots of times I wanted to stab her. . . . I wanted to kill my mother."[98]

The sudden recognition and acknowledgment of the murderous impulses and wishes from early childhood, originally arising from the painful assaults inflicted by the mother whom she needed to love, freed Sybil to acknowledge the fury within.

> Now, for the first time since she was three and a half years old, Sybil could get angry. The need for the selves who dealt with anger had therefore diminished, and those selves were now partially integrated with Sybil. Now, too, that Marcia's [an alternate personality] death wish for mother had become Sybil's wish, it was possible for Marcia and Sybil to move closer. But most remarkable of all was that once the capacity to get angry had been restored to Sybil, the pathways

had been cleared for other emotions. The very act of expressing rage against Hattie Dorset [her mother] had transformed Sybil into a woman no longer bereft of emotions. Sybil had begun to move away from depletion, toward wholeness.[99]

Wholeness, the opposite of the splitting experienced most dramatically by multiple personalities, is possible only when the memories of ancient traumas are made conscious and reexperienced. To greater and lesser degrees, many adults who experience dissociations, from the mildest to the most severe, are the victims of abuses in childhood that have created the need to survive through forgetting and disconnecting.

The complex process of reintegrating the fragmented selves with the core self is not only challenging for the therapists and patients, but reveals with the utmost clarity the general characteristics of dissociative states arising from abuse and traumas early in life. Bliss, who has treated many individuals suffering from multiple personalities, cautions:

> There are also formidable resistances to the therapeutic processes. The concealed experiences initially were forgotten because the patient could not consciously cope with them. As a result, these memories or functions have remained unacceptable and are feared. Some traumas can be rapidly identified and made conscious, but others are guarded or avoided relentlessly.[100]

He notes the crucial fact that

> the traumas, although they may have occurred decades earlier, are still virulent because they are unresolved and unprocessed by the conscious mind. In these patients, guilt, rage, neglect, or a rape is still frozen in its early form. Therefore, when reactivated and returned to consciousness, these old memories are experienced as events that have just occurred. . . . Personalities are fragments of an individual that are still anchored in the past. Adult learning residing in the conscious mind has not penetrated into this unconscious, so personalities also remain frozen as remnants of early experiences.[101]

The psychic past is also the psychic present, time being absent in the unconscious. The past thus survives intact in the psyche, creating the symptoms and causing the persistence of suffering long after the original suffering and traumas have passed. But the power of repression and amnesia can be broken, as Bliss and others have recognized, by helping patients see and acknowledge the realities of pain and fear that originally caused them to dissociate and then to split.

The key, always (as Alice Miller, Jeffrey Masson, Eugene Bliss, Bessel van der Kolk, and others have recognized), is to admit that real harm was done to the children whose adult selves bear the scars of the abuse experienced in infancy and childhood. As Bliss insists:

> Patients must accept the fact that these experiences, so artfully hidden, did occur. The hidden experiences, the concealed emotions, guilts, and urges are theirs. All must be recognized, accepted, and processed, usually by discovering and reexperiencing them in hypnosis. Although reality may be unfair, the truth must be faced; the past is unalterable and must be accepted.[102]

Only when the past is known, understood, and acknowledged can the recovery and healing come through the act of forgiveness. Alice Miller understands this process with rare insight and compassion:

> Genuine forgiveness does not deny anger but faces it head-on. If I can feel outrage at the injustice I have suffered, can recognize my persecution as such, and can acknowledge and hate my persecutor for what he or she has done, only then will the way to forgiveness be open to me. Only if the history of abuse in earliest childhood can be uncovered will the repressed anger, rage, and hatred cease to be perpetuated. Instead, they will be transformed into sorrow and pain at the fact that things had to be that way. As a result of this pain, they will give way to genuine understanding, the understanding of an adult who now has attained insight into his or her parents' childhood and finally, liberated from his own hatred, can experience genuine, mature sympathy. Such forgiveness cannot be coerced by rules and commandments; it is experienced as a form of grace and appears spontaneously when a repressed (because forbidden) hatred no longer poisons the soul.[103]

Few of us are so fortunate, for most of us have never had an opportunity to know ourselves and our pasts well enough to see, in the immediacy of total recall, the abuses and suffering that we experienced.

But dissociations and amnesias, from the mildest to the most devastating, frequently originate in the pain and suffering of childhood. The ability to forgive ancient assaults begins with the acknowledgment of the reality of physical and emotional abuse in their most ordinary forms. For many of us, this is not an easy thing to do.

Paranoia

The anticipation of pain often is as hard to bear as pain itself. The sense of vigilance rooted in that anticipation—captured in the familiar words "Go to your room and wait until your father comes home"—lays the groundwork for subsequent anticipations of harm, of injury, and of pain, as well as the persistent sense of threats and dangers to life, spirit, and limb that are characteristic of paranoid forms of being and behavior. Like dissociative disorders, paranoia comes in many guises and degrees, from the mildest to the most crippling and dangerous. Common to all forms, however, is a pervasive sense of being endangered. The anticipation of harm from outside is the core of paranoia.

For some people, such anticipations take the form of hypochondria, the sense that the body itself is threatened by internal disorders or diseases, which generates a constant sense of watchfulness and anxiety. But the body, in this instance, is perceived as "other" by the self and watched as though it were outside rather than inside the self. Hypochondriacs experience the anxiety, characteristic of paranoia, that is associated with the possibility of harm or even destruction and death by physiological means. The sense of being threatened by toxins or by poisonous foods, or by substances such as fluoride in water, is a common form of paranoia.

The sense of being endangered by other people is fundamental to paranoia. The generalized fear of assault or secretive machinations against the self is characteristic of paranoid forms of public beliefs and behaviors. But all of these expressions of paranoia, from the mildest to the most extreme, share the sense of being endangered and threatened, from within or without, a sense often rooted in the experiences of childhood. Paranoia arises from the keen and persistent sense that the body, the will, and the self are at risk. These are long-term consequences of abuse in infancy, childhood, and adolescence, the delayed expression of the anxieties associated with coercion, assault, and pain early in life.[104]

Until very recently, however, we had little awareness of the experiential roots of paranoia, having lived for the better part of a century with the misconceptions fostered by Sigmund Freud in his famous essay on the etiology of paranoia, based upon the autobiography of Dr. Daniel Paul Schreber.[105] Schreber's memoirs of his mental illness (generally diagnosed as paranoid schizophrenia) provided Freud with the evidence from which he constructed his hypotheses concerning the psychic roots of paranoia. Freud never met Schreber, although he certainly knew of his famous father, Daniel Gottlieb Moritz Schreber, one of the most influential writers on child-rearing and discipline in Germany in the mid-nineteenth century, a man whom Freud called "an excellent father."[106] Schreber's elder brother, also named Daniel after their father, never married and died by suicide at the age of thirty-eight. Freud, however, knew nothing about this brother, not even his name, although he intuited correctly that he was older than the schizophrenic Schreber.

Freud's "hypothesis" was "that the exciting cause of the illness was the appearance in him of a feminine (that is, a passive homosexual) wish-phantasy, which took as its object the figure of his physician. An intense resistance to this phantasy arose on the part of Schreber's personality, and the ensuing defensive struggle, which might perhaps just as well have assumed some other shape, took on, *for reasons unknown to us*, that of *a delusion of persecution* [emphasis added]."[107] Freud's basic assumption, which has persisted tenaciously to the present, is that repressed homosexual impulses are the basis of paranoia: "We consider, then, that what lies at the core of the conflict in cases of paranoia among males is a homosexual wish-phantasy of *loving a man*."[108] The mechanism by which such unconscious impulses are displaced is through projection and transformation into opposites. The love becomes hate, the beloved becomes the hater, the persecutor. As Freud noted: "In delusions of persecution the distortion consists in a transformation of affect; what should have been felt internally as love is perceived externally as hate."[109]

Schreber's paranoia thus became his own responsibility, an internal disorder arising in adulthood rather than being created by individuals or experiences that were originally external and beyond the control of the person who subsequently became paranoid. Freud's presumptions—that repressed homosexual impulses were at the root of paranoia and that love was transformed into hate, desire into persecution—made the victim into the victimizer, falsely accusing his innocent and "excellent" father, via the surrogate physician, of seeking to harm and even to destroy him. The fantasies of abuse thus became "delusions," without basis in the realities of experience in infancy and childhood. As with hysterics, Freud seemed to be unable to acknowledge the possibility that the paranoia of the adult could be rooted in the realities of persecution and harm in childhood. It was a serious misperception, with enduring consequences for our general understanding of the etiology and psychodynamics of paranoia.

In fact, we know now that Schreber's "delusions" mirrored, with un- canny accuracy, the varied forms of assault, control, and abuse that he suffered at the hands of his sadistic father, who practiced on his children what he preached in his writings. William Niederland explored many of the details in his pioneering analysis, *The Schreber Case: Psychoanalytic Profile of a Paranoid Personality.* In 1973, Morton Schatzman made these connections utterly clear in his analysis of Schreber in *Soul Murder: Persecution in the Family.* Both studies provide abundant evidence of the sadistic methods of child-rearing practiced in the Schreber household; these provided the roots of Daniel Paul Schreber's subsequent paranoia.

Schatzman points out that "Schreber's entire madness is an *image* of his father's war against his independence."[110] The elder Schreber's as- sault upon the will and the autonomy of his children (and on all children through the medium of his writings, a part of the German tradition that Alice Miller rightly labels "poisonous pedagogy") was precisely what gen- erations of evangelical and fundamentalist Christians have advocated. Niederland notes that "the Schreber family were devout Protestants," although he does not specify which form of Protestantism they prac- ticed.[111] Dr. Schreber's methods of discipline and control mirror those rationales for corporal punishment explored earlier.

Schreber's father invented a series of devices designed to shape and control children's bodies and physical movements, including head and neck braces, straps for shoulders, and harnesses to keep sleeping children from turning over in bed (a device still used in the mid-twentieth century in at least one Philadelphia household run by a Scottish Presbyterian nanny). The elder Schreber's impulse toward absolute physical and moral control was boundless, and it comes as no surprise that he was described in hospital records found after World War II as a man who " 'suffered from obsessional ideas with murderous impulses.' "[112] Schatzman perceptively observes that the elder Schreber preached "household totalitarianism."[113] Niederland notes that "he used a 'scientifically' elaborated system of relentless mental and corporeal pressure alternating with occasional indulgence, a methodical sequence of studiously applied terror interrupted by compensatory periods of seductive benevolence and combined with ritual observances that he as a reformer incorporated into his overall missionary scheme of physical education."[114] He recommended, for instance, that, when a small child cried for no apparent reason, the remedy was to " 'step forward in a positive manner: by quick distraction of the attention, stern words, threatening gestures, rapping against the bed . . . or when all this is of no avail—by moderate, intermittent, bodily admonishments consistently repeated until the child calms down or falls asleep.' " The goal was clear: " 'Such a procedure is necessary only once or at most twice and—one is master of the child *forever*.' "[115] Thus parents become masters, children slaves, the nexus of sadomasochism that often accompanies the creation of paranoia in years to come. Corporal punishments and other forms of coercion are the means by which this mastery is accomplished early in life.

In the case of Schreber, as in many individuals who become paranoid later in life, the crucial step in the creation of subsequent paranoia was the repression of all memories of abuse and coercion in childhood. This is what Freud failed to grasp: the forgetting, or the repression, of the consciousness of pain and terror that were frequent, if not constant, realities in infancy and childhood. Just as in the case of hysteria and in other dissociative phenomena, the ability to forget the feelings generated early in life by punishments and discipline and the inability to remember that they were inflicted by beloved adults is necessary for the subsequent development of paranoia. Schatzman observes:

> Schreber suffers from reminiscences. His body embodies his past. He retains memories of what his father did to him as a child; although part of his mind knows they are memories, "he" does not. He is considered insane not only because of the quality of his experiences, but because he misconstrues their *mode*: he *remembers*, in some cases perfectly accurately, how his father treated him, but thinks he *perceives* events occurring in the present for which he imagines God,

rays, little men, etc., are the agents. He knows what he most needs
to know, but does not know he knows it.[116]

This is precisely the same form of selective amnesia as in hysterias,
and both are rooted in the astonishing ability of children to deny their
own rage, aggression, hatred, and revengefulness when they are being
forced to suffer in the name of discipline by the parents or other adults
whom they love and on whom they must depend. Schreber believed even
as an adult that he adored his father. But he also believed that God and
his doctor were intent upon harming or destroying his very soul. He was
absolutely right in his assumption that his self and soul were in grave
danger, but he could not acknowledge from whom. Like other victims of
violence, assault, and abuse, he identified with his abuser and forgot
himself in the process.

His subsequent paranoia was a reenactment of the traumas he underwent throughout his childhood. Niederland assumes that "by the time
the child Schreber entered his third or fourth year of life, he had already
undergone a notable degree of traumatization."[117] Schatzman remarks:
"The son thinks the 'miracles' are enacted upon objective anatomical
organs of his body. He does not see that he is re-enacting his father's
behavior towards his body."[118] Like other forms of post–traumatic stress,
paranoia is a delayed and transformed reexperiencing of earlier threats
and dangers to the self, to the will, and to the body. Schatzman is surely
right when he observes that "many people whom psychiatrists call 'paranoid' have been persecuted, and know it, but they do not recognize their
real persecutors, nor how they have been persecuted. . . . To call them
paranoid which presupposes they are not 'really' persecuted, but imagine
it, is false and misleading."[119] The old joke remains as cogent as ever:
"Just because you're paranoid doesn't mean they aren't out to get you."

Children whose wills are assaulted and broken often become paranoid
as adults. The long-standing tradition of breaking children's wills, characteristic of evangelical and fundamentalist Protestantism, is paralleled
by an equally long-standing pattern of paranoid ideation and behavior,
evident both in countless individual lives and in the culture generally.
The historian George Marsden has documented the persistent paranoia
rooted in Protestant fundamentalism throughout the twentieth century,
but the wellsprings of anticipated danger and assault reach back to the
seventeenth century and beyond.[120] Richard Hofstadter once noted the

connections of fundamentalism and paranoia in the postscript to his brilliant essay "The Pseudo-Conservative Revolt."[121] Neither scholar, however, recognized the roots of paranoia in the early childhood experiences of the Christians whom they were analyzing.

The coercion and threats to the autonomy of the self inherent in the breaking of children's wills are often the seedbeds for subsequent paranoia. David Shapiro sees the will as the focal point of paranoia, although he, too, overlooks the realities of childhood trauma associated with the actual process of breaking wills. He recognizes that Dr. Schreber's "coercive regimen was [intended] to destroy one kind of autonomy and install another in its place and to force acceptance not only of the adult's command but also of the adult's standards and precepts—to force acceptance of them as his own and identification with their point of view. The result," Shapiro notes, "was not to be submissiveness but a new kind of will founded in authoritarian strictness and coercive self-control."[122] The roots of paranoia, Shapiro realizes, are to be found in struggles over the will, of being forced to give in to superior force and power and, we must add, pain and fear.

The pervasive sense of being threatened with harm, of being forced to surrender, of being manipulated or coerced into compliance with the will of another person or persons, persistent in paranoia, is rooted in the experience of aggression by adults against the wills, bodies, and selves of children. The pervasive suspiciousness and fear of subversion and of conspiracies, so characteristic of paranoia, reflect the earlier battles over the child's willfulness and autonomy, long submerged in the unconscious but still present in the minds of many people for the rest of their lives. Paranoia arises later because children are generally forbidden to react appropriately and effectively to aggression by adults; expressions of rage and of counteraggression that arise from self-defense are suppressed by both the adults and the children themselves. Later, however, these ancient feelings can be displaced, attributed to others, projected inappropriately onto persons and situations entirely removed from the earlier scenes of aggressive assaults and threatening encounters with discipline. American political and religious history is filled with examples of paranoid projections rooted in the childhood history that remains largely unexplored even now.

Aggression against the body, the will, and the self in childhood—not buried homosexual impulses—creates the central core of adult paranoia.

Paranoia thus continues to be one of the most widespread and disturbing consequences of the coercion, pain, and fear experienced as children by those grown-ups whose wills were bent or broken by violence and force many years earlier. Perhaps now we can begin to reckon with paranoia in terms of our knowledge about the actual violence directed by adults against so many children in our culture.

Sadomasochism

For many adults, sadomasochism in both erotic and nonerotic forms is a direct consequence of the confusions generated by the combination of love and pain in childhood, the long-term outcome of the normal assaults and abuse associated with physical punishment from infancy to adolescence.[123] Sadomasochism provides the most direct evidence for the enduring consequences of early corporal punishments, since the sexual forms that sadomasochism (or S&M) takes mirror the earlier encounters with discipline and pain with remarkable faithfulness.

The central core of sadomasochism in many of its manifestations is domination and submission, the imposition of power, control, and will by one person over another. Invariably some degree of coercion or force is involved, indeed required, since the degree of domination and submission sought generally requires actual, threatened, or imagined violence and pain (physical or verbal or both) to achieve the necessary goals of obedience and control. Sadomasochism is expressed and experienced in many ways, takes many forms, has many guises, comes in many degrees, but it also is one of the most common aftermaths of a childhood of suffering from the pains of punishments inflicted by those who are loved.

Spankings, whippings, and beatings are the painful origins of much adult sadomasochism. The astonishing absence of studies of sadomasochism in our history and culture is evidence of the denial that most people experience concerning the long-term consequences of physical punishments both for the psyche and sexuality. It is the early fusion of pain and love and the eroticization of coercion through the assaults upon the body and the anus that often shape the creation of sadomasochistic feelings, fantasies, and behaviors in adults.

Polarities are the hallmarks of sadomasochism, which itself is a word combining opposites—sadism and masochism.[124] Physical discipline and love combine to generate the persistent poles of S&M: domination and submission, pain and pleasure, punishments and rewards, fear and security, humiliation and power. The traumas of anxiety and suffering generated in the name of love form the nexus from which many forms of adult sadomasochism emerge.

The associations of love, fear, and pain begin early and remain embedded in the unconscious mind for life. Children from Island Pond, Vermont, who have been beaten for disobedience, have sometimes insisted that painful punishment is the proof of love. One father whose daughters had been subjected to such beatings said: "I have an eight-year-old girl who is a masochist. She equates love with beatings."[125] He taped his children's responses to his questions about their spankings:

On the tape, in squeaky, little-girl voices, the two older girls . . . earnestly try to make their father understand that they want to be spanked. . . . the five-year-old who was allegedly disciplined by a church elder for two days for lying about how many strawberries she had eaten, remained silent.

"We want to feel decent," say the voices on the tape. "If you don't discipline us then our hearts will never change. . . . Yeah, do something like that. Do something like spanking us, or hit us. . . . Yeah, do something."

[He] asks his daughters: "What do you want me to do?"

"Spank us. . . . Spank us or put us in the corner. . . . Do you rather put us in the corner, Papa? . . . Do you rather put us in the corner?"

"I want to love you children," says [their father]. "I want to do what the Lord would have me do for you."

"I know, the Lord wants you to spank us sometimes if we're disobedient. If you love us . . . then you'll spank us. If you spank us, then you love us. If you don't spank us, then you don't love us."

"Who told you that?" asks [their father].

"That's what it says in the Bible."[126]

These children were removed by their father from the Northeast Kingdom Community at Island Pond. They, like many other children, equate
spankings with love, pain with affection, coercion with obedience.

Love and fear, pain and suffering, power and authority, and unquestioning obedience—the leitmotifs of evangelical and fundamentalist
Protestantism for many centuries—are often the roots from which sadomasochism in all its beneficial and destructive manifestations arises.
The association of love and pain is inescapable when corporal punishments are used.

The Christian fundamentalist literature advocating corporal punishments can be read as guidebooks for the creation of sadomasochists. Many
of the books advocating the rod could provide apt titles for books on
bondage and discipline that many people might consider to be a form of
S&M pornography. What Christenson, Fugate, Tomczak (the author of
God, the Rod, and Your Child's Bod), Lessin, and many others advocate
as necessary forms of physical and moral coercion for children—through
corporal punishment and the application of the rod to their bodies—becomes taboo and "perverse" when acted out by adults. By simply substitut-
ing an adult for every child whose "bod" is being beaten by a loving adult
with a rod or any other implement (including hands), the scene suddenly
is transformed into a sadomasochistic encounter between two adults.

The pornography of sadomasochism—including the descriptions and
visual depictions of discipline, spankings, whippings, and other punishments and humiliations—often mirrors faithfully the childhood experiences so compellingly advocated by Christian apologists for corporal
punishments. Domination and submission, pain and punishment are the
usual hallmarks of S&M among many adults, the long-term reenactments
of the familiar equations of childhood.

What is most remarkable in terms of common reactions to S&M is
that people are generally shocked *only* when adults beat other adults or
inflict painful punishments on other adults by methods considered perfectly normal and ordinary when applied to children. When "The Rod:
The Way of Love" becomes eroticized and reenacted sexually between
adults, it clearly becomes a form of sadomasochistic behavior, unacceptable and profoundly disturbing to many of the same individuals who
advocate similar forms of coercive and painful discipline for children.
Much of Larry Townsend's *The Leatherman's Handbook*—a guide to
techniques of "discipline" and "punishment" for adult men to practice

with one another—parallels the religious literature on assaulting children with rods, belts, and paddles.[127] One major difference, however, is that Townsend advocates that such discipline be experienced by choice rather than through the coercion and force always used when children are being punished physically.

The crucial question, which ought to be asked (but rarely is), is this: Why is it a "perversion" when adults reenact physical punishments voluntarily, but "normal" when adults assault—hit and beat—children from infancy through adolescence? If anything is truly perverse, surely it has to be the striking and the hurting of children by adults.

The core paradigm for sadomasochism, which arises from the impulse to control and to break wills, is the relationship of masters and slaves: absolute power versus total powerlessness and obedience, the basic polarities of sadomasochism.[128] Too often people forget that slavery was embedded in American society and culture for many centuries; the aftermath—in terms of the persistence of sadomasochistic patterns of behavior, thought, and feeling—has yet to be fully fathomed.* Long after the formal abolition of slavery, the relationship of masters and slaves remains essential to S&M. It is now often grounded in the most painful experiences of childhood, the traumas of coercion and submission and pain that are invariably part of the experience of the rod inflicted as love.

Sadomasochism is also centrally expressive of aggression, for the key themes of power, control, domination, submission, and the breaking of the will all involve aggression, both directly and indirectly. The progenitors of these complex and variable forms of physical, verbal, and emotional expressions of aggression commonly are the disciplinary and punitive assaults by adults against children.

---

* See, however, Bertram Wyatt-Brown's fascinating essay, "The Mask of Obedience: Male Slave Psychology in the Old South," *American Historical Review*, vol. 93 (December 1988), pp. 1228–52. Wyatt-Brown notes that "From a psychological point of view, whippings had three major effects. They degraded the victim, shut down more normal communications, but, most important of all, compelled the victim to repress the inevitable anger felt toward those responsible for the pain and disgrace" (p. 1248).

Slavery can still take many forms even among people who believe they are free. See, for example, the memoir by Allen Wheelis; his boyhood experience with his domineering father—whose voice resonated for years in his head—made him "a psychological slave" for much of his adulthood. Allen Wheelis, *How People Change* (New York: Perennial Library, 1973), p. 76.

Flagellation is one of the most basic ways in which sadomasochism is acted out. The desires to punish and to be punished, to beat and to be beaten, find expressions in the sexual experiences and fantasies of vast numbers of people, past and present, as is amply evident both in America and elsewhere today. Often, however, adults whose psyches remain rooted in the ambiguous sensations of childhood punishments are considered aberrant and perverse. Nevertheless, their fantasies and actions—which are often judged by others to be obscene—frequently stem directly from the experiences of childhood.

John Mack, a psychoanalyst and a biographer of T. E. Lawrence, notes some of the connections between childhood punishments and subsequent flagellant compulsions in Lawrence himself. Lawrence was raised in an intensely evangelical Protestant household, the second of five sons. His elder brother became both a missionary and an apocalyptic, living in the expectation of the imminent return of Christ and the end of this world.[129] His mother singled her second son out for the most severe punishments, concentrated on his buttocks. According to Mack, "The beatings seem to have been brought on by nothing more than routine childhood misbehavior, such as T. E.'s resistance to learning to play the piano. In any case, what was unique about them," according to the youngest brother, "was that they seemed to be given for the purpose of breaking T. E.'s will."[130] For the remainder of his life, T. E. Lawrence was obsessed with issues associated with the will, obedience, authority, self-denial, and pain.

During his wartime campaigns in the Middle East in 1917, Lawrence was captured by the Turks, and suffered, as a helpless prisoner, from a traumatic experience both with beatings and anal rape by a number of Turkish soldiers who held him captive. Mack sees this assault at Der'a as the key to Lawrence's subsequent obsession with flagellation and bodily pain, the root of his sadomasochistic behavior for the remainder of his short life. In the midst of pain so intense that he thought he might die, he also experienced an erotic pleasure that confounded and tantalized him, from both the beatings and the forced anal intercourse. Mack says that he has "little doubt that Lawrence underwent a painful, humiliating assault at Der'a at the hands of the Turkish commander and his soldiers, and the element of sexual pleasure he experienced in the midst of such indignity, pain and degradation was particularly intolerable and shameful to him."[131] For years afterward, Lawrence suffered from terrible nightmares, indicative of the post–traumatic stress arising from both kinds of assaults. "Of the link between the Der'a assault and Lawrence's later flagellation problem there is little doubt."[132]

During his brutal captivity at Der'a, Lawrence's will was broken once more, and he thereafter sought to punish and degrade himself through a series of pains created by him and inflicted by other men, who whipped his bare body and buttocks on a regular basis. Mack notes that Lawrence described the "impact" of his experience at Der'a "in terms reminiscent of his brother's account of the mother's childhood beatings, done to break Lawrence's will."[133] Mack sets forth the parameters of the "flagellation disorder" in these words:

> His powerful identification with his guilt-ridden mother; the childhood experience of being beaten repeatedly by her in a manner to break his will; the lifetime fascination with, dread of, and need to master pain; the absence of any offsetting heterosexual adaptation; the guilt and shame which resulted from the war experience; and conceivably, a biologically rooted masochistic pre-disposition—all of these combined to make Lawrence vulnerable to this disorder, the form of which reflects his youthful familiarity with medieval flagellation practices.[134]

The beatings Lawrence arranged for himself evidently began in 1923, and continued to the end of his life. Mack reports: "The companion observed three beatings with a metal whip between 1931 and 1934. They were brutal, delivered on the bare buttocks, and a precise number of lashes was required. Lawrence . . . registered obvious fear and agony, but did not scream or cry out. He required that the beatings be severe enough to produce a seminal emission."[135] For Lawrence, "the humiliation of the self" was "as important an aspect of the penance as the physical pain," something that surely was rooted in his humiliating childhood experiences of being beaten by his mother.[136]

Central to such experiences was Lawrence's "elaborate imagination and rich fantasy life," which always shaped his impulses and actions.[137] Mack notes that "the link to his mother's childhood beatings is obvious, but the adult beaters are also associated with the Turkish soldiers who imposed the traumatic assault."[138] Mack concludes by noting that "the beatings, perverse, brutal and pathetic as they seem, are nevertheless a form of closeness, selected for the fusion of intimacy and simultaneous desecration they represent."[139] But Mack never describes the beatings that the boy Lawrence suffered at the hands of his loving but strict mother as "perverse," "brutal," or "pathetic"—these are descriptions characteristically applied only to adults driven to repeat the painful assaults inflicted upon their unwilling bodies and spirits as children.

What Lawrence's mother had done to him as a boy, however, was the indispensable preparation for his subsequent compulsion to be beaten and humiliated by other men, who took his mother's place and thus protected her from the full range of revengefulness and rage that Lawrence must surely have felt periodically toward his adored mother when she singled him out for will-breaking beatings. Lawrence, however, lived in a time and place in which homophobia was rampant; this may have precluded his becoming comfortable with his own attraction to other men, and made it impossible for him to cope with his impulses toward flagellation without feeling abased and ashamed. He appears to have had no choice in the matter, being driven by his experience of both pleasure and pain to fulfill his sexual fantasies through compulsions over which he had no control.*

Sadomasochism among adults often involves the repetition and the reenactment of childhood experiences—either suffered personally or wit-

* John Mack apparently was unaware when he wrote his biography of Lawrence that sadomasochism and flagellation have been an enduring part of English male culture for generations, indeed for centuries. Ian Gibson's remarkable study, *The English Vice: Beating, Sex and Shame in Victorian England and After* (London: Duckworth, 1978), which appeared after Mack's study of Lawrence, explores the complex culture of flagellation and sadomasochism that sustained Lawrence's secretive and private compulsions and made them commonplace.

The obsession with being beaten and punished was characteristic of innumerable British males, reared by strict, punitive nannies and subsequently inured to pain through the floggings and beatings endemic in boys' public schools, as Jonathan Gathorne-Hardy and others have made amply clear. The vast quantities of nineteenth- and twentieth-century pornography in Britain also revealed the obsession with flagellation, as both Steven Marcus and Gibson have noted in their studies. All this evidence confirms the continued presence of sadomasochistic forms of sexuality and behavior, both private and public, in Britain. The same is true for Americans, past and present, but we have paid even less heed to our collective impulses toward sadomasochism. See Jonathan Gathorne-Hardy, *The Unnatural History of the Nanny* (New York: Dial Press, 1973), and *The Public School Phenomenon, 597–1977* (London: Hodder and Stoughton, 1977). Also see Steven Marcus, *The Other Victorians: A Study of Sexuality and Pornography in Mid-Nineteenth Century England* (New York: Basic Books, 1966).

nessed—that involved coercion, pain, fear, and submission. These early traumas persist and remain active long after the experiences themselves have passed. Sadomasochism thus is often an invention of the imagination, arising from the deepest recesses of the unconscious, an enactment of fantasies that originate in childhood experiences.

The theatrical quality of S&M is crucial for many of the adults who engage in sadomasochistic play, particularly erotic and sexual play. David Shapiro, in his remarkable analysis of the sadomasochistic aspects of rigid character, observes that

> Sado-masochistic arrangements have something of the quality of theatrical productions. Whips, leather, the paraphernalia of sensuality and subjugation, are used essentially to create the erotic idea. Whips are not used only to produce pain; they are used more as props for the fantasy of pain and violence and the idea of erotic sensuality. . . . Altogether, sado-masochistic sexuality is a highly ideational matter, far more a product of the imagination than of the senses.[140]

Although Shapiro unfortunately never recognizes the role of corporal punishment in the creation of sadomasochism, he describes the imaginary scenario embedded in so much S&M with exceptional acuteness:

> There is no doubt that ideas of subjugation, of relationships of coercion and surrender, cruel power and humiliating obedience, and innumerable variations of these comprise the basic erotic theme, the basic sexual situation, of sado-masochistic fantasies. All the other elements—the inflicting of pain, struggle against restraint, and so on— are merely sensual particulars or embellishments of this basic situation. For the sado-masochistic person, ideas and images of such relationships are suffused with eroticism.[141]

The breaking of the will is often a primary aim of sadomasochism. Shapiro recognizes, as few others have, the centrality of the will to many forms of sadomasochism. Absolute authority and total obedience are the usual goals played out in S&M games and rituals, and pain and punishment are the means by which these goals are obtained. This is why the insistence on the breaking of children's wills, generation after generation, century after century, has been the foundation for sadomasochistic forms of feeling, thought, and behavior—private and public, social, religious, and political—for time out of mind.

Adults who are sadomasochistic find many ways to reenact and reexperience these earlier forms of violence and pain—often, but certainly not always, through forms of sexual play and fantasy, scenarios very much like those envisaged by David Shapiro and others.[142] Susan Farr, for example, has experienced what Shapiro imagined: sadomasochistic sexuality based upon love and pain and punishments. In her essay "The Art of Discipline: Creating Erotic Dramas of Play and Power" she explores her own experiences in language remarkably similar to Shapiro's:

> For the past three years I've been exploring my feelings through physically hurting my lover and through submitting to her physically hurting me. We spank each other with our hands, tie each other up and deliver a beating with a belt or paddle, discipline each other with a switch or whip. The punishment is always by mutual consent, and the severity, though most often mild, is sometimes sufficient to leave an occasional bruise or a faint welt the next day. It does hurt, and it feels very good to me, whether I'm on the giving or the receiving end.

Farr acknowledges that "Giving or getting a spanking is a sexual turn-on for me. Or, more accurately I should say, *imagining* giving or getting a spanking is a turn-on."

The crucial factor that permits such an experience, however, is that it is voluntary, a free choice by consenting adults and not something imposed and suffered without recourse, as is always true for children who are being corporally punished. The replaying of childhood experiences with punishments enables adults to transform repressed or consciously remembered childhood pain and terror into a game in which punishments can be stopped and controlled as well as being relived. In adult S&M, the child's fantasies of being in control and of stopping the pain can often be acted out relatively safely and by choice. This can empower the adult who chooses to play such games in ways never possible for children being victimized by adults who hit and hurt them while insisting that the discipline is being done out of love and concern for them.

Susan Farr's experience provides a mirror to some of the scenarios described by Christian advocates of physical punishment for the discipline of children. The crucial difference is that Farr is an adult, who is describing pain and punishment that she herself has chosen—though she acknowledges her own ambivalence about the pain that she invites and creates for herself: "When I'm to receive a spanking, I both love it and dread it, seek it and fear it, feel the pleasure and feel the pain."[143]

The imaginary scenarios Farr enacts with real pain and blows are centered around issues of discipline. One part involves "play-acting, with sexual foreplay, with imaginative rituals, with scary dramas of threat and pleading and relief." But the second, equally crucial part involves "power"—which, she notes, is "about dominance and submission, about anger and its expression, about distance and intimacy, about aggression. These two expressions," Farr acknowledges, "the playful and the powerful, come concretely together each time one of us feels the need to administer or submit to a spanking."[144]

For Farr, as for many individuals who express their sadomasochistic fantasies and impulses in their sexual imaginations and behavior, the creation of pleasure from pain through eroticism is the primary purpose of the drama that unfolds. She notes: "What is going on is a drama where the two principals . . . act at being master and slave, play at being fearsome and fearful." The key is the fluidity of the roles being played, something often overlooked and yet very common. As Farr points out, "One clue to how much of drama and how little of reality is involved is that the roles change. The vulnerable submissive of today is the firm and strict dominant of tomorrow. The other clue"—and a crucial one for all who engage in such activities—"is that the whole episode can be called off with a word."[145]

Although Susan Farr's experiences undoubtedly would be considered perverse and obscene by many people, there is actually nothing in her depiction of her sexual encounters with discipline, pain, and pleasure that cannot be paralleled directly with evidence from childhood—except for sexuality itself. The absence of sexuality has always been one of the central illusions of advocates of corporal punishments for children. Most advocates of physical punishment appear oblivious to the sexuality of children at any age prior to puberty. Having spent many centuries denying or prohibiting all forms of sexual experience and expression in children, Christian advocates of corporal punishment generally overlook the dimension of children's experience with punishment that subsequently transforms pain into pleasure: the erotic component of the assaults upon the buttocks and other parts of the body by people who say they love the child they are beating.

Corporal punishment commonly focuses upon a child's buttocks, the anal area in the back being the most frequently beaten part of the body. However, the anus, as Freud and many others have known, is one of the most erotic zones of the body, closely linked with the genitals and responsive to orgasms and erotic pleasures, a source of pleasure and pain for children and adults alike.[146] The assault upon the buttocks thus becomes far more consequential than most of us ever recognize.*

Long before Freud recognized the erotic and sexual natures of children, the connections between punishment and sexuality were evident to Jean-Jacques Rousseau. Reflecting in his *Confessions* about his own experiences with childhood punishment, he exclaimed: "How differently would one deal with youth, if one could more clearly see the remote effects of the usual method of treatment [corporal punishment], which is employed always without discrimination, frequently without discretion!"[147]

Rousseau's adult sadomasochism appears to have been the direct result of his encounters with physical punishments at the hands of the woman who raised him. He had previously witnessed his brother's brutal beating at the hands of their father. Although his brother was seven years older, Rousseau recalled once throwing himself "impetuously" between his father and brother, covering his brother's body with his own and receiving "the blows which were aimed at him." Several years later, after his brother had left home and disappeared, Rousseau was sent to live with a Protestant minister and his sister. Hitherto he had had a childhood

---

* Gay male literature on S&M often focuses on the anus as the source of both pain and pleasure through physical punishments and sexual intercourse. The opposite response is evident in the homophobia of fundamentalist Christians and many others as well, which is often rooted in the unrecognized connection of love with the painful assaults upon the buttocks and anus in childhood. The unconscious association of love with anal punishments is surely among the psychic sources of much of the fear and hatred of homosexuality and of sodomy rampant in the Christian right today. Homophobia is as central to the ideology and psychology of the Christian right today as anti-Semitism was to Nazis in the 1930s and 1940s.

Alice Miller makes the connections between physical and emotional abuse and anti-Semitism transparently clear in *For Your Own Good: Hidden Cruelty in Child-Rearing and the Roots of Violence*, trans. by Hildegarde and Hunter Hannum (New York: Farrar, Straus and Giroux, 1983).

blissfully free of harshness and punishments, unlike his elder brother's. Rousseau recalled that "the children of kings could not be more carefully looked after than I was during my early years—worshipped by all around me, and, which is far less common, treated as a beloved, never as a spoiled child." His "liveliest desire was to be loved by all who came near me." He was, he recalled, "of a gentle disposition," and was, for two years, "neither the witness nor the victim of any violent feelings." But in the Protestant minister's household, he too became subject to threats and to corporal punishments at the hands of a Mlle Lambercier. After his first encounter with painful punishments, he remembered that he "found the reality less terrible than the expectation; and, what was still more strange, this chastisement made me still more devoted to her who had inflicted it." He discovered that "I had found in the pain, even in the disgrace, a mixture of sensuality which had left me less afraid than desirous of experiencing it again from the same hand. No doubt some precocious sexual instinct was mingled with this feeling, for the same chastisement inflicted by her brother would not have seemed to me at all pleasant." He was only physically punished once more, yet the impact endured for his lifetime. Rousseau wonders:

> Who would believe that this childish punishment, inflicted upon me when only eight years old by a young woman of thirty, disposed of my tastes, my desires, my passions, and my own self for the re- mainder of my life, and that in a manner exactly contrary to that which should have been the natural result?

Forever after, his pleasure in flagellation and beatings was inextricably associated with his sexuality and his erotic pleasures. "My old childish taste, instead of disappearing, became so associated with the other, that I could never banish it from the desires kindled by my senses," but, being "Too bashful to declare my taste, I at least satisfied it in situations which had reference to it and kept up the idea of it. To lie at the feet of an imperious mistress," he observed, "to obey her commands, to ask her forgiveness—this was for me a sweet enjoyment," a pleasure directly rooted in the beatings and the submission that he experienced as an eight-year-old boy.[148] Such erotic pleasures and impulses are often the hallmarks of sadomasochistic individuals, for whom pain and beatings become essential components of erotic pleasures.

The roots of adult sadomasochism can often be traced back to the experiences of childhood, to actual encounters with punishment and pain, to the imposition of power and control by adults over the bodies and wills of children. These are the realities that most of us remain eager to deny, for their implications are troublesome and disturbing. Sadomasochism, however, shapes many lives and generates many fantasies, both private and public. So long as children are beaten by adults, the obsessions with domination and submission, with power and authority, with shame and humiliation, with painful pleasure—all hallmarks of sadomasochism— will remain an enduring consequence of the ordinary violence and coercion done in the name of discipline.

Sadomasochism is not an aberration; it is inherent in corporal punishment both psychically and culturally. Wherever children suffer from painful physical punishments and humiliating submission to more powerful authorities, sadomasochism will be present. Sadomasochism is thus one of the most enduring consequences of coercive discipline in childhood.

Domestic Violence

To a degree that few people fully appreciate, domestic violence emerges directly out of the experiences of childhood. Corporal punishment trains children to accept and to tolerate aggression and violence, since physical assaults are used by adults to teach obedience and submission. The feelings associated with such punishments—anger, rage, anxiety, fear, terror, hatred, hostility, and love—are carried into the domestic relationships of adults who were spanked, whipped, and beaten as children. The patterns of aggression and assault directed against children become the models of aggression and assault directed against other beloved adults, especially wives, husbands, or lovers.

Physical violence and verbal violence have been and still are present in many families.[149] Not only poor and marginal families experience these violent and painful impulses and act them out; middle- and upper-class families have their own versions of such violence, perhaps more often expressed in words than actions but hurtful nevertheless. Domestic aggression and violence are among the most pervasive consequences of the culture of childhood pain and punishment.

Only within the past two decades has the full extent of family aggression and pain begun to be recognized.[150] The first shelter for battered women and their children was the Chiswick Women's Aid in England, established in 1971 by Erin Pizzey and her colleagues, who set up a series of safe spaces for the victims of domestic violence and other male brutality.[151] Soon thereafter, the battered women's shelter movement came into being, and shelters have now been created throughout England and across America, as well as in other countries. They often remain marginal and fragile institutions, painful evidence of a vast sea of family suffering that most of us would prefer not to acknowledge. Throughout the country, though, there are many groups comparable to the Illinois Coalition Against Domestic Violence, which connects shelters for women and children throughout the state. But the number of shelters is vastly outweighed by the needs of the adults and children in jeopardy from assault and violence within the home. The great majority of domestic-violence victims—both adults and children—remain unsheltered and unprotected.

The first scholarly research on domestic violence was begun at about the same time that Erin Pizzey was setting up the first shelters for battered women in England. Richard Gelles's study *The Violent Home* (1974) was rejected by a series of publishers unprepared to deal with the topic of domestic violence; *The Violent Home* is now acknowledged to be both a pioneering analysis and a classic in the burgeoning study of family violence. Gelles interviewed families in a New Hampshire community and found an astonishing amount of evidence of physical violence in these households. Gelles "found that many of the respondents who had committed acts of violence towards their spouses had been exposed to conjugal violence as children and had been frequent victims of parental violence." He is convinced that "the family serves as basic training for violence by exposing children to violence, by making them victims of violence, and by providing them with learning contexts for the commission of violent acts." In addition, he notes, "the family inculcates children with normative and value systems that approve of the use of violence on family members in various situations."[152] Nearly all the families studied used corporal punishments; in violence between spouses, men generally assaulted women.[153] Gelles found ample evidence of a pattern of violence continuing over generations: "It was evident that many of the techniques of intrafamily violence are passed on from generation to generation. Where one mother used a belt on her children, we found that she had been hit with a belt by her parents. If a wife slaps her husband, she may have observed her mother do the same thing to her father."[154] The transmission of aggression and violence from generation to generation is a theme that recurs in many studies of family conflicts, violence, and crime.[155]

Gelles's observations have been confirmed by many others. In their powerful and disturbing analysis, *Behind Closed Doors: Violence in the American Family* (1980), Murray Straus, Richard Gelles, and Suzanne Steinmetz document in detail the fact that domestic violence is normal throughout the land. "Drive down any street in America. More than one household in six has been the scene of a spouse striking his or her partner last year." When assaults against children are included, "every other house in America is the scene of family violence at least once a year."[156] Physical punishments of children, these authors argue, are violent acts that underpin subsequent violence within families and between spouses. They estimate that in 1975 "between 3.1 and 4 million children" out of a total of "nearly 46 million children" in the United States "have been kicked, bitten, or punched by a parent at some time in their lives; while between 1 and 1.9 million were kicked, bitten, or punched in 1975. Between 1.4 and 2.3 million children have been 'beaten up' while growing up, and between 275,000 and 750,000 American children were 'beaten up' in 1975."[157]*

* A subsequent survey of family violence in 1985 by Richard Gelles and Murray Straus provided startling evidence "that, contrary to our expectations, the rates of abusive violence toward children and women had declined far more than we could have ever expected." Based upon their new rates, they estimate "that there were more than 700,000 fewer children victimized in 1985 than in 1975. Nearly 375,000 fewer women were victims of severe violence in 1985 than in 1975." Richard J. Gelles and Murray A. Straus, *Intimate Violence* (New York: Simon and Schuster, 1988), pp. 108–109. Not surprisingly, many people have been skeptical of their conclusions but, if they are correct, perhaps there is reason to hope that real change in levels of domestic violence can be achieved in the decades to come. See pp. 109–115 for their discussion of this issue. Most important, however, is their conclusion that "After nearly two decades of research on the causes and consequences of family violence, we are convinced that our society must abandon its reliance on spanking children if we are to prevent intimate violence" (p. 197). *Intimate Violence* provides a powerful series of arguments and an abundance of evidence in support of their conviction.

Punishments' long-term effects on adults are evident: "The relationship between punishment as a child and child abuse as an adult is clear for the mothers: the more they were punished physically as teen-agers, the higher the rate of violent acts which could cause serious injury they inflicted on their own child."[158] The connections between earlier punishments and later domestic violence are amplified by the authors' observations on wife-beating's links with previous punishments:

> We know that children who experienced physical punishment as teen-agers have higher rates of violence toward their spouses. Typically this is of the pushing, shoving, slapping variety. But does being hit as a teen-ager make people more prone to wife- or husband-beating? The answer is a clear yes. The wife-beating rate for men who were *not* physically punished in their teens was about two out of a hundred. The same "low" rates apply to husband-beating by women who had not been hit as teen-agers. As the amount of physical punishment experienced as a child goes up, the rates of wife-beating and husband-beating also go up. *The people who experienced the most punishment as teen-agers have a rate of wife-beating and husband-beating that is four times greater than those whose parents did not hit them.*[159]

Straus, Gelles, and Steinmetz also discuss aggression and violence among siblings where the children themselves have been victims of corporal punishments:

> the more often the parents in our study had hit their children, the more likely the child was to have *severely* attacked a brother or sister during the survey year. In fact, almost all the children who were on the receiving end of the most severe abuse from a parent also engaged in intensely violent acts. Had these acts occurred between two strangers rather than between two children in the same family, they would have been considered chargeable assault.[160]

Violence thus begets further violence, within the home as well as outside it, as will become evident shortly.[161] The American family is often a most dangerous place to be, something police have long known from bitter experience with domestic conflicts and battles. The kitchen and the bedroom are among the most lethal locales. As Straus, Gelles, and Steinmetz observe: "Americans run the greatest risk of assault, physical injury, and even murder in their own homes by members of their own families."[162]

Domestic violence thus is epidemic in our culture and society, as it is in Great Britain and other countries. But only recently, thanks largely to the feminist movement and the battered women's shelter movement, has the plight of women trapped in violent familial relationships become clear. No one who reads recent studies can doubt the reality of suffering scarring the lives of vast numbers of women both in America and abroad, who are caught in a cycle of physical and emotional violence that warps the life of every member of their families.[163]

Some feminists insist that males are by nature violent and aggressive; they argue that the battering of women is an inevitable consequence of patriarchalism and male domination in the culture at large. R. Emerson Dobash and Russell Dobash, for instance, "propose that the correct interpretation of violence between husbands and wives conceptualizes such violence as the extension of the domination and control of husbands over their wives. This control," they argue, "is historically and socially constructed." The Dobashes insist that "Men are socialized into aggression" and that "all men see themselves as controllers of women, and because they are socialized into the use of violence they are potential aggressors against their wives."[164] Many advocates of shelters for battered women are similarly convinced that men are naturally violent, and thus that battered women are not responsible for their victimization in any meaningful way. These arguments seem to deny that the men who batter and abuse women and children are themselves victims of prior abuse and violence.

The antimale ideology of some feminists fails to take sufficient note of the life histories of battering men. Recent studies of violent men reveal the same patterns over and over again, of childhood suffering and violence through punishments, assaults, and other forms of abuse, both physical and emotional, that leave permanent wounds and prepare the way for the violence these men subsequently practice as husbands and fathers. This is made utterly clear in the study of violent men by Anson Shupe, William Stacey, and Lonnie Hazlewood:

> This generational transfer of a proclivity for violence was frequently the case in the backgrounds of the men we encountered. The love/hurt/rage reactions that helpless young boys felt toward their abusive,

powerful parents (for whom the boys nevertheless felt affection) were replayed by these men in their own marriages. In other words, their own experiences of callous or even cruel treatment as children could be seen as an unfortunate legacy they carried with them into adulthood, often on a level below their own awareness.[165]

Battering men are usually victims of assaults and violence just as those whom they batter are victims; the evil that was once done to them, they do again to others whom they depend upon and often even love.

Erin Pizzey and Jeff Shapiro have worked for years with the victims of domestic violence in England through the shelters for battered women and children. In their book, *Prone to Violence* (1982), they have provided a powerful and compelling analysis of the personal roots and common experiences of familial violence. Pizzey and Shapiro understand, as too few yet have, that the early encounters of children with punishment, pain, and fear, and with inexpressible rage and resentment, provide the seedbed for the murderous violence—and the attachment to this violence—that mark so many lives. Erin Pizzey's personal encounters with violent men, the husbands or lovers of women being sheltered from the assaults and violence of their prior relationships, have provided her with an extraordinary range of experiences from which to assess the meaning of violence for the women and children she sought to protect.

At the core of Pizzey and Shapiro's observations is a recognition of the enduring impact that the early association of love and pain and the potent mixture of pleasure and pain have for all those whose adult lives are marked by continued aggression, violence, and pain. Although they never use the term "sadomasochism," the combination of pain and pleasure in physical violence and assaults clearly resonates with the themes I explored earlier. Pizzey and her colleagues had many opportunities to observe, both in children and in adults, the perplexing pleasure taken from pain, and the need so many individuals had for repeated encounters with painful beatings of all kinds and degrees. One such person was "Olga." She came to the shelter "in fear of her life from her boyfriend Jim," having been "repeatedly beaten" for many years. The beatings had left her face scarred and distorted.[166] The police inspector warned that she might be killed if she returned to her boyfriend. Careful questioning revealed Olga's early experiences with violence and pleasure:

Olga was born in Scotland. Her grandfather was a Bible-thumping Puritan bigot. The family lived in a small village, and Olga's mother was the only girl in a large family of boys. The beatings, always for religious reasons, did not spare her. The leather strap hung behind the door, both at home and at school. By the time she attended school, she was well used to the pain of it across her legs and buttocks.

The pattern was then repeated with Olga herself. She was illegitimate; her mother was sixteen when Olga was born, and became "an outcast" both in her family and in the village.

Olga too, was regularly beaten in this God-fearing family. And she does remember the first moments when pain evolved into pleasure. She was five, she thinks, and her mother removed her knickers and made her bend over her knee. She had not done anything very bad, so she was being smacked by hand, rather than strapped with the tawse. As usual, she felt a tremendous sense of fear and anxiety before bending over, but the difference this time was that as the pain in its crescendo reached its highest pitch, she suddenly felt a warm surge of tingling pleasure suffusing her whole body.

Olga was amazed and dreadfully embarrassed. Soon she began to look for that pleasure in further beatings. So she would definitely provoke her mother, and that was not difficult. She would fight at school until they whipped her and blood ran down her legs. "The Devil's in her," the teachers would tell her mother.[167]

Olga's relationship with her boyfriend subsequently was both violent and potentially lethal, her life being in constant danger from his assaults. As Pizzey and Shapiro observe, "She and Jim cannot live with each other, but they cannot live without each other. They are two badly abused and assaulted human beings endlessly acting out their past damage. It won't stop until one or [the] other of them gets killed."[168]

The persistence of such violent intimate relationships year after year, assault after assault, is profoundly puzzling on its face, but Pizzey and Shapiro draw a useful distinction between battered women, some of whom are nonviolent, others violent: "The difference between a non-violent woman and a violent woman is that a non-violent woman can get into a relationship with a man who is violent, and love the man but hate his violence. A violence-prone woman will look for a violent man with whom she will hate the man but cling to his violence."[169] Pizzey and Shapiro are convinced, from years of observation and encounters with men, women, and children in violent relationships, that many individuals who were abused as children become addicted to violence as adults, trained from early experiences to need the chemical highs from the adrenaline rush that terror and pain can produce. Children can become addicted to violence very early, since their bodies react biochemically to the assaults from "loving" adults while their emotions register their feelings and reactions in memories imprinted for life.

Addiction to violence and pain is evident in many lives. But, as Pizzey and Shapiro note, "The grave danger in these relationships is that since pleasure is found through pain, the ultimate orgasm is death." As they rightly point out, "In violent families . . . children grow up with death as a constant companion. They are reared on the language of death—'One of these days, I'll fucking kill you'—and, with violence all around, death becomes a very real and ever-present possibility."[170] Sadomasochism, too, often flirts with death, in one guise or another.[171]

Family violence brings death both to the spirit—"soul murder" in all its forms—and to the body.[172] Erin Pizzey knows this from her years of experience with the victims and the perpetrators of family violence, about whom she writes with immense insight and compassion. She knows, as many deny, that men who beat and batter their wives and children are as much victims as the women and children whom they hurt, violate, and terrify. She knows, too, that the best solution for violence is non-violence and love. The rages within cannot be quelled by counterviolence and aggression. That is why shelters for battered women and children prohibit corporal punishment, the foundation and model for all the violence that later brings pain, suffering, and danger to families everywhere.

Aggression and Delinquency

The most visible public outcome of early violence and coercion in the name of discipline is the active aggression that begins to shape character and behavior in childhood and continues, in far too many instances, throughout the lives of those who suffered most in their earlier years.[173] Aggressive children often become aggressive adults, who often produce more aggressive children, in a cycle that endures generation after generation.[174] Corporal punishments always figure prominently in the roots of adolescent and adult aggressiveness, especially in those manifestations that take an antisocial form, such as delinquency and criminality. Assaults upon children by adults in the name of discipline are the primary familial models for the aggression, assaults, and other forms of antisocial behavior, delinquency, and crime that emerge when children grow up.

Physical punishment of children consistently appears as one of the major influences shaping subsequent aggressiveness and delinquency of males.[175] The psychologists Ronald Slaby and Wendy Roedell, in "The Development and Regulation of Aggression in Young Children," note that "one of the most reliable predictors of children's level of aggression is the heavy use by parents of harsh, punitive discipline and physical punishment." They add that "Parental punitiveness has been found to be positively correlated with children's aggression in over 25 studies," which comes as no surprise to anyone familiar with the nature of the assaults done in the name of discipline. Slaby and Roedell define childhood aggression as "those actions that involve actual or intended physical or psychological injury to another individual"; they exclude "assertive behavior" and "fantasy or symbolic aggression." They note that aggression is the result of a complex set of factors, including physical punishments, rather than any single factor. But harsh physical punishments are always among the key factors fostering subsequent aggressiveness in children from infancy to adolescence. As Slaby and Roedell observe, "parental punishment is one important aspect of a general pattern of intercorrelated parental behaviors that influence the child's aggression. This pattern includes such additional factors as parental permissiveness for aggression, negativism or lack of warmth, low use of reasoning, and inconsistent application of discipline."[176]

The pattern often discerned in families in which boys are the most aggressive (and subsequently the most delinquent) usually involves both neglect or "permissiveness" and episodic, severe physical punishments. The emotional impact of such brutal and erratic discipline is often devastating, with enduring, dangerous consequences both for the children who suffer from these experiences and for the public, which suffers from their delinquency and criminality in the years that follow.

One of the most massive long-term studies of delinquency's origins and etiology, begun in 1940 by Sheldon and Eleanor Glueck, confirms the central role played by discipline and families in the shaping of anti-social aggressiveness enacted in male delinquency and criminality in adolescence and adulthood. Although the Gluecks' studies have been challenged and criticized by many scholars, James Wilson and Richard Herrnstein, in their illuminating synthesis of the scholarship on crime, *Crime and Human Nature* (1985), acknowledge that "most, if not all, of the distinguishing traits of the Gluecks' delinquent boys have been re-peatedly confirmed in other samples."[177] The Gluecks compared both delinquent and nondelinquent boys from English, Irish, and Italian fam-ilies in poor urban areas and discovered conclusive evidence that delin-quency is rooted in early childhood experiences, discipline and family life being of paramount importance.

What the Gluecks prove is that delinquency begins long before chil-dren become adolescents; signs are often visible by the time children are between three and six, and almost always before they are eleven:

> The onset of persistent misbehavior tendencies was at the early age of seven years or younger among 48 per cent of our delinquents, and from eight to ten in an additional 39 per cent; thus a total of almost nine-tenths of the entire group showed clear delinquent tendencies before the time when boys generally become members of organized boys' gangs.[178]

By the time most boys who become delinquent have either entered or left elementary school, the patterns of their subsequent aggressiveness and antisocial behavior have been set. Childhood experience within fam-ilies is often the matrix from which delinquency later emerges.

In their effort to understand the complex roots of delinquency and the many variables that shaped the lives of both delinquent and nonde-linquent boys, the Gluecks constructed a "Social Prediction Table," which focused on "five crucial factors," including "discipline of boy by father, supervision of boy by mother, affection of mother for boy, affection of father for boy," and "family cohesiveness."[179] They discovered that "71.8 per cent of the thousand boys included in *Unraveling* [*Juvenile Delin-quency*] whose fathers were overstrict or erratic in their disciplinary prac-tices turned out to be delinquent, compared with only 9.3 per cent of those whose fathers were firm but kindly. Those of lax discipline fell in between these extremes."[180] The Gluecks also found that

> in 95 per cent of these 2,000 offenders the disciplinary practices of one or the other parent were of a nature to be clearly assessed as inadequate, involving either extreme laxity or extreme rigidity, or inconsistency of control of the child. In only 4.5 per cent of the homes was the discipline essentially consistent and firm and entirely acceptable to the child because it was the product of sincerity and affection.[181]

Sheldon Glueck found "In far higher measure than was true of the parents of the non-delinquents, the fathers and mothers of the delinquents resorted to confusing extremes of laxity and harshness, instead of applying reasoned and just disciplinary practices."[182] As Slaby and Roedell point out, subsequent research has confirmed this view with remarkable consistency.[183] The Gluecks continued their analysis of discipline in their major study, *Unraveling Juvenile Delinquency* (1950), in which they assert: "All in all, the most marked difference between the disciplinary practices of the parents of the delinquents and those of the non-delinquents is found in the considerably greater extent to which the former resorted to physical punishment and in the lesser extent to which they reasoned with the boys about their misconduct." The Gluecks believe their analysis "is a revealing commentary on the relative effectiveness of physical punishment as opposed to an appeal to reason in the control of child behavior."[184]

The "mal-formations of personality and character" that Sheldon Glueck and many others have observed have long-term consequences.[185] Although corporal punishment is not the sole factor in the creating and sustaining of aggressive personalities and delinquency, it is almost always one of the major factors that must be reckoned with in any exploration of the roots of antisocial behavior and aggression in adolescence and adulthood, especially among males. The lowest incidence of delinquency and antisocial behavior in adolescence and beyond is always found among males who were loved, respected, cared for, and reasoned with in childhood. Most people eventually grow up without becoming delinquent or criminal, of course, as the Gluecks and others note repeatedly, but virtually every study done so far reveals that the early lives of nondelinquents have been significantly different from the lives of those who later act out their aggression, anger, and resentment against individuals and the public through delinquent or criminal behavior.

The infliction of pain through physical punishments is one of the causes of subsequent aggression, anger, and hostility, which often take the form of delinquency and criminality. Many people, including fundamentalist and Pentecostal preachers, argue that corporal punishment prevents delinquency and crime. Their apologias for physical assaults against children presume that the children subjected to painful punishments and parental violence will become obedient and law-abiding in later life. In case after case, however, life histories belie this assumption, for the theme that emerges frequently from the autobiographies and memoirs of many evangelical, fundamentalist, and Pentecostal Protestants during the years preceding their conversion and rebirth is disobedience and rebelliousness, sometimes including delinquent or even criminal behavior.[186] Their common adolescent rebelliousness or opposition to their parents, teachers, and other adults often reflects the intense feelings of rage and resentment stored up during a long childhood of pain and suffering. Their disobedience thus is cogent evidence of the failure of this method of discipline: If corporal punishment were successful, children would not persistently disobey and be punished time and time again.

The overwhelming evidence now available from scholarship on the roots of delinquency and crime suggests that corporal punishment—the application of the rod and other implements of discipline—is a major factor in the generation of the rage, aggression, and impulses for revenge that fuel the emotions, fantasies, and actions of individuals, mostly male, who become active delinquents or criminals. But it remains vital to recognize that delinquency generally is the outcome for only a small fraction of those assaulted by adults in childhood.

The vast majority of people find other means of expressing the anger, rage, and rebelliousness that stem from early encounters with assaultive, painful parental punishments. For many individuals who experience religious conversions, previous histories of delinquency and criminality can be overcome and behavior dramatically altered, although the theologies of such converts often continue to mirror their earlier experiences with violence, aggression, and punishments, transmuting these into acceptable beliefs and expressions.

For many American males, aggression and violence are channeled into the socially acceptable forms of sports, the spectacle of which enthralls millions in relatively harmless encounters. For equally vast numbers, television provides a nightly domestic theater of visual and verbal violence, through the assaults, mayhem, and murders that captivate so many viewers. Movies, too, provide surrogates for aggression and violence. But the most enduring and the most lethal expression of this aggressiveness and violence clearly is military "defense" and warfare.[187]

Authoritarianism

Authoritarianism has always been one of the most pervasive and enduring consequences of physical punishment, which creates the paradoxical subservience to and rebelliousness against authority that so often mark authoritarian personalities.[188] Authoritarianism—the familial, social, and political obsession with order, control, and obedience—is rooted in violence and coercion. Physical pain and abuse originating in discipline are consistent progenitors of authoritarianism. Coerced rather than voluntary obedience—"voluntary" meaning obtained through example, persuasion, and consent—is the rule among authoritarians of all descriptions. The polarities of order and disorder, obedience and rebelliousness—always present in authoritarians—are among the most enduring legacies of corporal punishments.[189]

The authoritarian Christian family is dependent upon coercion and pain to obtain obedience to authority within and beyond the family, in the church, the community, and the polity. Modern forms of Christian fundamentalism share the same obsessions with obedience to authority characteristic of earlier modes of evangelical Protestantism, and the same authoritarian streak evident among seventeenth- and eighteenth-century Anglo-American evangelicals is discernible today, for precisely the same reasons: the coercion of children through painful punishments in order to teach obedience to divine and parental authority.[190] Fear and suffering still shape the characters of children whose obedience is obtained involuntarily by physical punishments.

From the colonial period to the present, evangelical and fundamen-

talist Protestant treatises on child-rearing and discipline—treatises such
as those explored earlier—have been preoccupied with the necessity of
absolute and unquestioning obedience to authority—obedience obtained
by force rather than by persuasion, since it is assumed that no child
would obey without such intimidation and pain. Corporal punishment
often does force children to obey authority, but it does so by methods that
instill an enduring consciousness of the limitations of the very authorities
being obeyed. Consent plays little or no role in fundamentalist advocacy
of the rod as the proper and necessary mode of Christian discipline. The
rod coerces consent through suffering and fear. The fear of punishment
is the primary motivation for obedience and submission to both parental
and divine authority.

Fundamentalist authoritarianism is generally absolutist in its quest
for total obedience from children. As Larry Christenson writes with obvious approval, either paraphrasing or quoting his mid-nineteenth century German source, Heinrich Thiersch's *Christian Family Life*:

> In the command of obedience given to children, there is no mention
> made of any exception. It must be set forth and impressed upon them
> without any exception. "But what if my parents command something
> wrong?" This is precocious inquisitiveness. Such a question should
> perish on the lips of a Christian child.[191]

Given such a conviction, it would not have been inappropriate for Christenson to have called his book *The Authoritarian Family* instead of *The
Christian Family*, since the two appear virtually synonymous.

Alice Miller has explored remarkably similar attitudes toward obedience and authority among nineteenth- and twentieth-century Germans,
many of whom supported Adolf Hitler and his Nazi party during the
1920s, 1930s, and 1940s. She believes that the harsh discipline these
people experienced as children prepared them well for the absolute obedience sought by the totalitarian leader they obeyed. But such obedience,
as Miller knows well, becomes possible only after a series of hurtful
assaults upon the bodies, wills, and selves of children through spankings
and other punishments such as those advocated in this country for Christian parenting.[192]

One of the most enduring characteristics of authoritarianism is the
dominance of males, the assertion of patriarchy as the cornerstone of

authority and power. Fundamentalist Christianity always presupposes the domination of males and the subordination of both women and children to the absolute authority of fathers and husbands, who are themselves theoretically subject only to the will of other superior males and to that of God himself. Christenson, for example, believes that wives owe total obedience to their husbands' divinely ordained authority over the household: "Submission to authority means that you put yourself wholly at the disposal of the person who is set over you." This extends even to those situations in which women find themselves being tyrannized and abused by their husbands. Christenson says that such wives should "acknowledge this [Godly] guidance even in the sufferings which her husband may cause her. Let her yield herself to them with the certainty that this is the school wherein she has to learn patience, the hardest of Christian virtues."[193]

According to the Reverend Jack Hyles, girls are to be trained to absolute obedience from infancy. He believes that

> obedience is the most necessary ingredient to be required from the child. This is especially true in the life of a girl, for she must be obedient all her life. The boy who is obedient to his mother and father will someday become the head of the home; not so for the girl. Whereas the boy is being trained to be a leader, the girl is being trained to be a follower. Hence, obedience is far more important to her, for she must someday transfer it from her parents to her husband.

Hyles immediately points out the long-term implications of his conviction:

> This means that she should never be allowed to argue at all. She should become submissive and obedient. She must obey immediately, without question, and without argument. The parents who require this have done a big favor for their future son-in-law.[194]

The authoritarian patriarchal family is thus created in childhood, with the patterning of sex roles and the training in absolute, unquestioning obedience by children and by females of all ages. The complete domination of females by males and the belief that obedience must be total if it is to be effective are convictions characteristic of authoritarians everywhere.[195]

When we ignore the connections between corporal punishments and authoritarianism, however, as most of us generally do, the etiology of authoritarianism is often obscured and the childhood roots of adult authoritarianism remain unnoticed.[196] This was clearly the case with one of the most disturbing experiments ever undertaken in America to explore the nature of obedience—Stanley Milgram's experiments on submission to authority, which were designed and carried out by psychologists at Yale University in New Haven and at Bridgeport, Connecticut, during the early 1960s, before the Vietnam war transformed the American political and ideological scene.

In his remarkable study *Obedience to Authority* (1974), Milgram demonstrated the extraordinary lengths to which ordinary men and women from various walks of life and backgrounds were prepared to go in order to obey the commands of individuals whom they did not know in a situation made to appear life-threatening to another person. A person volunteered to participate in a learning experiment in which punishment would be applied to another "volunteer" (in fact a member of the experimental team) by a series of electric shocks whose voltages ranged from 0 to 450 (enough to do serious physical harm). The actual volunteer, called the "teacher," was led to believe that these electric shocks were being inflicted in response to incorrect answers to a series of questions. (In fact, no shocks were given to the "learner.") The experiment's true purpose was to discover the point at which an individual would refuse to obey and then actively disobey the insistent commands of the experimenter. Milgram found that in experimental situations in which the "learner" voiced his response to the increasing shocks, from mild discomfort to agonized screams and pleas to be released from the straps binding him to his chair, many of the "teachers" nevertheless continued to inflict the shocks.

> Painful groans were heard on administration of the 135-volt shock, and at 150 volts the victim cried out, "Experimenter, get me out of here! I won't be in the experiment any more! I refuse to go on!" Cries of this type continue with generally rising intensity, so that at 180 volts the victim cried out, "I can't stand the pain," and by 270 volts his response to the shock was definitely an agonized scream. Throughout, from 150 volts on, he insisted that he be let out of the experiment.

At 300 volts the victim shouted in desperation that he would no longer provide answers to the memory test.[197]

Silence followed for the remainder of the experiment. The subjects were told to continue to ask questions and provide the appropriate shocks if the learner did not respond, which many did right to the limit of 450 volts.

What astonished Milgram and his colleagues was the proportion of individuals willing to obey the command to inflict pain right to the limit even when, in at least one instance, the person inflicting the shock believed that the person apparently being shocked had died. After the termination of the experiment, this man commented: "Well, I faithfully believed the man was dead until we opened the door. When I saw him, I said, 'Great, this is great.' But it didn't bother me even to find that he was dead. I did a job."[198]

In most of the experiments, Milgram found that approximately half the people who volunteered to give the shocks were willing to obey the authority to the limit despite the anguished pleas, and subsequent silence, of the person they were helping to "teach." This result dismayed Milgram, whose book *Obedience to Authority* reflects his effort to comprehend the nature of obedience rendered even to authorities who instruct the infliction of pain beyond ordinary measures of tolerance. Milgram noted: "With numbing regularity good people were seen to knuckle under to the demands of authority and perform actions that were callous and severe. Men who are in everyday life responsible and decent were seduced by the trappings of authority, by the control of their perceptions, and by the uncritical acceptance of the experimenter's definition of the situation into performing harsh acts."[199]

In his quest to understand the motives for such extremely high levels of obedience to punitive authority, Milgram emphasized the role of "agency"—the sense of personal responsibility individuals may or may not have for their own actions and behavior—and the role of autonomy and selfhood. He also considered the role played by the "teacher's" relative distance from both the authority and the "learner" in influencing willingness to obey. But at no point in the entire study did Milgram ever ask explicitly about the childhood experiences of the individuals whose actions as adults he studied. In an appendix to *Obedience to Authority*, however, he observed: "I am certain that there is a complex personality basis to obedience and disobedience. But I know we have not found it."[200]

Not once, it appears, did Milgram ever ask the volunteers about their childhood encounters with authorities—with the parents, teachers, and others who first taught them to obey. Not once, it appears, did he ever ask directly about their childhood experiences with punishment and discipline, particularly with corporal punishments. Had he done so, undoubtedly he would have gained a range of information that might have enabled him to probe more deeply into the psyches of those whose obedience appears to have had no bounds and whose consciences remained either silent or muffled while the "victim" cried out in anguish, terror, and pain before lapsing into silence and noncompliance at the end of the experiment. These people were willing to obey authority far beyond any expected boundaries.

Quite clearly, Milgram was encountering the ordinary, everyday forms that authoritarianism takes now in New England and elsewhere, but his assumptions about the nature of authority in this country precluded his anticipation of such high levels of obedience. Had he been able to read Alice Miller's *For Your Own Good* or any of the Christian apologias for corporal punishment, perhaps he would not have been as astonished by his own discoveries. Without realizing it, Stanley Milgram tapped into the vast collective reservoir of earlier encounters with coercion and pain present in a culture that tolerates and even advocates assaults upon children's bodies, wills, and spirits as normal forms of discipline.

Child abuse is the primary means by which authoritarianism—in both its religious and secular forms—is created. Authoritarianism, in turn, is one of the most enduring of all the consequences—both internal and external, private and public—of corporal punishments. The persistent "conservatism" of American politics and society is rooted in large part in the physical violence done to children, for their autonomy and their very selves were threatened and suppressed by the adults who bore and nurtured them, and who educated them both at home and in school from infancy through adolescence.

Americans have always been far more prone to authoritarianism than the public ideology of participatory democracy would suggest, but the roots of this persistent tilt towards hierarchy, enforced order, and absolute authority—so evident in Germany earlier in this century and in the radical right in America today—are always traceable to aggression against children's wills and bodies, to the pain and the suffering they experience long before they, as adults, confront the complex issues of the polity, the society, and the world. Stanley Milgram's discoveries remain haunting revelations of this relatively uncharted territory of obedience and authority.[201]

Authoritarianism is usually a form of "order" that is actually a reaction to the hurtful violence children experience and the rage and hatred that violence creates. Authoritarianism is "order" built upon coercion rather than consent, upon self-alienation rather than empathy and love for one-self and others. Such efforts at control usually fail to achieve their goals in the long run, for the very impulses that create authoritarian person-alities create aggressive, violent, and antisocial feelings and behavior that subvert and betray the wish for "order" and "power" and "uniformity" characteristic of authoritarianism. Without violence, there would be less authoritarianism, since it is violence itself that both creates and sustains authoritarianism in many of its guises.

But authoritarianism has another side—even deeper, darker, and far more dangerous—that is present even when it is most covert and hidden from view: the destructive and murderous impulse to destroy life itself, the alliance with death that is always present in authoritarianism. Living in the age in which nuclear annihilation is always a possibility, we must reckon with the impulses toward destruction of life and the end of history and the earth itself that arise from the abuse of children—impulses that have, for the past two millennia, been expressed most powerfully and persuasively in the apocalyptic imagery and dire threatenings of the Gos-pels and the Book of Revelation.

The Apocalyptic Impulse

For the last four centuries, the apocalyptic impulse has continually been present in this land, waxing and waning in intensity, taking various forms, but often anticipating the imminent end of this world and the inaugu-ration of the millennium, the thousand years of peace promised in the Book of Revelation to those who survive the horrors of the tribulation marking the end of humanity and history. Only "true" Christians, obedient and submissive children of God, are expected to survive the ultimate holocaust and the Last Judgment and to become the eternal inhabitants of the New Jerusalem on this earth or elsewhere.

Today, many millions of Americans live in daily expectation of the end of this world, eagerly anticipating the return of Jesus and their removal from this earth prior to the onset of the period of devastation and destruction, punishment and horror, set forth in vivid detail in the prophetic texts of the Old and New Testaments. Evangelical and fundamentalist Protestant bookstores are filled with books prophesying the imminent end of the world.* The apocalyptic fantasies set forth in bestselling books, in sermons preached in churches and meetinghouses across the land and throughout the day and night on television and radio, hymn the approaching holocaust, keenly expectant of the Second Coming and the subsequent destruction of this world and most of its inhabitants.

Vast numbers of Americans are expecting the end at any moment. Even Ronald Reagan, both before and during his presidency, has been an apocalyptic, believing that he, too, has been living in the End Times. As the President told an Israeli lobbyist in October 1983: "You know, I turn back to your ancient prophets in the Old Testament and the signs foretelling Armageddon, and I find myself wondering if—if we're the generation that's going to see that come about. I don't know if you've noted any of those prophecies lately, but believe me, they certainly describe the times we're going through."[202] Caspar Weinberger, Secretary of Defense during much of the Reagan administration, told an audience at Harvard University in 1982: "I have read the Book of Revelation and, yes, I believe the world is going to end—by an act of God, I hope—but every day I think that time is running out."[203] When A. G. Mojtabai, a novelist and writer, went to Amarillo, Texas, to study the lives and reactions of people living next to Pantex, the assembly plant which puts

---

* Hal Lindsey has sold more than fifteen million copies of his book *The Late Great Planet Earth* (1970), which has been followed by a series of apocalyptic titles such as *The Terminal Generation, The 1980's: Countdown to Armageddon,* and *There's a New World Coming.* The John Walvoords published *Armageddon: Oil and the Middle East Crisis* in 1974. David Wilkerson published his apocalyptic study, *The Vision,* in 1974, followed by *Racing Toward Judgment* in 1976. In 1977, John Wesley White published *WW III: Signs of the Impending Battle of Armageddon.* Other such books include William Goetz's *Apocalypse Next* (1980), Harold Lindsell's *The Gathering Storm* (1980), Billy Graham's *Approaching Hoofbeats: The Four Horsemen of the Apocalypse* (1983), and many others.

together all American nuclear weapons, she found that the community was immersed in apocalyptic biblical imagery and the anticipation of the end of the world.[204]

The apocalyptic impulse has been and continues to be an integral part of American conciousness and culture, both religious and political, although very few of us seem aware of this profoundly disturbing fact. What are its roots? Why are so many people enthralled by the imagery and the fantasies of punishment, devastation, destruction, and doom set forth in the Book of Revelation and other New Testament texts? Why are so many individuals and groups captivated by the fantasies of rescue implicit in the doctrine of the "Rapture"? (According to this doctrine, common to most fundamentalist and Pentecostal Protestants today, all twice-born Christians will be spared the horrors of the tribulation that will precede the world's end, by being lifted bodily up from the earth when Jesus returns.) As A. G. Mojtabai asks, "Out of what felt life does it come?"[205]

The apocalyptic impulse generally emerges from a life history of pain and suffering, and is grounded in the assaults against the body, the will, and the spirit of children that are rationalized as discipline. It is surely no accident that so many of the Protestant Christians who are ardent advocates of corporal punishment for children are also intensely apocalyptic.

The painful punishment of children creates the nuclear core of rage, resentment, and aggression that fuels fantasies of the apocalyptic end of the world. This has been true at least from the early seventeenth century to the present. The most consistent thread connecting apocalyptics generation after generation has been the experience of pain, assault, and physical coercion resulting from harsh corporal punishments in childhood.

For vast numbers of people, however, the anxieties, fears, and sufferings of childhood through various forms of discipline and punishment have been augmented and intensified by other forms of suffering, such as poverty, transiency, marginality, and the constant humiliations and anguish and stress inherent in poverty or the economic and personal struggles of the middling ranks in our society. The first few generations of Pentecostals in the early twentieth century were emblematic of such generalized deprivation and suffering.[206] Throughout our history, the lives of vast numbers of apocalyptics have borne the scars of suffering from many sources, including illnesses and personal experiences of all kinds.

The outer sources of apocalypticism, important as they undoubtedly were and are, only fuel the inner impulses toward the apocalypse that are generated in apocalyptics' most formative experiences early in life.[207] Central among these psychological sources, I believe, is the pain of punishment and the experience of domination and submission inherent in assaults by adults upon children. Alice Miller has explored the implications of such physical and emotional violence in the context of German-speaking cultures, especially in her portraits of Nazis, including Adolf Hitler, whose rage, nihilism, and hatred provided the impulses and the ideas that ultimately generated the mass murder of six million Jews and millions of others in the Holocaust, and the wartime death and destruction of many millions more. Miller traces the roots of this holocaust ultimately to the abuse of children and the denial of selfhood inherent in the coercions of corporal punishments.[208]

The end of the world envisaged two millennia ago in the Book of Revelation—if it comes about—will be the ultimate holocaust. After a series of horrendous events that millions of people currently anticipate happening, the final battle at Armageddon, which most contemporary Protestant apocalyptics believe will be located in Israel, is expected to occur.[209] This is the fantasy—for it can only be a fantasy unless it is acted out and brought into being. Hal Lindsey has provided lurid details of the end, as he, like so many others, interprets the scenario unfolded in Revelation. "It staggers the imagination," he observes, "to realize that one-fourth of the world's population will be destroyed within a matter of days. According to projected census figures this will amount to nearly one billion people! Since one of these grim reapers of death is Hades, it means that only *unbelievers* will perish in this phase of the holocaust."[210] Later he writes: "The horrors of the first five seals seem to be the inevitable results of what will happen when men's evil natures are totally unrestrained. The *sixth seal* unleashes a worldwide nuclear holocaust and is God's judgment on the world for its persecution of His saints."[211]

David Wilkerson has had a similar fantasy of the End Times:

These are exciting days for true Christians. God, in His love and mercy, is allowing disasters to strike the earth to warn all who will hear that Jesus is coming back, and that it's time to get ready. He

loves His children too much to bring His new kingdom to pass without
warning. . . . These disasters are a kind of countdown, too painful to
ignore, choreographed by God to set the stage for the final moments
of time.[212]

Wilkerson was convinced in 1974 that "God has it all preprogrammed.
He knows the exact moment Christ will return. The final tribulation, the
judgment, and the battle of Armageddon are all on His calendar." He
was confident, however, "that God is suddenly going to deliver His true
children from His final fury that will be outpoured on the earth. He will
deliver His children from the most gruesome hour of disaster that the
Bible predicts will fall upon the earth."[213]

The fundamental assumption shaping the prophetic convictions of
such writers and preachers is that *only* twice-born Christians will be
rescued from the coming holocaust. (This belief excludes, of course, most
Catholics, many Protestants, Jews, and virtually all non-Christians of
every persuasion—the vast majority of the world's population thus being
expected to suffer in the tribulations to come and in the fires of hell
thereafter.) Not all Protestant apocalyptics share this assumption, since
not all believe in the doctrine of the Rapture, but the great majority today
seem confident that they will not be present at the end, having been
rescued by the returned Christ just prior to the final tribulation.[214] In
1977, Billy Graham believed that Jesus would reappear just in time to
save the world from nuclear holocaust. He wrote, in the foreword to John
Wesley White's *WW III: Signs of the Impending Battle of Armageddon*:
"All of this will plunge the world to its nadir—the war of all time, which
will universally involve all mankind in a holocaust more horrendous than
anything man has experienced since his appearance on this planet. With
humanity locked irretrievably into Armageddon, with sure annihilation
beckoning, Christ will suddenly come and miraculously save man from
himself, and set up His kingdom throughout the whole world."[215] This
is faith, but faith in a fantasy. It assumes that nuclear annihilation, the
ultimate holocaust by fire, will not occur even if it is set in action by men
prior to the miraculous intervention of Jesus himself.

Billy Graham, however, has had second thoughts, and has committed
himself publicly to preventing the nuclear annihilation that he seemed
to take for granted earlier. In 1983, in his book on the apocalypse, Graham
noted that "it is important to remember this: though Christ warned us

there will constantly be wars and rumors of wars, it does not follow that we should sit silently by while the peoples of the world destroy each other. We must not by our silence give approval to such devastation with weapons of mass destruction. We must warn the nations of the world that they must repent and turn to God while there is yet time."[216] He is now convinced that "evangelicals cannot afford to stay isolated in a world where nuclear holocaust threatens to destroy us. We must leave our safe enclaves and journey into the world, standing for what we believe— in love, in strength, in openness and in trust." Graham acknowledges that he does not "plan to be a leader in a peace movement or organization. I am an evangelist. But I am a man who is still in process."[217] That sets him apart now from many other apocalyptics. Being "in process" is being fully alive and committed to the preservation, not the destruction, of life on this earth. His acknowledgment of his personal responsibility for the preservation of life has propelled Graham, as it has so many other people, into becoming an active opponent of nuclear warfare.

What is most dismaying about the vast majority of American apocalyptics today is that they appear to be both prepared and willing to witness the demise of life on this earth in the immediate future. Many Christian apocalyptics seem to be joyous at the prospect of Armageddon, because they believe it to be the necessary and inevitable prelude to their salvation and the end of Satan's reign on this earth. After the tribulation has passed, Hal Lindsey believes that "Christ will lead His rescued followers into God's Kingdom of peace and righteousness on a beautiful new earth." Convinced that all signs point to this imminent end, Lindsey reassures his readers: "Even though many of these signs are appalling in themselves, their tremendous significance should gladden the heart of every true believer in Christ."[218] Similarly, David Wilkerson once declared that "when you have God's glory, you can rejoice in God's doom. You and I may live to see the wreck of matter and the crash of worlds—nevertheless, we will not fear."[219]

For apocalyptics such as these, the fundamental assumption shaping their fantasies of the end is that God the Father is filled with wrath against the sinners of this world and is about to punish sinners and the world itself in one culminating series of catastrophic blows, the seven vials of wrath set forth in the Book of Revelation. Rage and retribution by the divine Father against his sinful and disobedient children on earth are the primary reasons for God's long-planned punishments and destruction of life on earth. Perhaps it will come as no surprise that Lindsey once informed his readers that his own father "gave me my share of lickings, too, and I know now that it really was for my good, though at the time I didn't think so!"[220] Although Lindsey's punitive God seems to be a projection of his own father, his earthly father, unlike his heavenly Father, could not destroy the entire world and nearly every person living on this planet.

God, however, according to the visions of Revelation, is planning to destroy his own earthly creation once again. The images of wrathful and murderous destructiveness ascribed to God's will by the Book of Revelation haunt the consciousness of apocalyptics, who are obsessed by the fantasies of destruction and suffering set forth, in the familiar language of the King James translation, by this prophetic text:

> And I heard a great voice out of the temple saying to the seven angels, Go your ways, and pour out the vials of the wrath of God upon the earth. And the first went, and poured out his vial upon the earth; and there fell a noisome and grievous sore upon the men which had the mark of the beast, and upon them which worshipped his image. And the second angel poured out his vial upon the sea; and it became as the blood of a dead man: and every living soul died in the sea. And the third angel poured out his vial upon the rivers and fountains of waters; and they became blood. And I heard the angel of the waters say, Thou art righteous, O Lord, which art, and wast, and shalt be, because thou has judged thus. . . . And I heard another out of the altar say, Even so, Lord God Almighty, true and righteous are thy judgments. And the fourth angel poured out his vial upon the sun; and power was given unto him to scorch men with fire. . . . And the fifth angel poured out his vial upon the seat of the beast; and his kingdom was full of darkness; and they gnawed their tongues for pain, And blasphemed the God of heaven because of their pains and their sores, and repented not of their deeds. And the sixth angel poured out his vial upon the great river Euphrates; and the water thereof was dried up, that the way of the kings of the east might be prepared. And I saw three unclean spirits like frogs come out of the mouth of the dragon, and out of the mouth of the beast, and out of the mouth of the false prophet. For they are the spirits of devils, working miracles, which go forth unto the kings of the earth and of the whole world, to

gather them to the battle of that great day of God Almighty. Behold, I come as a thief. Blessed is he that watcheth, and keepeth his garments, lest he walk naked, and they see his shame. And he gathered them together into a place called in the Hebrew tongue Armageddon. And the seventh angel poured out his vial into the air; and there came a great voice out of the temple of heaven, from the throne, saying, It is done (Revelation 16:1–5, 7, 9–17).

The Apocalypse is thus to be the final solution to sin and disobedience on this earth. It will entail mass murder and annihilation of life both in the sea and on land on a scale without precedent in human history. The god responsible for this apocalypse, wrathful and pitiless as he appears to be, is surely the ultimate authoritarian.

Punishment has always been at the core of this apocalyptic scenario. Apocalyptics are usually people who have been hurt and harmed early in life, who have suffered, often far more than they themselves realize or can acknowledge. Their eagerness for the end is grounded in the anguish, and the sorrows, and the pains of their own lives. Fundamentalist Protestant forms of apocalyptic Christianity mirror theologically the violence and abuse that so many once experienced in childhood, transforming their earlier pain and fear and terror into fantasies of rescue and triumph.

The Apocalypse of the Book of Revelation has been one of the most enduring sadomasochistic fantasies obsessing many Protestants. It has provided and still provides endless pleasure and satisfaction to those who consider themselves safe from the punishments that will be meted out to so many others by the all-powerful master of the universe. Only in heaven will such pain and suffering cease for those who have submitted themselves to the will of the master of the universe and become obedient children forever. The rest will be tortured in hell eternally.

The apocalyptic impulse, which arises from the violence suffered in childhood, is far more common than we generally realize. It is one thing to have an impulse, however, but entirely another to act upon it. The common impulses to punish and to destroy need not become the alternatives most of us will wish to choose, once we become conscious of the power of the buried rage, hate, and murderous aggression that so often find displaced expression in apocalyptic visions of the End Times. There have always been other alternatives available to the vast majority of Christians and others who have rejected the image of God as the Father who is the wrathful punisher and destroyer of life on this earth.

As we enter the final decade of the twentieth century, we have only begun to reckon with the consequences of the pain and suffering inflicted upon successive generations of children by the abuse and violence associated with physical punishments. The consequences, both personal and collective, are so complex, so massive, so intertwined with our consciousness, our feelings, our thoughts, our lives, our culture, and our society that we have much still to do before we can have any confidence that we understand the full implications of such commonplace hitting and hurting. Yet even though our understanding and our knowledge remain limited, we face choices for ourselves, our children, our families, our communities, our nation, and our world that need to be explored and confronted. It is to these choices that we now must turn our attention.

PART V

Choices

Physical punishment is both a practice and a choice. Most of us have chosen, sometimes consciously, sometimes unconsciously, to use some form of bodily assault in the rearing and disciplining of our children. That is what makes it so difficult for most of us to imagine not using corporal punishments. Our own childhood experiences and the experiences of countless generations before us legitimate physical punishment and seem to obligate us to perpetuate the suffering that we once knew ourselves.

We often feel and act as though we have no alternatives to such choices. Yet once we begin to recognize the long-term personal and collective consequences of such ordinary punishments, many of us surely will begin to refuse to hit children in the name of discipline. Once we understand that physical assaults against children are abusive and that they often cut to the core of life itself, threatening individuals and humanity as a whole with harm, suffering, and even death, we will begin to act less aggressively, less coercively, less violently, and less painfully against the children whose lives will unfold on this earth long after we ourselves have gone. The future will be shaped by our choices and actions now.

Consider these alternative attitudes toward punishment: One alternative, ardently pro–physical punishment, has always been extraordinarily gripping and powerful in its enduring appeal to many individuals. Many advocates today, as in the past, often are apocalyptic, feeling and believing that this world will shortly come to a catastrophic end. Another alternative, equally powerful and enduring, is associated with people who, while committed to the preservation of life on this earth for the foreseeable future, combine a respect for self and others with a willingness to use occasional violence against children. The third alternative, far less common but deeply committed to the sustaining and preserving of life and humanity, is rooted in nonviolent methods of child-rearing. This alternative has recognized the dangers of physical assault against children and opposes the use of all forms of corporal punishments.

Each of these alternatives reflects choices that have been shaped and formed by our own pasts, our encounters with discipline and punishment, and with adult authority in childhood. Given the power of the unconscious mind, however, many of these "choices" are hardly choices at all; they are not the result of actively discriminating between distinct alternatives. Far more often, these alternatives appeal to us because they express most directly and effectively what we have known all our lives, from earliest childhood, and because they articulate—in theology, culture, and politics—the most basic feelings and impulses that we have towards ourselves and the world, towards life and towards death.

These alternatives, however, can form two primary polarities, stark but clear. One points to the annihilation of life on this earth, the other leads to its preservation. These are real choices each of us faces daily, now and for the foreseeable future. But many already have chosen the route towards the Apocalypse and are truly eager for the end.[1]

The crucial question, therefore, is which choices will the vast majority of us who place ourselves in the middle—both religious and secular—make in the years to come: to prepare for the end or to commit ourselves to the nurturing and sustaining of life on this planet Earth for generations and centuries yet to come? The ambivalence of the middle, which simultaneously has doubted and embraced physical punishments and painful discipline of children, needs to be resolved through a choice that will foster life rather than succumb, however passively, to the apocalyptic impulses that emerge so often from aggression and abuse in childhood.

Once we understand what was done to us and what we have done to ourselves, to our children, and to others through the infliction of pain by physical punishments, and once we understand why this has always been done, generation after generation, we can choose not to use violence against the young. We can begin to choose to nurture and preserve life, our own and others', rather than to abuse life and to destroy it. Our collective addiction to pain and suffering can be overcome through conscious decisions and actions, however difficult such transformation seems to be. We can step off the endless Möbius strip of punishment into a new, unfamiliar, but far more sustaining world in which violence against children will not be taken for granted. Once the middle ground ceases to be filled with ambivalence about violence, coercion, and pain, we can foresee a new era in our lives and our culture in which nonviolence will be preferred to violence, in which discipline will not involve physical punishment.

We now have an opportunity far greater than has ever been possible before, because we have an awareness, which previous generations lacked, of the harmful consequences of physical violence against children. We need to act upon our new consciousness and to begin to chart a new course for our individual and collective futures. We need to oppose the Apocalypse in all its mutations by choosing life and the preservation of life over the impulses, profound and powerful as they always are in so many of us, to hasten the end of humanity and history on this earth.

Nonviolent child-rearing is the way to begin. Since the vast majority of Americans have experienced physical punishments and practiced them in turn, we as a people lack precedents to confirm our commitment to nonviolent methods of child-rearing. But they exist; they have existed for a long while; and they need to be considered before bringing this exploration to a close. If the middle ground in American society and culture is to become a place in which children no longer will experience the fear and hurt generated by adults' assaults against them, we need to recognize that there are real alternatives to traditional, violent modes and begin to accept them, advocate them, and practice them. Only then will it be possible for those of us who feel ambivalent about such physical punishments to resolve our ambivalence and opt for less harmful and dangerous methods of disciplining and rearing children.

For many people, the place to begin is with the conviction that God is loving, not wrathful and vengeful and punitive. The text familiar to many Christians from the first Epistle of John provides one of the keys to this form of life-sustaining theology:

God is love, and he who abides in love abides in God, and God abides in him. In this is love perfected with us, that we may have confidence for the day of judgment, because as he is so are we in this world. There is no fear in love, but perfect love casts out fear. For fear has to do with punishment, and he who fears is not perfected in love. We love, because he first loved us. If any one says, "I love God," and hates his brother, he is a liar; for he who does not love his brother whom he has seen, cannot love God whom he has not seen. And this commandment we have from him, that he who loves God should love his brother also (I John, 4:16–21 [Revised Standard Version]).

The pivotal premise of John's message is the distinction between love and fear, precisely the polarities that are central to rationales for physical violence and assault against children. Advocates of corporal punishments usually insist that love and fear go together in tandem, one being inconceivable without the other. As Larry Christenson contends, "Fear acts as a catalyst for love."[2] But John here says the opposite: "There is no fear in love, but perfect love casts out fear." He adds the crucial observation, which advocates of painful discipline generally ignore, that "fear has to do with punishment, and he who fears is not perfected in love." People who are open to the possibility of change in their commitments to physical punishments and violence against children might wish to take note of this biblical passage, which recognizes that fear is inconsistent with love, parental and divine alike.

If God is love, as John insists and many believe, then the ambivalence felt by so many parents about inflicting pain and using physical assaults in their discipline of children can be resolved, once and for all, by heeding these words. Fear should be banished from child-rearing and discipline since "fear has to do with punishment, and he who fears is not perfected in love." Everything that we are beginning to know about punishment confirms this ancient observation. Fear stifles love and constricts our ability to feel and to live. Fear also limits our ability to put ourselves in the place of others, to have empathy, to feel compassion, to know pity, and to extend ourselves openly and freely toward other lives and other people.

Despite all the efforts by advocates of the rod and the belt to convince us that physical punishment is the "Christian" method of discipline, we must reject this confusion of fear with love and begin to act upon our knowledge that the physical violence against children urged by so many Christians is not truly "Christian" at all. Although one father, after spanking his small son for some act or attitude of disobedience, told him, "You know how much I love you, but when you don't obey, Jesus teaches that you must receive the rod," we need to remember that Jesus never taught any such thing.[3]

Jesus never once spoke a word recorded in any gospel that can be interpreted as advocating physical assaults against children or urging the infliction of painful punishments on any child. Yet so much pain has been inflicted on so many children for so many centuries in the name of Jesus Christ! So many tears shed, so much suffering experienced, so much anger and hatred generated, so much aggression and violence summoned forth, so much destruction and death brought about—all because of the oft-repeated but misguided belief that physical discipline is indispensable to "Christian" child-rearing and soul-saving and salvation.

The core issue, however, is the enduring ambivalence which so many of us have felt and still feel about the infliction of pain on children and the use of physical blows as at least occasional forms of discipline, our last resort when all other methods seem to fail us. This is where the continuum must be broken, and the majority of us begin to dissociate ourselves from the commitment to and the advocacy of hitting and hurting as an acceptable form of discipline. To do this is not easy, or it would have been done often by many of us long before now.

The task and the challenge confronting us is to take that vital step, to commit ourselves to nonviolence as the basis for rearing and disciplining children from infancy through adolescence. Only then will the continuum of violence and pain be narrowed down to the hard core of those for whom violence is necessary and addictive. For most of us, nonviolence will be possible once we see that physical punishments are not only harmful and dangerous to children and to ourselves, but are also unnecessary. We will realize that there is no need for a last resort at all.

The Swedes have done this already, despite a long-standing tradition, rooted in familiar biblical texts, of physical violence against children. In 1979, the Swedish parliament passed a law declaring "A child may not be subjected to physical punishment or other injurious or humiliating treatment." The law carried no criminal penalties yet has succeeded— in the space of only one decade—in transforming the ways in which Swedes discipline and rear their children. Adrienne Ahlgren Haeuser's observations suggest that many Swedes in recent years have chosen modes of discipline and child-rearing that we might place in the "moderate" or "middling" category, setting limits and bounds and advocating firmness without physical or verbal violence.[4]

Sweden, of course, is a small country with a relatively well-educated and wealthy population that historically has been quite homogeneous. Sweden's experience clearly demonstrates what can be done to radically alter traditional methods of child-rearing and discipline, through the combination of legislation and education, when the desire and intention are present. But Sweden also has a tradition in this century of neutrality and nonbelligerency in international affairs, and thus cannot be compared readily to our own country or many others. Still, given the punitive Germanic traditions embedded in Swedish culture throughout much of this century (the tradition of "poisonous pedagogy" which Alice Miller has explored), the Swedish experience is notable: An entire society can choose to change the ways in which children are disciplined and to reject, both in private and in public, the last resort to assault and violence still characteristic of most American families and schools today.

Perhaps in the not-too-distant future many voices heard throughout the United States and many works found in religious and secular bookstores across the nation will provide persuasive and practical alternatives to assault and violence. Anyone now willing to make the commitment to nonviolent child-rearing can find alternative methods of child-rearing and discipline, useful and effective means of coping with the virtually infinite variety of situations and circumstances influencing character, temperament, and development that make parenting so challenging and complex.[5]

Among the most popular alternatives to physical punishment discussed in many books currently available are: reasoning; discussion; demonstration of logical consequences; setting of boundaries, rules, and limits; and time out and isolation—methods of child-rearing and discipline that seek to foster a sense of responsibility, of conscience, and of self-governance in children. At the same time, some of these methods also recognize the value of moderate levels of guilt and shame in the quest for self-discipline and self-direction. Most of their writers seem to agree with the conviction voiced by Horace Bushnell more than a century ago: "A wise parent understands that his government is to be crowned by an act of emancipation; and it is a great problem, to accomplish that emancipation gracefully."[6] This is why, time and time again, issues of authority, power, and control remain at the center of these discussions of discipline.

These nonviolent alternatives to physical punishment generally share a deep commitment to nonassaultive, nonaggressive, and noncoercive methods of discipline. Since such alternatives already exist, they now need to be acted upon and explored further so that even skeptics—of whom there are vast numbers—can be convinced that violence against children is harmful. The last resort of hitting, used by so many parents, is clearly not a satisfactory solution to the problems of discipline and child-rearing. We have much still to learn, however, before we can begin to be as comfortable and as confident with nonviolence as most of us always have been with violence in our disciplining of children. The place to begin, surely, is with an enduring sense of respect for the bodies, wills, and selves of children and with a commitment to their right to remain unhurt and inviolate, just as most adults would wish to be.

*   *   *

In recent years, we have seen our own planet from afar, with astonishingly beautiful—awesome—pictures of the Earth floating in the blackness of space, the encircling blue and white of water and clouds, the green and yellow and red and brown of vegetation and landscape visible to us now as never before in human history.[7] We are learning again through science and technology what many people have always known—that all life is interconnected and that all the parts form a whole web of existence. The concept of Gaia, the living planet, being articulated by some contemporary scientists, is a modern, organic and nonhierarchical, version of the ancient concept of the Great Chain of Being.[8]

Although we are nearing the end of the second millennium after Christ, we have only begun to grapple with the immensity of our interconnectedness with one another and with all forms of life on earth. We have yet to fathom fully the implications for our collective future of the wholeness of life on our planet. Yet the end of the world may well come about, at least in terms of the world as we have known it for many, many generations. The death of the world is a possibility now as never before in human history—death from nuclear annihilation; from ecological collapse due to the pollution and acid rain silently destroying the forests, the fresh waters, and the seas; from catastrophes such as the destruction of the ozone layer in the upper atmosphere, the transformation of climates by the greenhouse effect, or earthquakes attributable to the movement of the tectonic plates that encircle the planet.[9]

None of this potential destruction and devastation—much of it long under way and now extremely difficult to forestall or repair—can be attributed to God or to transcendental causes. We ourselves are responsible for most of the dangers that humanity currently confronts, and it is our own technology and science, our own individual and collective lives, our own automobiles, air conditioners, plastics, and spray cans, among many other manmade things, including genetic engineering, that threaten us with unprecedented dangers and with potential destruction and death. But if the world does end, it will not be because of God's wrath or vengeance or retribution or punishment, as set forth in the prophecies of the Book of Revelation. We will have ourselves to blame for most of what befalls us in the decades to come.[10]

I believe that if we can begin to see and understand that the end of the world begins with the striking of a single child, we can act differently towards future generations by finding alternatives to the painful assaults of corporal punishments. The abuse of any child is a terrible thing. It is hard to love life fully when one has been hit and hurt. We need to decide now—person by person, family by family, church by church, community by community, state by state, nation by nation—to embrace nonviolent methods of discipline, which can begin to reshape our lives, our consciousness, and our world, and to alter the course of our future and the futures of generations yet to come.

If we can spare the child and spoil the rod, reversing the old adage that has justified so much pain and suffering for so many centuries, perhaps we can find the will and the way to forestall the Apocalypse itself and to make the twenty-first century and the third millennium after Christ significantly different from what we always have known. By consciously deciding not to inflict pain, not to cause suffering, not to coerce, and not to assault a child in the name of discipline, we will be making choices that will enhance and sustain life, not deny it. Love and nurture, empathy and understanding—not fear, not hate, not anger, and not revenge— must be our goal. If we are determined to protect and not to destroy life on this unique and precious planet we call Earth, these are choices we can make.

NOTES

1. The epigraph is taken from Adrienne Ahlgren Haeuser, "Reducing Violence Towards U.S. Children: Transferring Positive Innovations from Sweden [Report from Sweden Study Visit, May 14–June 16, 1988]" (unpublished report for the U.S. Department of Health and Human Services, 1987–1989), p. 1.

PART I   THE PROBLEM

1. Morrow C. Graham, *They Call Me Mother Graham* (Old Tappan, N.J.: Fleming H. Revell Co., 1977), pp. 27–28.

2. Barbara T. Roessner, "Obedience, Diligence, and Fun: Bush's 'Extraordinary Family Life' Recalled by Brother Prescott," Jacksonville, Florida, *Times-Union*, January 15, 1989, p. A3. My thanks to David Courtwright for bringing this article to my attention.

3. Alice Miller, *For Your Own Good: Hidden Cruelty in Child-Rearing and the Roots of Violence*, Hildegarde and Hunter Hannum, trans. (New York: Farrar, Straus & Giroux, 1983), p. ix.

4. Alfred Kadushin and Judith A. Martin, *Child Abuse: An Interactional Event* (New York: Columbia University Press, 1981), p. 5.

5. For an alternative view, see John Demos, "Child Abuse in Context: An Historian's Perspective," *Past, Present, and Personal: The Family and the Life Course in American History* (New York: Oxford University Press, 1986), p. 75 and *passim*. Also see Lloyd de Mause, ed., *The History of Childhood* (New York: Harper Torchbooks, 1975).

PART II   EXPERIENCES

1. See Linda Pollock, *Forgotten Children: Parent-Child Relations from 1500 to 1900* (Cambridge, England: Cambridge University Press, 1983) and *A Lasting Relationship: Parents and Children over Three Centuries* (Hanover, N.H.: University Press of New England, 1987); Elizabeth Pleck, *Domestic Tyranny: The*

Making of Social Policy Against Family Violence from Colonial Times to the Present (New York: Oxford University Press, 1987).

2. See Philip Greven, *The Protestant Temperament: Patterns of Child-Rearing, Religious Experience, and the Self in Early America* (New York: Alfred A. Knopf, 1977; Chicago: University of Chicago Press, 1988). Also see William R. Hutchison, "Cultural Strain and Protestant Liberalism," *American Historical Review*, vol. 76 (1971), pp. 386–411.

3. Lyman Abbott, *Reminiscences* (Boston: Houghton Mifflin Co., 1915), p. 143.

4. Ira V. Brown, *Lyman Abbott, Christian Evolutionist: A Study in Religious Liberalism* (Cambridge: Harvard University Press, 1953), p. 233.

5. For Jacob Abbott's views, see Bernard Wishy, *The Child and the Republic: The Dawn of Modern American Child Nurture* (Philadelphia: University of Pennsylvania Press, 1968), pp. 94–104.

6. William R. Moody, *The Life of Dwight L. Moody* (New York: Fleming H. Revell Co., 1900), p. 24.

7. Paul D. Moody, *My Father: An Intimate Portrait of Dwight Moody* (Boston: Little, Brown and Co., 1938), pp. 82–83.

8. Moody, *My Father*, p. 83.

9. Harry Emerson Fosdick, *The Living of These Days: An Autobiography* (New York: Harper & Brothers, 1956), p. 32.

10. Fosdick, *The Living of These Days*, pp. 32–33.

11. The Fosdicks were patterned after the mold set by Horace Bushnell as well as being twentieth-century versions of the Moderates examined in my book *The Protestant Temperament*. See Robert Moats Miller, *Harry Emerson Fosdick: Preacher, Pastor, Prophet* (New York: Oxford University Press, 1985), pp. 17–18.

12. Raymond B. Fosdick, *Chronicle of a Generation: An Autobiography* (New York: Harper & Brothers, 1958), pp. 12–13.

13. Benjamin Spock and Mary Morgan, *Spock on Spock: A Memoir of Growing Up with the Century* (New York: Pantheon, 1989), p. 10.

14. Benjamin Spock, *Dr. Spock on Parenting: Sensible Advice from America's Most Trusted Child-Care Expert* (New York: Simon and Schuster, 1988), p. 150.

15. Spock, *Dr. Spock on Parenting*, pp. 150–51.

16. See C. Henry Kempe *et al.*, "The Battered-Child Syndrome," *Journal of the American Medical Association*, vol. 181 (1962), pp. 105–112, and Ray E. Helfer and C. Henry Kempe, eds., *The Battered Child* (Chicago: University of Chicago Press, 1968).

17. See Greven, *The Protestant Temperament*, p. 36.

18. Philip J. Greven, Jr., ed., *Child-Rearing Concepts, 1628–1861: Historical Sources* (Itasca, Ill.: F. E. Peacock, 1973), p. 47.

19. Greven, *Child-Rearing Concepts*, p. 51.

20. Greven, *Child-Rearing Concepts*, pp. 77–78.

21. Carol F. Karlsen and Laurie Crumpacker, eds., *The Journal of Esther Burr 1754–1757* (New Haven, Conn.: Yale University Press, 1984), p. 95. Also see Greven, *The Protestant Temperament*, pp. 35–36.

22. John Pollock, *Moody Without Sankey: A New Biographical Portrait* (London: Hodder and Stoughton, 1963), p. 16; Moody, *My Father*, pp. 74–75.

23. Moody, *The Life of Dwight L. Moody*, p. 24.

24. Jack Hyles, *How to Rear Children* (Hammond, Ind.: Hyles-Anderson Publishers, 1972), p. 97.

25. N[ickels]. J. Holmes and Wife, *Life Sketches and Sermons* (Royston, Ga.: The Pentecostal Holiness Church Press, 1920), pp. 11–13.

26. [Aimee Semple McPherson], *Aimee: [The] Life Story of Aimee Semple McPherson* (Los Angeles, Calif.: Foursquare Publications, 1979), p. 13.

27. [McPherson], *Aimee*, p. 8.

28. John Pollock, *Billy Graham: The Authorized Biography* (New York: McGraw-Hill Book Co., 1966), p. 4.

29. Marshall Frady, *Billy Graham: A Parable of American Righteousness* (Boston: Little, Brown and Co., 1979), p. 49.

30. Frady, *Billy Graham*, p. 49.

31. See Morrow C. Graham, *They Call Me Mother Graham* (Old Tappan, N.J.: Fleming H. Revell Co., 1977), pp. 27–28.

32. See Billy Graham, "Why Have Homes?" Southeastern Michigan Crusade, October 20, 1976. Billy Graham Evangelistic Association, Films and Video Tapes, 1955–1977, Archives of the Billy Graham Center, Wheaton, Illinois, Collection 113, v. 51.

33. Oral Roberts, *Oral Roberts' Life Story* (Tulsa, Okla.: Oral Roberts, 1952), pp. 24–26.

34. Evelyn Roberts, *His Darling Wife, Evelyn: The Autobiography of Mrs. Oral Roberts* (New York: Dial Press, 1976), p. 96.

35. Jamie Buckingham, *Daughter of Destiny: Kathryn Kuhlman . . . Her Story* (Plainfield, N.J.: Logos International, 1976), p. 14.

36. Buckingham, *Daughter of Destiny*, pp. 16, 19. See Kathryn Kuhlman, taped interview [with Jamie Buckingham], n.d., CN212, tape A, Billy Graham Center Archives, Wheaton, Illinois.

37. David Wilkerson, with John and Elizabeth Sherrill, *The Cross and the Switchblade* (Lincoln, Va.: Chosen Books, 1963), p. 83.

38. Ruth Wilkerson Harris, *It was Good Enough for Father: The Story of the Wilkerson Family* (Old Tappan, N.J.: Fleming H. Revell Co., 1969), p. 97.

39. Harris, *Good Enough for Father*, p. 96.

40. See David Wilkerson's account of his own experience: "Woodshed Revival," quoted in Larry Christenson, *The Christian Family* (Minneapolis: Bethany House Publishers, 1970), pp. 106–107.

41. Christenson, *The Christian Family*, p. 107.

42. Harris, *Good Enough for Father*, pp. 96–97.

43. A. E. Humbard, *My Life Story (Just a Little Bit Different) from the Plow Handle to the Pulpit* (Cleveland, Ohio: Union Gospel Press, 1945), pp. 163–64.

44. Finlay Lewis, *Mondale: Portrait of An American Politician*, rev. ed. (New York: Perennial Library, 1984), p. 13.

45. C. Allyn Russell, *Voices of American Fundamentalism: Seven Biographical Studies* (Philadelphia: The Westminster Press, n.d.), p. 22.

46. Tammy Bakker, *I Gotta Be Me* (Harrison, Ark.: New Leaf Press, 1978), p. 19.

47. A. A. Allen with Walter Wagner, *Born to Lose, Bound to Win: An Autobiography* (Garden City, N.Y.: Doubleday & Co., 1970), p. 1.

48. Allen and Wagner, *Born to Lose*, p. 40.

49. Allen and Wagner, *Born to Lose*, p. 41.

50. Allen and Wagner, *Born to Lose*, p. 44.

51. Allen and Wagner, *Born to Lose*, p. 48.

52. Allen and Wagner, *Born to Lose*, pp. 48–49.

53. Allen and Wagner, *Born to Lose*, p. 52.

54. Allen and Wagner, *Born to Lose*, p. 54.

55. Allen and Wagner, *Born to Lose*, p. 58.

56. Arnold L. White, *The Almighty and Us: The Inside Story of Shiloh, Maine* (Ft. Lauderdale, Fla.: Arnold L. White [privately printed], 1979), pp. 115–16. For additional information on Sandford and Shiloh, see: Frank S. Murray, *The Sublimity of Faith: The Life and Work of Frank W. Sandford* (Amherst, N.H.: The Kingdom Press, 1981); Frank W. Sandford, *The Golden Light upon the Two Americas* (Amherst, N.H.: The Kingdom Press, 1974).

57. *Lewiston* [Maine] *Evening Journal*, October 21, 1904, p. 9, quoted in White, *Almighty and Us*, pp. 94–95.

58. *Lewiston Evening Journal*, February 3, 1904, p. 1, also quoted in White, *Almighty and Us*, p. 170. The *Journal* contains a partial transcript and description of the trial, which provide additional details.

59. *Lewiston Evening Journal*, February 3, 1904, p. 1, also quoted in White, *Almighty and Us*, p. 171.

60. For details, see White, *Almighty and Us*, pp. 171–73, and *State* v. *Sandford*, January 3, 1905, in *Maine Reports 99. Cases Argued and Determined in the Supreme Judicial Court of Maine 1905* (Portland, Me.: William W. Roberts, 1905), pp. 441–52.

61. Quoted in John D. Burchard [Commissioner], "Children at Risk: Why Protective Action in Island Pond Was Necessary" (Ms., Social and Rehabilitation Services, Vermont Agency of Human Services, July 17, 1984), p. 6 [a news release document]. For additional information, see: "Children of Sect Seized in Vermont," *The New York Times*, June 23, 1984, p. 1; Barbara Grizzuti Harrison, "The Children and the Cult," *The New England Gazette*, vol. 1 (December 1984), pp. 56–70; Yvonne Daley, "Who's Minding the Children in Island Pond?," *Yankee* (January 1985), pp. 78–158.

62. Burchard, "Children at Risk," p. 5.

63. *Open Letters from the Church in Island Pond* (Island Pond, Vt.: Parchment Press, n.d.), pp. 24–25.

64. Sharon Sexton, "Suffer the Children: A Vermont Sect Believes It's Wrong to Spare the Rod," *The Boston Phoenix*, April 19, 1983, p. 6.

65. Sexton, "Suffer the Children," p. 1.

66. Colin Nickerson, "Affidavits Allege Sect Beatings," *The Boston Globe*, July 14, 1984, p. 31.

67. Sexton, "Suffer the Children," p. 34.

68. Sexton, "Suffer the Children," p. 34.

69. Sexton, "Suffer the Children," p. 34.

70. Nickerson, "Affidavits," p. 31.

71. *McClellan* v. *West Virginia*, "Petition for a Writ of Certiorari to the Circuit Court of Jefferson County, West Virginia," United States Supreme Court Records & Briefs, No. 86–575 [microfiche], "Statement of the Case," pp. 13, 4.

72. *McClellan* v. *West Virginia*, pp. 4–5

73. *McClellan* v. *West Virginia*, p. 12.

74. *McClellan* v. *West Virginia*, pp. 55–56.

75. *McClellan* v. *West Virginia*, appendix, pp. 10–11. Also see the brief account in *The New York Times*, January 28, 1987, p. B7.

PART III   RATIONALES

1. This and other biblical quotations are taken from the King James Version, unless otherwise noted.

2. *The New English Bible* (New York: Cambridge University Press, 1970), p. 98.

3. The aphorism is from Samuel Butler's poem "Hudibras" (1664). See Ian Gibson, *The English Vice: Beating, Sex and Shame in Victorian England and After* (London: Duckworth, 1978), p. 49.

4. There are very close parallels to these proverbs in Egyptian and Assyrian texts. R. N. Whybray notes that

> the *Words of Ahikar*, a book which is probably of Assyrian origin, is particularly important. Much of its contents is very similar to passages in Proverbs: for example, its teaching on parental discipline is very close indeed: "The son who is educated and disciplined and whose feet are fettered will do well. Do not hesitate to take the rod to your son if you cannot restrain him from wickedness. If I strike you, my son, you will not die, and if I leave you to your own devices you will not live."

He notes the parallel with Proverbs 23:13–14. R. N. Whybray, *The Book of Proverbs* (Cambridge, England: Cambridge University Press, 1972), p. 6. Also see Whybray's comment on p. 80 concerning Egyptian attitudes toward corporal punishment of students. Clearly these attitudes were widespread throughout the Middle East in this period. Whybray assumes "that much of Proverbs as we have it now is the product of a continuous development of literary wisdom throughout the period of the monarchy, that is from the tenth to the sixth century B.C." (p. 5). No one actually knows how much, if any, of Proverbs actually derives from Solomon himself. For additional information, see: A. Cohen, *Proverbs: Hebrew Text and English Translation with an Introduction and Commentary* (London: The Soncino Press, 1946).

5. See, for instance, Michael Grant, *Jesus: An Historian's Review of the Gospels* (New York: Charles Scribner's Sons, 1977), chapter 6.

6. For the general issue of punishment in relation both to Jesus and to Christians, see J. Arthur Hoyles, *Punishment in the Bible* (London: Epworth Press, 1986).

7. Jonathan Edwards, *The Freedom of the Will*, Paul Ramsey, ed. (New Haven: Yale University Press, 1957), pp. 406–407.

8. Larry Tomczak, *God, the Rod, and Your Child's Bod: The Art of Loving Correction for Christian Parents* (Old Tappan, N.J.: Fleming H. Revell Co., 1982), p. 104.

9. See, for example, Simon J. Kistemaker, *New Testament Commentary: Exposition of the Epistle to the Hebrews* (Grand Rapids, Mich.: Baker Book House, 1984), pp. 6–8; Thomas Hewitt, *The Epistle to the Hebrews: An Introduction and Commentary* (Grand Rapids, Mich.: Wm. B. Eerdmans Publishing Co., 1960). See also Norman Perrin and Dennis C. Duling, *The New Testament, An Introduction: Proclamation and Parenesis, Myth and History*, 2nd ed. (New York: Harcourt Brace Jovanovich, 1974), pp. 227–28, for discussion of the authorship of Hebrews.

10. See Perrin & Duling, *The New Testament*, pp. 209–212, 218. For a discussion of "Punishment According to St. Paul," see Hoyles, *Punishment in the Bible*, pp. 61–76.

11. See Martha Himmelfarb, *Tours of Hell: An Apocalyptic Form in Jewish and Christian Literature* (Philadelphia: Fortress Press, 1985).

12. Michael Wigglesworth, *The Day of Doom or a Poetical Description of the Great and Last Judgment with Other Poems*, Kenneth B. Murdock, ed. (New York: Russell & Russell, 1966), p. 15.

13. Wigglesworth, *Day of Doom*, p. 42.

14. Wigglesworth, *Day of Doom*, p. 44.

15. Wigglesworth, *Day of Doom*, p. 61.

16. See Philip Greven, " 'Some Root of Bitterness': Corporal Punishment, Child Abuse, and the Apocalyptic Impulse in Michael Wigglesworth," in James A. Henretta, Michael Kammen, and Stanley N. Katz, eds., *The Transformation of Early American History: Society, Authority, and Ideology* (New York: Alfred A. Knopf, 1991).

17. See Norman Fiering, *Jonathan Edwards's Moral Thought and Its British Context* (Chapel Hill: University of North Carolina Press, 1981), chapter 5, "Hell and the Humanitarians." Edwards's literalism and his personal involvement with these doctrines are apparent from this study, despite Fiering's evident discomfort with the subject of Edwards's pleasure in the eternal torment of sinners. In a footnote on p. 254, Fiering links Edwards's concerns with those of the Marquis de Sade, thus recognizing, however obliquely and hesitantly, the sadomasochism of Edwards's vision.

18. However, James Joyce's brilliant reconstruction of the sermon on hell by a Catholic priest in Dublin (which parallels the fiery pains of the paddling Stephen Dedalus suffers at the hands of another priest in school) is equally explicit. See James Joyce, *A Portrait of the Artist as a Young Man*, in Harry Levin, ed., *The Portable James Joyce* (New York: The Viking Press, 1947), pp. 293–96, 358–403.

19. Jonathan Edwards, "The Future Punishment of the Wicked Unavoidable and Intolerable" (1741), in Clarence H. Faust and Thomas H. Johnson, eds., *Jonathan Edwards: Representative Selections* (New York: American Book Co., 1935), pp. 146–47.

20. Jonathan Edwards, "The Eternity of Hell Torments" (1739), *The Works of President Edwards* (Leeds, England: Edward Baines, 1811), vol. VII, p. 524.

21. [Morris Cerullo], *Portrait of a Prophet: The Amazing Story of Morris Cerullo* (San Diego, Calif.: World Evangelism, Inc., 1965), pp. 69–70.

22. Lester Sumrall with J. Stephen Conn, *Run with the Vision* (Plainfield, N.J.: Logos International, 1977), p. 21.

23. Roy Lessin, *Spanking: Why When How?* (Minneapolis: Bethany House Publishers, 1979), p. 30.

24. Larry Christenson, *The Christian Family* (Minneapolis: Bethany House Publishers, 1970), p. 91.

25. Christenson, *The Christian Family*, p. 98.

26. J. Richard Fugate, *What the Bible Says about . . . Child Training* (Garland, Tex.: Aletheia Publishers, 1980), p. 137.

27. Philip J. Greven, Jr., ed., *Child-Rearing Concepts 1628–1861: Historical Sources* (Itasca, Ill.: F. E. Peacock, 1973), pp. 48–49.

28. Jack Hyles, *How to Rear Children* (Hammond, Ind.: Hyles-Anderson Publishers, 1972), pp. 95–96.

29. Christenson, *The Christian Family*, p. 112.

30. Lessin, *Spanking*, p. 21.

31. Lessin, *Spanking*, p. 93.

32. Hyles, *How to Rear Children*, p. 96. The Reverend Billy Graham, in his book on the Apocalypse, declares:

As God, our loving Father, looks on, we, His disobedient children, continue to disobey. It would not be *just* for him to let our sins go unpunished. Justice requires judgment. But God loves us and works to save us from the results of our own disobedience.

(Billy Graham, *Approaching Hoofbeats: The Four Horsemen of the Apocalypse* [Waco, Tex.: Word Books, 1983], p. 214.)

33. Greven, *Child-Rearing Concepts*, pp. 126–27.

34. Greven, *Child-Rearing Concepts*, p. 129.

35. Christenson, *The Christian Family*, p. 100.

36. Christenson, *The Christian Family*, pp. 101–102.

37. Greven, *Child-Rearing Concepts*, p. 13.

38. Greven, *Child-Rearing Concepts*, p. 14.

39. Greven, *Child-Rearing Concepts*, p. 48.

40. Anonymous, "Importance of Family Discipline," *The Mother's Magazine*, vol. 10 (January 1842), pp. 12–14.

41. For a discussion of breaking wills in early America, see Philip Greven, *The Protestant Temperament: Patterns of Child-Rearing, Religious Experience, and the Self in Early America* (New York: Alfred A. Knopf, 1977; Chicago: University of Chicago Press, 1988), pp. 32–43, 87–99. Also see Alice Miller, *For Your Own Good: Hidden Cruelty in Child-Rearing and the Roots of Violence*, Hildegarde and Hunter Hannum, trans. (New York: Farrar, Straus and Giroux, 1983), "Poisonous Pedagogy," pp. 3–91, and *passim*.

42. Fugate, *What the Bible Says about . . . Child Training*, p. 143.

43. Hyles, *How to Rear Children*, pp. 99–100.

44. Lessin, *Spanking*, p. 82.

45. See James Dobson's *The Strong-Willed Child: From Birth to Adolescence* (Wheaton, Ill.: Tyndale House, 1978), pp. 25, 31–33, 46, 58, 74–75, 78 and *passim* for his views on the will, corporal punishment, and methods of discipline. Also see Peter Steinfels's article on Dobson: "Why Psychologist Without a Pulpit

Is Called Religious Right's New Star," *The New York Times* (June 5, 1990), p. A22, for further details concerning his organization, activities, and ideology.

46. James Dobson, *Dare to Discipline* (Wheaton, Ill.: Tyndale House; and Glendale, Calif.: Regal Books, 1970), p. 13.

47. Dobson, *Dare to Discipline*, p. 45. Also see Dobson, *Strong-Willed Child*, pp. 31–33.

48. Fugate, *What the Bible Says about . . . Child Training*, pp. 142–43. Also see the experience of Francis Wayland, in Greven, *The Protestant Temperament*, pp. 39–42.

49. Tomczak, *God, the Rod, and Your Child's Bod*, p. 110. His viewpoint surely reflects his own experiences as the child who grew up in "a good, Polish Catholic family." He describes his father's punishments vividly:

> A religious man, Dad had deep pride in his Catholicism and always insisted on our worshiping together as a family. If there was ever any objection to this or any other of Dad's rules, out came the razor strop. Pop felt that the best way to straighten kids out was to bend them over, and when he got all his weight behind it, he could pack an awful wallop.

Larry Tomczak, *Clap Your Hands!* (Plainfield, N.J.: Logos International, 1973), p. 3.

50. Greven, *Child-Rearing Concepts*, pp. 105–106.

51. Anonymous, "Parental Government," *The Mother's Magazine*, vol. II (1834), pp. 7–8.

52. Hyles, *How to Rear Children*, p. 145.

53. Hyles, *How to Rear Children*, p. 144.

54. Lessin, *Spanking*, p. 49.

55. Christenson, *The Christian Family*, p. 57.

56. Christenson, *The Christian Family*, p. 100.

57. Christenson, *The Christian Family*, p. 108.

58. Christenson, *The Christian Family*, p. 93.

59. See Lessin, *Spanking*, pp. 88–89.

60. Fugate, *What the Bible Says about . . . Child Training*, pp. 103–104.

61. Paul D. Meier, *Christian Child-Rearing and Personality Development* (Grand Rapids, Mich.: Baker Book House, 1977). Quote is from the book's cover.

62. Meier, *Christian Child-Rearing*, pp. 121, 129.

63. Meier, *Christian Child-Rearing*, p. 124.

64. Meier, *Christian Child-Rearing*, p. 124.

65. Christenson, *The Christian Family*, p. 104.

66. Lessin, *Spanking*, pp. 88–89.

67. Fugate, *What the Bible Says about . . . Child Training*, p. 141.

68. Meier, *Christian Child-Rearing*, pp. 169–70.

69. Dobson, *Dare to Discipline*, p. 47.

70. Greven, *Child-Rearing Concepts*, p. 97.

71. Christenson, *The Christian Family*, pp. 99, 103. For a history which is surprisingly informative, see the Rev. William M. Cooper's *Flagellation and the Flagellants: A History of the Rod in All Countries from the Earliest Period to the Present Time*, rev. ed. (London: William Reeves, n.d. [ca. 1870s?]).

72. Tomczak, *God, the Rod, and Your Child's Bod*, p. 117.

73. Fugate, *What the Bible Says about . . . Child Training*, p. 141.

74. Lessin, *Spanking*, pp. 67–68.

75. Dobson, *Dare to Discipline*, pp. 16, 217–19. Also see Dobson, *The Strong-Willed Child*, p. 46.

76. See Dobson, *The Strong-Willed Child*, p. 58.

77. See Lessin, *Spanking*, pp. 69–70, and Dobson, *The Strong-Willed Child*, p. 47.

78. Fugate, *What the Bible Says about . . . Child Training*, p. 103 and *passim*.

79. Fugate, *What the Bible Says about . . . Child Training*, p. 145.

80. Hyles, *How to Rear Children*, p. 98.

81. Lessin, *Spanking*, pp. 74–75.

82. Fugate, *What the Bible Says about . . . Child Training*, p. 143.

83. Tomczak, *God, the Rod, and Your Child's Bod*, p. 118.

84. Fugate, *What the Bible Says about . . . Child Training*, p. 139.

85. Fugate, *What the Bible Says about . . . Child Training*, pp. 142–43.

86. Lessin, *Spanking*, p. 79.

87. Lessin, *Spanking*, p. 79.

88. Christenson, *The Christian Family*, p. 118.

89. Christenson, *The Christian Family*, pp. 117–18.

90. Dobson, *Dare to Discipline*, p. 38.

91. See Beverly La Haye, *How to Develop Your Child's Temperament* (Irvine, Calif.: Harvest House Publishers, 1977), pp. 82–83.

92. For La Haye's views on the will and on rods, see *How to Develop Your Child's Temperament*, pp. 18–19, 39, 145–47.

93. Dobson, *Dare to Discipline*, p. 21.

94. Lessin, *Spanking*, p. 69. For similar views, see Hyles, *How to Rear Children*, p. 97.

95. Tomczak, *God, the Rod, and Your Child's Bod*, p. 113.

96. Christenson, *The Christian Family*, p. 116.

97. Fugate, *What the Bible Says about . . . Child Training*, p. 144.

98. See Dobson, *The Strong-Willed Child*, pp. 74–75.

99. Lessin, *Spanking*, p. 24.

100. Lessin, *Spanking*, p. 24.

101. Meier, *Christian Child-Rearing*, p. 169.

102. Greven, *Child-Rearing Concepts*, p. 22.

103. Greven, *Child-Rearing Concepts*, p. 31.

104. Greven, *Child-Rearing Concepts*, p. 33.

105. Greven, *Child-Rearing Concepts*, p. 35.

106. Greven, *Child-Rearing Concepts*, p. 28.

107. Greven, *Child-Rearing Concepts*, p. 44.

108. [Lydia Maria] Child, *The Mother's Book* (Boston: Carter, Hendee and Babcock, 1831), p. 46. Another influential author, Jacob Abbott, John Abbott's brother, was also an advocate of gentle measures of discipline, but, like Child, invoked a range of methods, including corporal punishments. For a good discussion of his views, see Anne L. Kuhn, *The Mother's Role in Childhood Education: New England Concepts 1830–1860* (New Haven, Conn.: Yale University Press, 1947), pp. 167–70.

109. Child, *Mother's Book*, p. 37.

110. For further information, see *Life and Letters of Horace Bushnell* (London: Sampson Low, Marston, Searle, & Rivington, 1880), and Barbara M. Cross, *Horace Bushnell: Minister to a Changing America* (Chicago: University of Chicago Press, 1958).

111. Horace Bushnell, *Christian Nurture* (New Haven, Conn.: Yale University Press, 1916) [original edition, 1861], p. 23.

112. Bushnell, *Christian Nurture*, p. 205.

113. Bushnell, *Christian Nurture*, p. 211.

114. Bushnell, *Christian Nurture*, p. 211.

115. Bushnell, *Christian Nurture*, pp. 208–209.

116. Bushnell, *Christian Nurture*, p. 255.

117. Bushnell, *Christian Nurture*, p. 44.

118. Bushnell, *Christian Nurture*, p. 284–85.

119. Bushnell, *Christian Nurture*, p. 285.

120. One fascinating connection between Bushnell's brief advocacy of physical punishment, however controlled and limited it might be, and the advocacy of the rod by Larry Christenson in *The Christian Family* is the fact that both Bushnell and Christenson cite the same source for their arguments: Dr. H.W.J. Thiersch's *Christian Family Life*, first published in German in 1854 and then in English translation in 1856. See Bushnell, *Christian Nurture*, pp. 258–59, 276–77, 285. Also see Christenson, *Christian Family*, pp. 6–7 and *passim*. Readers might note that Christenson only marks his borrowings from Thiersch with an asterisk rather than quoting him in quotation marks. A comparison of Bushnell's and Christenson's texts suggests, however, that Christenson often quotes Thiersch at length, rather than paraphrasing him, thus making it difficult for readers to judge which views are Thiersch's and which Christenson's—unless, of course, they are identical.

Anyone familiar with Alice Miller's *For Your Own Good* would not be too surprised to find a German theologian being cited by two Americans, one mid-nineteenth century, the other mid-twentieth century, who are arguing for the use of physical punishments. Miller's book is filled with comparable examples from German and other European writers from the eighteenth century to the twentieth.

121. Bushnell, *Christian Nurture*, p. 286.

122. D. Ross Campbell, *How to Really Love Your Child* (Wheaton, Ill.: Victor Books, 1977), p. 29.

123. Campbell, *How to Really Love Your Child*, p. 36.

124. Campbell, *How to Really Love Your Child*, p. 84.

125. Campbell, *How to Really Love Your Child*, pp. 84–85.

126. Campbell, *How to Really Love Your Child*, pp. 87–88.

127. Campbell, *How to Really Love Your Child*, p. 88.

128. Campbell, *How to Really Love Your Child*, p. 89.

129. Campbell, *How to Really Love Your Child*, p. 95.

130. Campbell, *How to Really Love Your Child*, pp. 106–107.

131. Campbell, *How to Really Love Your Child*, p. 107.

132. Campbell, *How to Really Love Your Child*, p. 109.

133. Campbell, *How to Really Love Your Child*, pp. 109–110.

134. Benjamin Spock, *Baby and Child Care* (Montreal: Pocket Books of Canada, 1957), p. 331.

135. Spock, *Baby and Child Care*, p. 332.

136. Spock, *Baby and Child Care*, p. 334.

137. Benjamin Spock and Michael B. Rothenberg, *Baby and Child Care* (New York: Pocket Books, 1985), p. 407.

138. Spock and Rothenberg, *Baby and Child Care*, p. 408.

139. Benjamin Spock, *Dr. Spock on Parenting: Sensible Advice from America's Most Trusted Child-Care Expert* (New York: Simon and Schuster, 1988), p. 26.

140. Spock, *Dr. Spock on Parenting*, pp. 151–52.

141. For additional information, see Ronald A. Paquet, *Judicial Rulings, State Statutes and State Administrative Regulations Dealing with the Use of Corporal Punishment in Public Schools* (Palo Alto, Calif.: R & E Research Associates, 1982). In addition, see Irwin A. Hyman and James H. Wise, eds., *Corporal Punishment in American Education* (Philadelphia: Temple University Press, 1979), which provides a valuable overview of the subject as well as several essays specifically devoted to *Ingraham* v. *Wright*.

Corporal punishment is traditional in schools in English-speaking cultures around the world. See, for example, Jonathan Gathorne-Hardy, *The Public School Phenomenon, 597–1977* (London: Hodder and Stoughton, 1977), and Joseph A. Mercurio, *Caning: Educational Rite and Tradition* (Syracuse, N.Y.: Syracuse University Press, 1972), which studies corporal punishment in New Zealand schools.

142. *Ingraham* v. *Wright*, 498 F.2d 248 (5th Cir. 1974), p. 255.

143. *Ingraham* v. *Wright*, 498 F.2d 248 (1974), p. 255.

144. *Ingraham* v. *Wright*, 498 F.2d 248 (1974), p. 256.

145. *Ingraham* v. *Wright*, 498 F.2d 248 (1974), pp. 256–59.

146. *Ingraham* v. *Wright*, 498 F.2d 248 (1974), pp. 259–65, 269.

147. *Ingraham* v. *Wright*, 498 F.2d 248 (1974), p. 269.

148. *Ingraham* v. *Wright*, 525 F.2d 909 (5th Cir. 1976), p. 912.

149. *Ingraham* v. *Wright*, 525 F.2d 909 (1976), p. 915.

150. *Ingraham* v. *Wright*, 525 F.2d 909 (1976), p. 915n.

151. *Ingraham* v. *Wright*, 525 F.2d 909 (1976), p. 917.

152. *Ingraham* v. *Wright*, 525 F.2d 909 (1976), p. 919.

153. *Ingraham* v. *Wright*, 97 S.Ct. 1401 (1977), p. 1405. For the transcript of the Court's consideration of *Ingraham* v. *Wright*, see Philip B. Kurland and Gerhard Casper, eds., *Landmark Briefs and Arguments of the Supreme Court of the United States: Constitutional Law 1976 Term Supplement*, vol. 93 (Washington, D.C.: University Publications of America, 1978), pp. 1–348.

154. *Ingraham* v. *Wright*, 97 S.Ct. 1401 (1977), p. 1419.

155. *Ingraham* v. *Wright*, 97 S.Ct. 1401 (1977), p. 1406.

156. *Ingraham* v. *Wright*, 97 S.Ct. 1401 (1977), p. 1411.

157. *Ingraham* v. *Wright*, 97 S.Ct. 1401 (1977), p. 1414.

158. *Ingraham* v. *Wright*, 97 S.Ct. 1401 (1977), p. 1407.

159. *Ingraham* v. *Wright*, 97 S.Ct. 1401 (1977), p. 1408.

160. *Ingraham* v. *Wright*, 97 S.Ct. 1401 (1977), p. 1407.

161. *Ingraham* v. *Wright*, 97 S.Ct. 1401 (1977), p. 1411.

162. *Ingraham* v. *Wright*, 97 S.Ct. 1401 (1977), p. 1423.

163. *Ingraham* v. *Wright*, 525 F.2d 909 (5th Cir. 1976), p. 924.

164. *Ingraham* v. *Wright*, 525 F.2d 909 (1976), p. 924.

165. *Ingraham* v. *Wright*, 525 F.2d 909 (1976), p. 925.

166. *Ingraham* v. *Wright*, 525 F.2d 909 (1976), p. 926.

167. *Ingraham* v. *Wright*, 525 F.2d 909 (1976), p. 927.

168. B. F. Skinner, *A Matter of Consequences: Part Three of an Autobiography* (New York: Alfred A. Knopf, 1983), p. 403. For a discussion of his general views on punishment and nonpunishment, see B. F. Skinner, *Beyond Freedom and Dignity* (New York: Alfred A. Knopf, 1971), especially chapters 4 and 5.

169. B. F. Skinner, *Particulars of My Life* (New York: Alfred A. Knopf, 1976), p. 60.

170. Skinner, *A Matter of Consequences*, p. 404.

171. Skinner, *Particulars of My Life*, p. 61.

172. Skinner, *A Matter of Consequences*, pp. 403–404.

173. Skinner, "Origins of a Behaviorist," *Psychology Today*, vol. 17 (September 1983), p. 31.

174. See, for instance, Skinner's letter to the editor, *Educational Leadership* (October 1973), p. 61, in which he states his opposition to physical punishments in schools. Also see *A Matter of Consequences*, pp. 332–33, for further discussion of this matter.

175. Ron Van Houten, "Punishment: From the Animal Laboratory to the Applied Setting," in Saul Axelrod and Jack Apsche, eds., *The Effects of Punishment on Human Behavior* (New York: Academic Press, 1983), p. 39.

176. Edward G. Carr and O. Ivar Lovaas, "Contingent Electric Shock as a Treatment for Severe Behavior Problems," in Axelrod and Apsche, *The Effects of Punishment on Human Behavior*, p. 221.

177. Van Houten, "Punishment," p. 27.

178. Van Houten, "Punishment," p. 28.

179. Crighton Newsom, Judith E. Favell, and Arnold Rincover, "The Side Effects of Punishment," in Axelrod and Apsche, *The Effects of Punishment on Human Behavior*, pp. 286–87.

180. Van Houten, "Punishment," p. 20.

181. Van Houten, "Punishment," p. 20.

182. Van Houten, "Punishment," p. 31.

183. Van Houten, "Punishment," p. 33.

184. Newsom, Favell, and Rincover, "Side Effects of Punishment," p. 288. However, this may be changing. See: H. Rutherford Turnbull, III, and Doug Guess *et al.*, "A Model for Analyzing the Moral Aspects of Special Education and Behavioral Interventions: The Moral Aspects of Aversive Procedures," in P. R. Dokecki and R. M. Zaner, eds., *Ethics of Dealing with Persons with Severe Handicaps* (Baltimore: Brookes, 1986), pp. 167–208.

185. Newsom, Favell, and Rincover, "Side Effects of Punishment," p. 288.

186. Newsom, Favell, and Rincover, "Side Effects of Punishment," p. 301.

187. Van Houten, "Punishment," pp. 33–34.

188. Van Houten, "Punishment," pp. 34–35.

189. Skinner, *A Matter of Consequences*, p. 399.

190. Van Houten, "Punishment," p. 33.

191. Newsom, Favell, and Rincover, "Side Effects of Punishment," p. 289.

192. Newsom, Favell, and Rincover, "Side Effects of Punishment," p. 290.

193. Newsom, Favell, and Rincover, "Side Effects of Punishment," p. 291.

194. Newsom, Favell, and Rincover, "Side Effects of Punishment," pp. 291–92.

195. Newsom, Favell, and Rincover, "Side Effects of Punishment," p. 306.

196. Newsom, Favell, and Rincover, "Side Effects of Punishment," p. 309.

197. Newsom, Favell, and Rincover, "Side Effects of Punishment," p. 310.

198. Saul Axelrod, "Doing It Without Arrows: A Review of Lavigna and Donnellan's *Alternatives to Punishment: Solving Behavior Problems with Non-Aversive Strategies*," in *The Behavior Analyst*, vol. 10 (Fall 1987), p. 251. Also see: V. Mark Durand, "In Response: 'Look Homeward Angel': A Call to Return to Our (Functional) Roots," in *The Behavior Analyst*, vol. 10 (Fall 1987), pp. 299–302, and Brian A. Iwata, "The Development and Adoption of Controversial Default Technologies," *The Behavior Analyst*, vol. 11 (Fall 1988), pp. 149–57.

199. Edward G. Carr, personal communication.

200. Edward G. Carr and V. Mark Durand, "See Me, Help Me," *Psychology Today* (November 1987), p. 64. Also see Edward G. Carr, Sarah Robinson, Jill C. Taylor, and Jane I. Carlson, "Positive Approaches to the Treatment of Severe Behavior Problems in Persons with Developmental Disabilities: A Review and Analysis of Reinforcement and Stimulus-Based Procedures," in *Monographs of the Association for Persons with Severe Handicaps* (forthcoming), and Edward G. Carr, Sarah Robinson, and Laura Wray Palumbo, "The Wrong Issue: Aversive Versus Nonaversive Treatment. The Right Issue: Functional Versus Nonfunctional Treatment," in A. Repp and N. Singh, eds., *Current Perspectives in the Use of Nonaversive and Aversive Interventions with Developmentally Disabled Persons* (Sycamore, Ill.: Sycamore, 1990).

201. Crighton D. Newsom, personal communication.

PART IV CONSEQUENCES

1. See Colleen McDannell and Bernhard Lang, *Heaven: A History* (New Haven, Conn.: Yale University Press, 1988). The index contains no reference to punishment.

2. See Philip Greven, *The Protestant Temperament* (New York: Alfred A. Knopf, 1977; Chicago: University of Chicago Press, 1988), pp. 109–124, for a discussion of anger among evangelicals; see also the innovative study by Carol Zisowitz Stearns and Peter N. Stearns, *Anger: The Struggle for Emotional Control in America's History* (Chicago: University of Chicago Press, 1986). Alice Miller, as always, has much to say about anger in *For Your Own Good: Hidden Cruelty in Child-Rearing and the Roots of Violence*, Hildegarde and Hunter Hannum, trans. (New York: Farrar, Straus and Giroux, 1983).

3. See Miller, *For Your Own Good*, esp. pp. 248–49.

4. Edmund Gosse, *Father and Son: A Study of Two Temperaments* (London: Penguin Books, 1970; originally published 1907), pp. 37–38.

5. Allen Wheelis, *How People Change* (New York: Perennial Library, Harper & Row, 1973), pp. 60–63.

6. Wheelis, *How People Change*, p. 68.

7. Miller, *For Your Own Good*, p. 61.

8. See, For example, Arnold P. Goldstein and Gerald Y. Michaels, *Empathy: Development, Training, and Consequences* (Hillsdale, N.J: Erlbaum, 1985), pp. 53–61; Carolyn Zahn-Waxler, E. Mark Cummings, and Ronald Iannotti, eds., *Altruism and Aggression: Biological and Social Origins* (Cambridge, England: Cambridge University Press, 1986); Martin L. Hoffman and Herbert D. Saltzstein, "Parent Discipline and the Child's Moral Development," *Journal of Personality and Social Psychology*, vol. 5 (1967), pp. 45–57; Kiki V. Roe, "Toward a Contingency Hypothesis of Empathy Development," *Journal of Personality and Social Psychology*, vol. 39 (1980), pp. 991–94.

9. Richard Fugate, *What the Bible Says about . . . Child Training* (Garland, Tex.: Aletheia Publishers, 1980), p. 141.

10. See, for instance, Roe, "Toward a Contingency Hypothesis"; also see Goldstein and Michaels, *Empathy*, pp. 58–59.

11. Jessica Benjamin, *The Bonds of Love: Psychoanalysis, Feminism, and the Problem of Domination* (New York: Pantheon, 1988), p. 48.

12. Daniel Goleman, "Great Altruists: Science Ponders Soul of Goodness," *The New York Times*, March 5, 1985, p. C2. Also see Ervin Straub, "A Conception of the Determinants and Development of Altruism and Aggression: Motives, the Self, and the Environment," in Zahn-Waxler *et al.*, *Altruism and Aggression*, pp. 135–64.

13. See, for example: Ronald G. Slaby and Wendy Conklin Roedell, "The Development and Regulation of Aggression in Young Children," *Psychological Development in the Elementary Years*, J. Worell, ed. (New York: Academic Press, 1982), pp. 97–149; Ross D. Parke and Ronald G. Slaby, "The Development of Aggression," in P. H. Mussen, ed., *Handbook of Child Psychology*, 4th ed. (New York: Wiley, 1983), vol. 4, pp. 547–641.

14. See Justin Aronfreed, *Conduct and Conscience: The Socialization of Internalized Control over Behavior* (New York: Academic Press, 1968), esp. pp. 302–323.

15. Ruth S. Kempe and C. Henry Kempe, *Child Abuse* (Cambridge, Mass.: Harvard University Press, 1978), p. 32.

16. Parke and Slaby, "The Development of Aggression," p. 605.

17. For a general perspective on the history of depression, see Stanley W. Jackson, *Melancholia and Depression: From Hippocratic Times to Modern Times* (New Haven, Conn.: Yale University Press, 1986). Also see: Aaron T. Beck, *Depression: Causes and Treatment* (Philadelphia: University of Pennsylvania Press, 1967), and John Bowlby's classic work *Attachment and Loss* (New York: Basic Books, 1969–1980).

18. Sigmund Freud, "Mourning and Melancholia," in *Collected Papers*, Joan Riviere, trans. (New York: Basic Books, 1959), vol. 4, p. 153.

19. Sigmund Freud, " 'A Child Is Being Beaten': A Contribution to the Study of the Origin of Sexual Perversions" (1919), in *Collected Papers*, Joan Riviere, trans., vol. 2, pp. 172–201.

20. Freud, "Mourning and Melancholia," p. 158.

21. Freud, "Mourning and Melancholia," pp. 158–59.

22. Freud, "Mourning and Melancholia," p. 162.

23. Freud, "Mourning and Melancholia," p. 162.

24. See Greven, *The Protestant Temperament*, especially pp. 65–86.

25. See Philip Greven, " 'Some Root of Bitterness': Corporal Punishment, Child Abuse, and the Apocalyptic Impulse in Michael Wigglesworth," in James A. Henretta, Michael Kammen, and Stanley N. Katz, eds., *The Transformation of Early American History: Society, Authority, and Ideology* (New York: Alfred A. Knopf, 1991).

26. John Owen King III, *The Iron of Melancholy: Structures of Spiritual Conversion in America from the Puritan Conscience to Victorian Neurosis* (Middletown, Conn.: Wesleyan University Press, 1983).

27. Kenneth Silverman, *The Life and Times of Cotton Mather* (New York: Harper & Row, 1984), pp. 35, 392, 414, 433. Also see Robert Middlekauff, *The Mathers: Three Generations of Puritan Intellectuals* (New York: Oxford University Press, 1971), especially chapter 18.

28. Frank E. Manuel, *A Portrait of Isaac Newton* (Cambridge, Mass.: The Belknap Press of Harvard University Press, 1968), pp. 57–58, 343, 348.

29. For an important modern study that demonstrates the long-term impact of physical punishments on depression, see S. J. Holmes and L. N. Robins, "The Influence of Childhood Disciplinary Experience on the Development of Alcoholism and Depression," *Journal of Child Psychology and Psychiatry*, vol. 28 (1987), pp. 399–415.

30. See, for example, James Barr, *Fundamentalism* (London: SCM Press, 1977); Nancy Tatom Ammerman, *Bible Believers: Fundamentalists in the Modern World* (New Brunswick, N.J.: Rutgers University Press, 1987); Alan Peshkin, *God's Choice: The Total World of a Fundamentalist Christian School* (Chicago: University of Chicago Press, 1988).

31. David Shapiro, *Autonomy and Rigid Character* (New York: Basic Books, 1981), p. 73.

32. Shapiro, *Autonomy and Rigid Character*, p. 86.

33. Stuart C. Henry, *George Whitefield: Wayfaring Witness* (Nashville, Tenn.: Abingdon Press, 1957), p. 75, quoted in Greven, *The Protestant Temperament*, p. 142; Philip J. Greven, ed., *Child-Rearing Concepts, 1628–1861: Historical Sources* (Itasca, Ill.: F. E. Peacock, 1973), pp. 68, 71.

34. David Leverenz, *The Language of Puritan Feeling: An Exploration in Literature, Psychology, and Social History* (New Brunswick, N.J.: Rutgers University Press, 1980), p. 3. See also chapter 4, "Obsessive Dependence." King's *The Iron of Melancholy* brilliantly explores the persistence of obsessive-compulsive behavior and experience from the Puritans to the Victorians in complex detail through both individual life histories and collective biographical analyses. But he never grapples with the problem of the origins of the long-standing prevalence of obsessive-compulsive character.

35. Leverenz, *Language of Puritan Feeling*, p. 111.

36. Leverenz, *Language of Puritan Feeling*, p. 117. In his denial that Puritanism was "the product of strong patriarchs breaking the child's will, at least at the start," he is surely mistaken.

37. See, for example, Graham F. Reed, *Obsessional Experience and Com-

pulsive Behaviour: A Cognitive-Structural Approach (New York: Academic Press, 1985). Reed acknowledges that "we are no nearer to understanding today than our forebears were at the beginning of the century" (p. xii). As a description of the phenomena, however, the book is excellent. It is the etiology that remains mysterious.

38. See, for example, Stuart Schneiderman's Lacanian study *Rat Man* (New York: New York University Press, 1986). The closest he comes to making a connection is his statement that "From other cases of obsessional neurosis we know of the extent to which these patients live in constant fear of punishment" (p. 26).

39. Larry Wolff, *Postcards from the End of the World* (New York: Atheneum, 1988), chapter 3.

40. Sigmund Freud, "Notes Upon a Case of Obsessional Neurosis" (1909), in *Collected Papers*, Alix and James Strachey, trans. (New York: Basic Books, 1959), vol. 3, p. 304.

41. Freud, "Notes Upon a Case of Obsessional Neurosis," pp. 343, 345–46.

42. Freud, "Notes Upon a Case of Obsessional Neurosis," pp. 329–30. In his subsequent essay "The Predisposition to Obsessional Neurosis: A Contribution to the Problem of the Option of Neurosis" (1913), Freud again called attention to "The all-important part played by hate impulses and anal eroticism in the symptomatology of the obsessional neurosis," and noted that his "patient's sexual life began with sadistic beating-phantasies in her earliest childhood." He does nothing further with this observation, however. Freud, *Collected Papers*, vol. 2, p. 127.

43. Freud, "Notes Upon a Case of Obsessional Neurosis," p. 327.

44. Erik H. Erikson, *Young Man Luther: A Study in Psychoanalysis and History* (New York: W. W. Norton & Co., 1958), p. 40.

45. Erikson, *Young Man Luther*, p. 61. Also see pp. 156, 174, 196 for further details about Luther's obsessional character.

46. Erikson, *Young Man Luther*, p. 137.

47. Erikson, *Young Man Luther*, p. 64.

48. Erikson, *Young Man Luther*, p. 64, quoting Roland H. Bainton, *Here I Stand* (New York: Abingdon-Cokesbury Press, 1930), p. 23.

49. Erikson, *Young Man Luther*, p. 65.

50. Erikson, *Young Man Luther*, p. 68.

51. Silverman, *Life and Times of Cotton Mather*, pp. 254–56.

52. Manuel, *Portrait of Isaac Newton*, p. 64.

53. Manuel, *Portrait of Isaac Newton*, p. 343.

54. Michael Wigglesworth, *Meat out of the Eater: Or, Meditations Concerning the Necessity, End, and Usefulness of Afflictions unto God's Children*, 5th ed. (Boston: J. Allen, 1717), pp. 41–42.

55. Alfred Kadushin and Judith A. Martin, *Child Abuse: An Interactional Event* (New York: Columbia University Press, 1981), pp. 210–12.

56. Wigglesworth, "Carriage of a Child of God," in *Meat out of the Eater*, reprinted in Perry Miller and Thomas H. Johnson, eds., *The Puritans* (New York: American Book Company, 1938), pp. 620–23. Also see Greven, " 'Some Root of Bitterness.' "

57. Anne Sexton, "Red Roses," *The Complete Poems* (Boston: Houghton Mifflin, 1981), pp. 492–93.

58. Miller, *For Your Own Good*, p. 118.

59. See Eugene L. Bliss, *Multiple Personality, Allied Disorders, and Hypnosis* (New York: Oxford University Press, 1986); Ernest R. Hilgard, *Divided Consciousness: Multiple Controls in Human Thought and Action* (New York: John Wiley & Sons, 1977); Bessel A. van der Kolk, *Psychological Trauma* (Washington, D.C.: American Psychiatric Press, 1987).

60. For definitions and studies of hysteria, see: Josef Breuer and Sigmund Freud, *Studies on Hysteria*, James Strachey, trans. and ed. (New York: Basic Books, n.d.); Ilza Veith, *Hysteria: The History of a Disease* (Chicago: University of Chicago Press, 1965); Alan Krohn, *Hysteria: The Elusive Neurosis* (New York: International Universities Press, 1978). For definitions of borderline character disorders, see: John G. Gunderson and Margaret T. Singer, "Defining Borderline Patients: An Overview," in Michael H. Stone, ed., *Essential Papers on Borderline Disorders: One Hundred Years at the Border* (New York: New York University Press, 1986), pp. 453–74.

61. One fascinating study done in the Bible Belt reveals the frequent presence of dissociative experiences. See James T. Proctor, "Hysteria in Childhood," *American Journal of Orthopsychiatry*, vol. 28 (April 1958), pp. 394–405, and the follow-up of his research in V. R. Hensley, "Hysteria in Childhood: A Note on Proctor's Incidence Figures 27 Years Later," *American Journal of Orthopsychiatry*, vol. 55 (January 1985), pp. 140–42.

62. Quoted in Bliss, *Multiple Personality*, p. 51.

63. Bliss, *Multiple Personality*, p. 79.

64. See Van der Kolk, *Psychological Trauma*.

65. Ellen Hale, "Inside the Divided Mind," *The New York Times Sunday Magazine* (April 17, 1983), p. 102.

66. See Alice Miller, *Prisoners of Childhood*, Ruth Ward, trans. (New York: Basic Books, 1981), pp. 71–72. Also see Ingmar Bergman's *The Magic Lantern: An Autobiography*, Joan Tate, trans. (New York: Viking, 1988), p. 8.

67. Ingmar Bergman, *Fanny and Alexander*, Alan Blair, trans. (New York: Pantheon, 1982), p. 32. This interpretation of *Fanny and Alexander* stems from a conversation that I had in 1984 with Virginia Demos.

68. Bergman, *Fanny and Alexander*, p. 106.

69. Bergman, *Fanny and Alexander*, pp. 135–39.

70. Bergman, *Fanny and Alexander*, pp. 184, 198–202.

71. Bergman, *Fanny and Alexander*, p. 141.

72. Gosse, *Father and Son*, pp. 30, 33–34.

73. Hilgard, *Divided Consciousness*, chapters 9 and 10.

74. Jeffrey Moussaieff Masson, *The Assault on Truth: Freud's Suppression of the Seduction Theory* (New York: Penguin, 1985).

75. Sigmund Freud, "The Aetiology of Hysteria" (1896), in *Collected Papers*, Joan Riviere, trans., vol. 1, pp. 198, 202, 204.

76. Freud, "The Aetiology of Hysteria," p. 205.

77. Freud, "The Aetiology of Hysteria," pp. 208, 217.

78. Sándor Ferenczi, "Confusion of Tongues Between Adults and the Child (The Language of Tenderness and the Language of [Sexual] Passion)," Jeffrey M. Masson and Marianne Loring, trans., in Masson, *The Assault on Truth*, pp. 291–303.

79. This essay should be supplemented, however, with the astonishing per-

sonal notes in his diary. See Judith Dupont, ed., *The Clinical Diary of Sándor Ferenczi*, Michael Balint and Nicola Zarday Jackson, trans. (Cambridge, Mass.: Harvard University Press, 1988).

80. Ferenczi, "Confusion of Tongues," pp. 296–98.

81. Ferenczi, "Confusion of Tongues," p. 298.

82. Ferenczi, "Confusion of Tongues," p. 298.

83. Quoted in Greven, *The Protestant Temperament*, p. 79.

84. Ferenczi, "Confusion of Tongues," pp. 300–301.

85. Ferenczi, "Confusion of Tongues," p. 300.

86. Jean Goodwin, "Credibility Problems in Multiple Personality Disorder Patients and Abused Children," in Richard P. Kluft, ed., *Childhood Antecedents of Multiple Personality* (Washington, D.C.: American Psychiatric Press, 1985), p. 5.

87. Richard P. Kluft, "The Natural History of Multiple Personality Disorder," in Kluft, ed., *Childhood Antecedents*, p. 204.

88. Bessel van der Kolk, "The Psychological Consequences of Overwhelming Life Experiences," in Van der Kolk, *Psychological Trauma*, p. 6.

89. Bessel van der Kolk and William Kadish, "Amnesia, Dissociation, and the Return of the Repressed," in Van der Kolk, *Psychological Trauma*, p. 185.

90. Bliss, *Multiple Personality*, p. 70. Also see pp. 121–23.

91. Bliss, *Multiple Personality*, p. 93.

92. Bliss, *Multiple Personality*, p. 146.

93. Chris Costner Sizemore and Elen Sain Pittillo, *I'm Eve* (New York: Jove Publications, 1983), pp. 165 (italics omitted), 332. Also see pp. 30–31, 69–70, 89–90, 92, 101, 183, and 187 for other examples of corporal punishments.

94. Cornelia B. Wilbur, "The Effect of Child Abuse on the Psyche," in Van der Kolk, *Psychological Trauma*, p. 33.

95. Wilbur, "Effect of Child Abuse on the Psyche," p. 27.

96. Flora Rheta Schreiber, *Sybil* (New York: Warner Books, 1973), pp. 292, 207, 209, 222–23.

97. Schreiber, *Sybil*, pp. 220–21.

98. Schreiber, *Sybil*, pp. 401–402.

99. Schreiber, *Sybil*, p. 403.

100. Bliss, *Multiple Personality*, p. 195.

101. Bliss, *Multiple Personality*, p. 195.

102. Bliss, *Multiple Personality*, p. 195.

103. Miller, *For Your Own Good*, p. 248.

104. Many observers have noted the hypervigilance of abused children, a foreshadowing, in many instances, of the varying degrees of paranoia of adulthood. See, for instance: Harold P. Martin and Martha A. Rodeheffer, "The Psychological Impact of Abuse on Children," in Gertrude J. Williams and John Money, eds., *Traumatic Abuse and Neglect in Children at Home* (Baltimore: Johns Hopkins University Press, 1980), p. 257. They note:

> A common form of this survival adaptation is hypervigilance. In an attempt to stay out of harm's way the child becomes a "watcher," an observer acutely sensitive to adults and to any sudden change in the environment that is inexplicable to him. This behavior is particularly noticeable in situations such as during developmental testing [p. 257].

This anticipation of danger often extends beyond the household and family in which the anxiety and apprehension is most immediately justified, becoming a pervasive means of defense against danger and abuse.

105. See, for example: Harold P. Blum, "Paranoia and Beating Fantasy: An Inquiry into the Psychoanalytic Theory of Paranoia," *Journal of the American Psychoanalytic Association*, vol. 28 (1980), pp. 331-61. "There will be efforts to repair, reverse, and revenge the fantasied injury, and these mechanisms may be discerned in the paranoid beating fantasy and in derivative action" (p. 357).

106. Sigmund Freud, "Psycho-analytic Notes upon an Autobiographical Account of a Case of Paranoia (Dementia Paranoides)" (1911), in *Collected Papers*, Alix and James Strachey, trans., vol. 3, p. 465.

107. Freud, "Psycho-analytic Notes," p. 431.

108. Freud, "Psycho-analytic Notes," p. 448.

109. Freud, "Psycho-analytic Notes," p. 452.

110. Morton Schatzman, *Soul Murder: Persecution in the Family* (London: Allen Lane, 1973), p. 21. In addition, see: Han Israëls, *Schreber: Father and Son*, H. S. Lake, trans. (Amsterdam: Han Israëls, 1981); Louis A. Sass, "Schreber's Panopticism: Psychosis and the Modern Soul," *Social Research*, vol. 54 (Spring 1987), pp. 101-147.

111. William G. Niederland, *The Schreber Case: Psychoanalytic Profile of a Paranoid Personality* (New York: Quadrangle/The New York Times Book Co., 1974), p. 70.

112. Quoted in Morton Schatzman, "Paranoia or Persecution: The Case of Schreber," *The History of Childhood Quarterly*, vol. 1 (Summer 1973), p. 73.

113. Schatzman, "Paranoia or Persecution," p. 84.

114. Niederland, *The Schreber Case*, p. 70.

115. Schatzman, "Paranoia or Persecution," p. 74.

116. Schatzman, "Paranoia or Persecution," p. 71.

117. Niederland, *The Schreber Case*, p. 72.

118. Schatzman, "Paranoia or Persecution," p. 71.

119. Schatzman, "Paranoia or Persecution," p. 82.

120. George M. Marsden, *Fundamentalism and American Culture: The Shaping of Twentieth-Century Evangelicalism: 1870-1925* (New York: Oxford University Press, 1980), pp. 210-11 and *passim*. See also Greven, *The Protestant Temperament*, pp. 110, 352.

121. Richard Hofstadter, "Pseudo-Conservativism Revisited: A Postscript (1962)," in Daniel Bell, ed., *The Radical Right: The New American Right*, rev. ed. (Garden City, N.Y.: Anchor Books, 1964), pp. 99-103.

122. Shapiro, *Autonomy and Rigid Character*, p. 164.

123. See Jane E. Brody, "Scientists Trace Aberrant Sexuality," *The New York Times* (January 23, 1990), pp. C1, C12, which reports on a pioneering study of the childhood origins of deviant adult sexual behaviors: John Money and Margaret Lamacz, *Vandalized Lovemaps: Paraphilic Outcome of Seven Cases in Pediatric Sexology* (Buffalo, N.Y.: Prometheus Books, 1989).

124. See Wilhelm Stekel, *Sadism and Masochism: The Psychology of Hatred and Cruelty*, Louise Brink, trans. (New York: Liveright Publishing Corp., 1929); Gerald Greene and Caroline Greene, *S-M: The Last Taboo* (New York: Grove Press, 1974).

125. Sharon Sexton, "Suffer the Children," *The Boston Phoenix* (April 19,

1983), p. 36. Also see Barbara Grizzuti Harrison, "The Children and the Cult," *New England Monthly* (December 1984), p. 63.

126. Sexton, "Suffer the Children," p. 36.

127. Larry Townsend, *The Leatherman's Handbook II* (New York: Modernismo Publications, 1972).

128. See, for example, Townsend's essay "Masters and Slaves," in *The Leatherman's Handbook*, chapter 5. Also see Ronald V. Sampson, *The Psychology of Power* (New York: Vintage Books, 1968), and Money and Lamacz, *Vandalized Lovemaps.*

129. John E. Mack, *A Prince of Our Disorder: The Life of T. E. Lawrence* (Boston: Little, Brown and Co., 1976), pp. 14–15.

130. Mack, *Prince of Our Disorder*, p. 33. Also see p. 455 for a similar observation on the breaking of Lawrence's will.

131. Mack, *Prince of Our Disorder*, p. 233.

132. Mack, *Prince of Our Disorder*, p. 234.

133. Mack, *Prince of Our Disorder*, p. 419.

134. Mack, *Prince of Our Disorder*, p. 427.

135. Mack, *Prince of Our Disorder*, p. 433.

136. Mack, *Prince of Our Disorder*, p. 436.

137. Mack, *Prince of Our Disorder*, p. 440.

138. Mack, *Prince of Our Disorder*, p. 440.

139. Mack, *Prince of Our Disorder*, p. 440.

140. Shapiro, *Autonomy and Rigid Character*, pp. 128–29.

141. Shapiro, *Autonomy and Rigid Character*, p. 130.

142. See, for example, Robert J. Stoller, *Perversion: The Erotic Form of Hatred* (New York: Pantheon Books, 1975); Thomas Weinberg and G. W. Levi Kamel, eds., *S and M: Studies in Sadomasochism* (Buffalo, N.Y.: Prometheus Books, 1983); and Greene and Greene, *S-M: The Last Taboo.*

143. Susan Farr, "The Art of Discipline: Creating Erotic Dramas of Play and Power," in *Coming to Power: Writings and Graphics on Lesbian S/M*, 3rd ed. (Boston: Alyson Publications, 1987), pp. 184–85. For alternative perspectives, see Robin Ruth Linden, Darlene R. Pagano, Diana E. H. Russell, and Susan Leigh Star, eds., *Against Sadomasochism: A Radical Feminist Analysis* (San Francisco: Frog in the Well, 1982). For male experiences and fantasies that bear the imprint of S&M, see Klaus Theweleit, *Male Fantasies*, Stephen Conway, trans., vol. 1 (Minneapolis: University of Minnesota Press, 1987).

144. Farr, "The Art of Discipline," p. 185.

145. Farr, "The Art of Discipline," p. 187.

146. See Ian Gibson, "Flagellation and Anal Eroticism," in *The English Vice: Beating, Sex and Shame in Victorian England and After* (London: Duckworth, 1978), pp. 288–94. Also see Erikson's discussions of anality and corporal punishments in *Young Man Luther*, pp. 79, 245–48. Jane Ritchie and James Ritchie also note the sadomasochistic implications of physical punishments in *Spare the Rod* (Sydney, Australia: George Allen & Unwin, 1981), p. 58. For homophobia and the fundamentalist Christian Right, see Perry Deane Young, *God's Bullies: Native Reflections on Preachers and Politics* (New York: Holt, Rinehart and Winston, 1982), and Flo Conway and Jim Siegelman, *Holy Terror: The Fundamentalist War on America's Freedoms in Religion, Politics and Our Private Lives* (Garden City, N.Y.: Doubleday, 1982).

147. *The Confessions of Jean-Jacques Rousseau* (New York: The Modern Library, n.d.), pp. 8, 12–13.

148. Rousseau, *Confessions*, pp. 14–16.

149. See especially Linda Gordon, *Heroes of Their Own Lives: The Politics and History of Family Violence—Boston 1880–1960* (New York: Viking, 1988), and Elizabeth Pleck, *Domestic Tyranny: The Making of Social Policy Against Family Violence from Colonial Times to the Present* (New York: Oxford University Press, 1987). Also see: Ann Taves, ed., *Religion and Domestic Violence in Early New England: The Memoirs of Abigail Abbot Bailey* (Bloomington: Indiana University Press, 1989); Dickson Bruce, *Violence and Culture in the Antebellum South* (Austin: University of Texas Press, 1979); Bertram Wyatt-Brown, *Southern Honor: Ethics and Behavior in the Old South* (New York: Oxford University Press, 1982).

150. Among the studies are the pioneering analysis by David G. Gil, *Violence Against Children: Physical Child Abuse in the United States* (Cambridge, Mass.: Harvard University Press, 1970); Jean Renvoize, *Web of Violence: A Study of Family Violence* (London: Routledge & Kegan Paul, 1978); Mildred Daley Pagelow with Lloyd W. Pagelow, *Family Violence* (New York: Praeger, 1984); Richard J. Gelles and Murray A. Straus, *Intimate Violence* (New York: Simon and Schuster, 1988).

151. See Erin Pizzey's *Scream Quietly or the Neighbors Will Hear* (Hillside, N.J.: Enslow, 1977) and *Infernal Child: A Memoir* (London: Victor Gollancz Ltd., 1978). Also see Erin Pizzey and Jeff Shapiro, *Prone to Violence* (Feltham, England: Hamlyn Paperbacks, 1982), and Lenore E. Walker's pioneering study, *The Battered Woman Syndrome* (New York: Springer Publishing Co., 1984).

152. Richard Gelles, *The Violent Home*, rev. ed. (Newbury Park, Calif.: Sage Publications, 1987), pp. 169–70.

153. See Gelles, *The Violent Home*, pp. 58–78 and *passim*.

154. Gelles, *The Violent Home*, pp. 175–76.

155. See, for instance, L. Rowell Huesmann, Leonard D. Eron, Monroe M. Lefkowitz, and Leopold O. Walder, "Stability of Aggression over Time and Generations," *Developmental Psychology*, vol. 20 (1984), pp. 1120–34. Unfortunately, they do not recognize the role played by corporal punishments in the phenomena they observe.

156. Murray A. Straus, Richard J. Gelles, Suzanne K. Steinmetz, *Behind Closed Doors: Violence in the American Family* (Garden City, N.Y.: Anchor Books, 1981), p. 3.

157. Straus, Gelles, and Steinmetz, *Behind Closed Doors*, p. 62.

158. Straus, Gelles, and Steinmetz, *Behind Closed Doors*, p. 107.

159. Straus, Gelles, and Steinmetz, *Behind Closed Doors*, pp. 109–110.

160. Straus, Gelles, and Steinmetz, *Behind Closed Doors*, p. 117.

161. See David Finkelhor with Gerald T. Hotaling and Kersti Yllo, *Stopping Family Violence: Research Priorities for the Coming Decade* (Newbury Park, Calif.: Sage Publications, 1988).

162. Straus, Gelles, and Steinmetz, *Behind Closed Doors*, p. 4.

163. Among these studies are the following: R. Emerson Dobash and Russell Dobash, *Violence Against Wives: A Case Against the Patriarchy* (New York: The Free Press, 1979); Pizzey and Shapiro, *Prone to Violence*; Walker, *The Battered Woman Syndrome*; Anson Shupe, William A. Stacy, and Lonnie R. Hazlewood,

Violent Men, Violent Couples: The Dynamics of Domestic Violence (Lexington, Mass.: Lexington Books, 1987). Shupe *et al.* discuss the role of violence both in the military and in fundamentalist religious contexts, noting that "in fact the relation of religion to family violence has been virtually ignored" (p. 87).

164. Dobash and Dobash, *Violence Against Wives*, pp. 15, 22.

165. Shupe, Stacy, and Hazlewood, *Violent Men, Violent Couples*, p. 35.

166. Pizzey and Shapiro, *Prone to Violence*, p. 35.

167. Pizzey and Shapiro, *Prone to Violence*, pp. 36–37.

168. Pizzey and Shapiro, *Prone to Violence*, p. 38.

169. Pizzey and Shapiro, *Prone to Violence*, p. 38. Also see pp. 173–74.

170. Pizzey and Shapiro, *Prone to Violence*, pp. 170–71.

171. See, for example, Benjamin, *Bonds of Love*, pp. 62–74.

172. See Leonard Shengold, *Soul Murder: The Effects of Childhood Abuse and Deprivation* (New Haven, Conn.: Yale University Press, 1989).

173. The long-term impact of early aggressiveness has been studied in Sweden, confirming the enduring consequences of earlier patterns of aggression, particularly in males. See Daniel Goleman, "Taming Unruly Boys: Old Techniques and New Approaches," *The New York Times*, February 1, 1990, p. B10. Goleman reports that these studies show that "highly aggressive boys are roughly three times as likely to become criminals as are their less aggressive peers." Also see Albert Bandura, *Aggression: A Social Learning Analysis* (Englewood Cliffs, N.J.: Prentice-Hall, 1973).

174. See, for instance, Huesmann, Eron, Lefkowitz, and Walder, "Stability of Aggression over Time and Generations," and Monroe M. Lefkowitz, Leonard D. Eron, Leopold O. Walder, and L. Rowell Huesmann, *Growing Up to Be Violent: A Longitudinal Study of the Development of Aggression* (New York: Pergamon Press, 1977), one of the few longitudinal studies yet done.

175. See James Q. Wilson and Richard J. Herrnstein, *Crime and Human Nature* (New York: Simon and Schuster, 1986), chapters 4 and 8.

176. Ronald G. Slaby and Wendy Conklin Roedell, "The Development and Regulation of Aggression in Young Children," in Judith Worell, ed., *Psychological Development in the Elementary Years* (New York: Academic Press, 1982), pp. 106, 98, 107.

177. Wilson and Herrnstein, *Crime and Human Nature*, p. 179.

178. Sheldon Glueck, "Ten Years of 'Unraveling Juvenile Delinquency': An Examination of Criticisms," in Sheldon Glueck and Eleanor Glueck, *Ventures in Criminology: Selected Recent Papers* (London: Tavistock Publications, 1964), p. 285.

179. Sheldon Glueck and Eleanor Glueck, "Predictive Techniques in the Prevention and Treatment of Delinquency," in Glueck and Glueck, *Ventures in Criminology*, p. 89.

180. Glueck and Glueck, "Predictive Techniques," p. 89.

181. Eleanor T. Glueck, "Role of the Family in the Etiology of Delinquency," in Glueck and Glueck, *Ventures in Criminology*, p. 63.

182. Sheldon Glueck, "The Home, the School, and Delinquency," in Glueck and Glueck, *Ventures in Criminology*, p. 23.

183. Slaby and Roedell, "The Development and Regulation of Aggression." Also see John D'Allesandro, "Child Abuse and Violent Juvenile Offenders: Some

Cogent Parallels with Implications for Prevention" (paper delivered at the Twelfth Annual Juvenile Justice Conference, March 11, 1985, Philadelphia); William McCord and Joan McCord, *Origins of Crime: A New Evaluation of the Cambridge-Somerville Youth Study* (New York: Columbia University Press, 1959), especially pp. 74–95. The McCords conclude that "a combination of lax or erratically punitive discipline with a lack of maternal affection greatly increases a tendency to criminality. On the other hand, consistent discipline coupled with maternal love greatly reduces the chances of criminality" (p. 102).

184. Sheldon Glueck and Eleanor Glueck, *Unraveling Juvenile Delinquency* (New York: The Commonwealth Fund, 1950), p. 133.

185. Glueck, "The Home, the School, and Delinquency," p. 27.

186. See, for example, A. A. Allen with Walter Wagner, *Born to Lose, Bound to Win: An Autobiography* (Garden City, N.Y.: Doubleday, 1970). Also see Greven, *The Protestant Temperament*, for examples earlier in our history.

187. See especially Jonathan Schell, *The Fate of the Earth* (New York: Alfred A. Knopf, 1982).

188. The classic analysis is T. W. Adorno, Else Frenkel-Brunswik, Daniel J. Levinson, and R. Nevitt Sanford, *The Authoritarian Personality* (New York: W. W. Norton, 1969 [originally published 1950]). Also see Herbert C. Kelman and V. Lee Hamilton, *Crimes of Obedience: Toward a Social Psychology of Authority and Responsibility* (New Haven, Conn.: Yale University Press, 1989), which entirely ignores the issue of childhood discipline and punishment; and Bob Altemeyer, *Enemies of Freedom: Understanding Right-Wing Authoritarianism* (San Francisco: Jossey-Bass, 1988).

189. See Miller, *For Your Own Good*, pp. 67–91, as well as her extraordinary analysis of the childhood roots of Adolf Hitler's psyche and politics, pp. 142–97; also see Claudia Koonz, *Mothers in the Fatherland: Women, the Family, and Nazi Politics* (New York: St. Martin's Press, 1987).

190. See Greven, *The Protestant Temperament*, pp. 32–43, 99–109, 339–347.

191. Larry Christenson, *The Christian Family* (Minneapolis: Bethany House Publishers, 1970), p. 59.

192. Many of the examples provided by Miller are from Christians, including individuals such as Rudolf Höss, the commandant at Auschwitz, who was raised as a devout Catholic. See Miller, *For Your Own Good*, pp. 67–68 and *passim*.

193. Christenson, *The Christian Family*, pp. 43, 52.

194. Jack Hyles, *How to Rear Children* (Hammond, Ind.: Hyles-Anderson, 1972), p. 158.

195. The pattern of patriarchy and obedience evident in many fundamentalist Protestant treatises on Christian child-rearing and family life bears a disturbing resemblance to the authoritarian families explored in Claudia Koonz's *Mothers in the Fatherland*, which examines the assumptions about gender roles shaping Nazi ideology concerning women and the family during the 1930s and 1940s.

196. See, for example, Paul M. Sniderman, *Personality and Democratic Politics* (Berkeley: University of California Press, 1975), and Rupert Wilkinson, *The Broken Rebel: A Study in Culture, Politics, and Authoritarian Character* (New York: Harper & Row, 1972). Wilkinson mentions strict discipline but does not explore it in any detail. Also see Kelman and Hamilton, *Crimes of Obedience*,

which has no apparent awareness of the childhood roots of authoritarianism. On the other hand, Adorno *et al.*, *The Authoritarian Personality*, pp. 351–53, 372–75, and *passim*, does make clear the connections between harsh punishments and authoritarianism. Also see Altemeyer, *Enemies of Freedom*.

197. Stanley Milgram, *Obedience to Authority: An Experimental View* (New York: Harper Torchbooks, 1975), p. 23.

198. Milgram, *Obedience to Authority*, p. 88.

199. Milgram, *Obedience to Authority*, p. 123.

200. Milgram, *Obedience to Authority*, p. 133, Appendix II, p. 205.

201. For some case studies, see Joachim C. Fest, *The Face of the Third Reich: Portraits of the Nazi Leadership*, Michael Bullock, trans. (New York: Pantheon, 1970); Hannah Arendt, *Eichmann in Jerusalem: A Report on the Banality of Evil* (New York: Penguin, 1964); Miller, *For Your Own Good*.

202. *The Jerusalem Post*, October 28, 1983, p. 3.

203. Quoted in A. G. Mojtabai, *Blessed Assurance: At Home with the Bomb in Amarillo, Texas* (Boston: Houghton Mifflin, 1986), p. 152.

204. See Mojtabai, *Blessed Assurance*, especially chapters 7–14.

205. Mojtabai, *Blessed Assurance*, p. xii.

206. Robert Mapes Anderson, *The Vision of the Disinherited: The Making of American Pentecostalism* (New York: Oxford University Press, 1979), p. 113 and *passim*. Also see Ruth H. Bloch, *Visionary Republic: Millennial Themes in American Thought, 1756–1800* (New York: Cambridge University Press, 1985); James K. Hopkins, *A Woman to Deliver Her People: Joanna Southcott and English Millenarianism in an Era of Revolution* (Austin: University of Texas Press, 1982); J. F. C. Harrison, *The Second Coming: Popular Millenarianism 1780–1850* (New Brunswick, N.J.: Rutgers University Press, 1979); Timothy P. Weber, *Living in the Shadow of the Second Coming*, rev. ed. (Grand Rapids, Mich.: Academie Books, 1983).

207. Anderson, *Vision of the Disinherited*, p. 103.

208. Miller, *For Your Own Good*, pp. 67–91, 142–97. Also see the suggestive and insightful essay by Charles B. Strozier: "Christian Fundamentalism, Nazism, and the Millennium," in *The Psychohistory Review*, vol. 18 (Winter 1990), pp. 207–217.

209. See, for example, Grace Halsell, *Prophecy and Politics: Militant Evangelists on the Road to Nuclear War* (Westport, Conn.: Lawrence Hill & Co., 1986), and Hal Lindsey with C. C. Carlson, *The Late Great Planet Earth* (New York: Bantam Books, 1973), among many others.

210. Hal Lindsey, *There's a New World Coming: A Prophetic Odyssey* (Eugene, Or.: Harvest House Publishers, 1973), p. 106.

211. Lindsey, *There's a New World Coming*, pp. 126–27.

212. David Wilkerson, *The Vision* (New York: Jove Books, 1974), p. 114.

213. Wilkerson, *The Vision*, pp. 119–21.

214. See, for example, Jim McKeever, *Christians Will Go Through the Tribulation and How to Prepare for It* (Medford, Or.: Omega Publications, 1978).

215. John Wesley White, *WWIII: Signs of the Impending Battle of Armageddon* (Grand Rapids, Mich.: Zondervan Publishing House, 1977), foreword, n.p.

216. Billy Graham, *Approaching Hoofbeats: The Four Horsemen of the Apocalypse* (Waco, Texas: World Books, 1983), pp. 124–25.

217. Graham, *Approaching Hoofbeats*, p. 144.

218. Lindsey, *There's a New World Coming*, pp. 80–81.

219. David Wilkerson, *Racing Toward Judgment* (Old Tappan, N.J.: Fleming H. Revell Co., 1976), p. 134.

220. Lindsey, *There's a New World Coming*, p. 294.

PART V   CHOICES

1.. See, for example, Norman O. Brown, *Life Against Death: The Psychoanalytical Meaning of History* (Middletown, Conn.: Wesleyan University Press, 1959); Brigid Brophy, *Black Ship to Hell* (New York: Harcourt, Brace & World, 1962); Erich Fromm, *The Anatomy of Human Destructiveness* (New York: Holt, Rinehart and Winston, 1973); William Griffin, ed., *End-Time: The Doomsday Catalog* (New York: Collier Books, 1979).

2. Larry Christenson, *The Christian Family* (Minneapolis: Bethany House Publishers, 1970), p. 101.

3. Larry Tomczak, *God, the Rod, and Your Child's Bod: The Art of Loving Correction for Christian Parents* (Old Tappan, N.J.: Fleming H. Revell Co., 1982), p. 104.

4. See Adrienne Ahlgren Haeuser, "Reducing Violence Towards U.S. Children: Transferring Positive Innovations from Sweden (Report from Sweden Study Visit, May 14–June 16, 1988)" (unpublished report for the U.S. Department of Health and Human Services, 1987–1989). Also see: Richard J. Gelles and Murray A. Straus, *Intimate Violence* (New York: Simon and Schuster, 1988), pp. 194–98.

5. Two psychiatrists, both refugees from Nazism—Alfred Adler and his disciple Rudolf Dreikurs—wrote extensively in the 1930s and 1940s on alternatives to physical punishments. Their viewpoints have continued to influence advocates of nonviolent methods of child-rearing in this country in recent decades as well. Dreikurs insisted that "Every person who was beaten as a child shows the marks of the blows in his character." He understood why corporal punishment continued to be practiced despite "its uselessness, absurdity, and downright harmfulness," and set forth his alternatives in a series of books, including *The Challenge of Parenthood*, rev. ed. (New York: Hawthorn Books, 1958). More recently, Bruno Bettelheim, a psychoanalyst who survived a Nazi concentration camp, also provided alternatives in *A Good Enough Parent: A Book on Child-Rearing* (New York: Alfred A. Knopf, 1987).

Other advocates of alternative, nonviolent methods of child-rearing and discipline include Haim G. Ginott, *Between Parent & Child* (New York: Macmillan, 1956; Avon Books, 1969), chapter 5; Benjamin Spock, whose recent book *Dr. Spock on Parenting: Sensible Advice from America's Most Trusted Child-Care Expert* (New York: Simon and Schuster, 1988) takes a strong stand against all forms of physical punishments; Thomas Gordon, one of the founders of the system of nonviolent child-rearing described in *P.E.T. Parent Effectiveness Training: The Tested New Way to Raise Responsible Children* (New York: New American Library, 1975); Selma Fraiberg, whose *The Magic Years: Understanding and Handling the Problems of Early Childhood* (New York: Charles Scribner's Sons,

1959) continues to be helpful and insightful; Jane Nelsen, who draws upon Adler and Dreikurs, in *Positive Discipline* (Fair Oaks, Calif.: Sunrise Press, 1981); Michael Popkin, who recommends another system known as *Active Parenting: Teaching Cooperation, Courage, and Responsibility* (San Francisco: Perennial Library, 1987). Also see Jane Ritchie and James Ritchie, *Spare the Rod* (Sydney, Australia: George Allen & Unwin, 1981), Nancy Samalin with Martha Moraghan Jablow, *Loving Your Child Is Not Enough: Positive Discipline That Works* (New York: Penguin Books, 1987), and Penelope Leach, *Your Growing Child: From Babyhood Through Adolescence* (New York: Alfred A. Knopf, 1984), and *Your Baby and Child: From Birth to Age Five*, rev. ed. (New York: Alfred A. Knopf, 1989).

Some advocates of nonviolence draw upon the field of behaviorism for alternative methods of discipline and child-rearing: Jerry Wyckoff and Barbara Unell in *Discipline Without Shouting or Spanking: Practical Solutions to the Most Common Preschool Behavior Problems* (New York: Meadowbrook Books, 1984); Elizabeth Crary, *Without Spanking or Spoiling: A Practical Approach to Toddler and Preschool Guidance* (Seattle, Wash.: Parenting Press, 1979).

6. Horace Bushnell, *Christian Nurture* (New Haven, Conn.: Yale University Press, 1916), p. 281.

7. See the stunningly beautiful book of photographs edited by Kevin W. Kelley for the Association of Space Explorers: *The Home Planet* (Reading, Mass.: Addison-Wesley Publishing Co., 1988; Moscow: Mir Publishers, 1988).

8. Bushnell, too, had a profound sense of organicism in the mid-nineteenth century. See *Christian Nurture*, pp. 18–23 and *passim*. Also see Philip Greven, *The Protestant Temperament* (New York: Alfred A. Knopf, 1977; Chicago: University of Chicago Press, 1988), pp. 194–98, for the theme of organicism among Moderates in early America.

9. See, for example, Jonathan Weiner, *The Next Hundred Years: Shaping the Fate of Our Living Earth* (New York: Bantam Books, 1990).

10. See Jonathan Schell's eloquent and disturbing book *The Fate of the Earth* (New York: Alfred A. Knopf, 1982).

PERMISSIONS
ACKNOWLEDGMENTS

Grateful acknowledgment is made to the following for permission to reprint previously published material:

Academic Press: Excerpts from "Contingent Electric Shock as a Treatment for Severe Behavior Problems" by Edward G. Carr and O. Ivar Lovaas; excerpts from "The Side Effects of Punishment" by Crighton Newsom, Judith E. Favell, and Arnold Rincover; and excerpts from "Punishment: From the Animal Laboratory to the Applied Setting" by Ron Van Houten from *The Effects of Punishment on Human Behavior*, edited by Saul Axelrod and Jack Apsche. Published in 1983. Reprinted by permission of Academic Press and the authors.

Alyson Publications: Excerpts from "The Art of Discipline: Creating Erotic Dramas of Play and Power" by Susan Farr from *Coming to Power: Writings and Graphics of Lesbian S/M* (Boston, 1987). Reprinted by permission of Alyson Publications.

American Psychiatric Press: Excerpts from *Psychological Trauma* by Bessel A. van der Kolk (Washington, 1987). Reprinted by permission of American Psychiatric Press.

Baker Book House: Excerpts from *Christian Child-Rearing and Personality Development* by Paul D. Meier (Grand Rapids, MI, 1977). Reprinted by permission of Baker Book House.

Basic Books, Inc., Publishers: Excerpts from *Autonomy and Rigid Character* by David Shapiro. Copyright © 1981 by Basic Books, Inc. Reprinted by permission of Basic Books, Inc., Publishers, New York.

Basic Books, Inc., Publishers and *The Hogarth Press Ltd.:* Excerpts from "The Aetiology of Hysteria" from *Collected Papers*, Vol. I, and excerpts from "Mourning and Melancholia" from *Collected Papers*, Vol. IV, by Sigmund Freud. Authorized translations under the supervision of Joan Riviere. Excerpts from "Notes upon a Case of Obsessional Neurosis (1909)" and excerpts from "Psychoanalytic Notes upon an Autobiographical Account of a Case of Paranoia" from *Collected Papers*, Vol. III, by Sigmund Freud. Authorized translations under the supervision of Alix and James Strachey. Published by Basic Books, Inc. by arrangement with The Hogarth Press Ltd. and the Institute of Psychoanalysis, London. Reprinted by

The Journal of Psychohistory: Excerpts from "Paranoia or Persecution: The Case of Schreber" by Morton Schatzman (*The History of Childhood Quarterly,* Summer, 1973). Reprinted by permission of *The Journal of Psychohistory,* formerly *The History of Childhood Quarterly.*

Houghton Mifflin Company and *Sterling Lord Literistic, Inc.:* Excerpt from "Red Roses" from *45 Mercy Street* by Anne Sexton. Copyright © 1976 by Linda Gray Sexton and Loring Conant Jr., Executors of the Estate of Anne Sexton. Reprinted by permission of Houghton Mifflin Company and Sterling Lord Literistic, Inc.

Hyles Publications: Excerpts from *How to Rear Children* by Dr. Jack Hyles (Hyles-Anderson Publishers, 1972). Reprinted by permission of Hyles Publications, First Baptist Church, Hammond, IN.

Little, Brown and Company: Excerpts from *My Father: An Intimate Portrait of Dwight Moody* by Paul Moody. Reprinted by permission of Little, Brown and Company.

Little, Brown and Company and *Russell & Volkening, Inc.:* Excerpts from *A Prince of Our Disorder: The Life of T. E. Lawrence* by John Mack. Copyright © 1976 by John Mack. Reprinted by permission of Little, Brown and Company and Russell & Volkening, Inc. as agents for the author.

National Council of the Churches of Christ: Scripture quotations from *The Revised Standard Version Bible.* Copyright 1946, 1952, © 1971 by the Division of Christian Education of the National Council of the Churches of Christ in the U.S.A. Used by permission.

W. W. Norton and Company: Excerpts from *Young Man Luther: A Study in Psychoanalysis and History* by Erik H. Erikson (New York, 1958). Reprinted by permission of W. W. Norton and Company.

Oxford University Press: Excerpts from *Multiple Personality, Allied Disorders, and Hypnosis* by Eugene L. Bliss. Reprinted by permission of Oxford University Press, New York.

Pantheon Books: Excerpts from *Fanny and Alexander* by Ingmar Bergman, translated by Alan Blair. English translation copyright © 1982 by Alan Blair. Reprinted by permission of Pantheon Books, a division of Random House, Inc.

Erin Pizzey and *Jeff Shapiro:* Excerpts from *Prone to Violence* by Erin Pizzey and Jeff Shapiro (Hamlyn Paperbacks, 1982). Reprinted by permission of the authors.

Fleming H. Revell Company: Excerpts from *It Was Good Enough for Father: The Story of the Wilkerson Family* by Ruth Wilkerson Harris (Old Tappan, NJ, 1969). Excerpts from *God, the Rod, and Your Child's Bod: The Art of Loving Correction for Christian Parents* by Larry Tomczak (Old Tappen, NJ, 1982). Reprinted by permission of Fleming H. Revell Company.

Sharon A. Sexton: Excerpts from "Suffer the Children" by Sharon A. Sexton (*The Boston Phoenix,* April 19, 1983). Reprinted by permission of the author.

Simon & Schuster, Inc., Lescher & Lescher, Ltd., and Michael Joseph Ltd.: Excerpts from *Dr. Spock on Parenting: Sensible Advice from America's Most Trusted Child-Care Expert* by Benjamin Spock, M.D. Copyright © 1988 by Benjamin Spock. Reprinted by permission of Simon & Schuster, Inc., Lescher & Lescher, Ltd., and Michael Joseph Ltd.

Murray A. Straus and *Richard J. Gelles:* Excerpts from *Behind Closed Doors: Violence in the American Family* by Murray A. Straus, Richard J. Gelles, and Suzanne K. Steinmetz (Anchor Books, 1980, now available through Sage Publications, Newbury Park, CA 91320). Reprinted by permission of Murray A. Straus and Richard J. Gelles.

Victor Books: Excerpts from *How to Really Love Your Child* by D. Ross Campbell (Wheaton, IL, 1977). Reprinted by permission of Victor Books.

INDEX

A NOTE ABOUT THE AUTHOR

Philip Greven was born in New Orleans in 1935. He received his B.A. from Harvard College in 1957, his M.A. from Columbia University in 1958, and his Ph.D. from Harvard University in 1965. He was a recipient of the Rockefeller Foundation's Humanities Fellowship in 1982–1983. He is currently Professor of History at Rutgers—The State University of New Jersey in New Brunswick, where he teaches courses on the history of the family (including child-rearing and discipline), Protestant religious experience and thought, and the use of psychology in historical biography, writing, and analysis, among other subjects. His previous books include *Four Generations* and *The Protestant Temperament*.

A NOTE ON THE TYPE

This book was set on the Linotype in a face called Primer, designed by Rudolph Ruzicka (1883–1978). Mr. Ruzicka was earlier responsible for the design of Fairfield and Fairfield Medium, Linotype faces whose virtues have for some time been accorded wide recognition.

The complete range of sizes of Primer was first made available in 1954, although the pilot size of 12-point was ready as early as 1951. The design of the face makes general reference to Linotype Century—long a serviceable type, totally lacking in manner or frills of any kind—but brilliantly corrects its characterless quality.

Composed by PennSet, Inc., Bloomsburg, Pennsylvania
Printed and bound by The Haddon Craftsmen, Scranton, Pennsylvania